"Much Madness is divinest Sense"

MUCH
MADNESS
IS DIVINEST
SENSE

Wisdom in Memoirs of Soul-Suffering

Kathleen J. Greider

THE PILGRIM PRESS   CLEVELAND

❀ *For all who suffer anguish of soul*

The Pilgrim Press, 700 Prospect Avenue, Cleveland, Ohio 44115-1100
thepilgrimpress.com
©2007 by Kathleen J. Greider

Cover image: "Adagio: A Movement in Slow Time" 1998. Chalk pastel, 12 x 9 in. The artist, a seventeen-year-old female, writes: "When I drew this tree, I felt intense emotions. The tree is me. It lacks color and has a sense of anger, sadness, and regret. The tree like me is dark, but still gives off life and energy. It is strong, highlighted with color and goodness. It is self-sufficient and firmly grounded." From *Childhood Revealed: Art Expressing Pain, Discovery, and Hope*, ed. Harold S. Koplewicz and Robin F. Goodman (New York: Harry N. Abrams, 1999), 6.

12   11   10   09   08   07   5   4   3   2   1

Library of Congress Cataloging-in-Publication Data

Greider, Kathleen J., 1954–
    Much madness is divinest sense : wisdom in memoirs of soul-suffering / Kathleen J. Greider.
        p. cm.
    ISBN 978-0-8298-1570-2 (alk. paper)
    1. Mental health—Religious aspects—Christianity.   2. Emotions—Religious aspects—Christianity.   3. Mentally ill—Case studies.   4. Mentally ill—Religious aspects.   I. Title.
BT732.4.G74 2007
248.8'62—dc22   2007024216

CONTENTS

FREQUENTLY REFERENCED MEMOIRISTS

Numerous memoirists are cited in this study. A few are referenced repeatedly, and an alphabetical list of the most frequently cited memoirists is provided here to help the reader trace the memoirists' stories as they emerge throughout this book.

MERI NANA-AMA DANQUAH is the author of *Willow Weep for Me: A Black Woman's Journey through Depression*. She is a native of Ghana who, from the age of six, was reared in the Washington, D.C., area. She is a poet, playwright, performance artist, author, and editor. She and her daughter divide their time between Ghana and the United States.

JYL LYNN FELMAN is a professor, author, performance artist, and lawyer. She teaches in the Judaic Studies Program and the Commonwealth College of the University of Massachusetts, Amherst. The recipient of several writing fellowships, performance grants, and literary awards, she is the author of *Never A Dull Moment: Teaching and the Art of Performance, Cravings,* a memoir, and *Hot Chicken Wings*, a collection of short stories. *If Only I'd Been Born A Kosher Chicken*, her autobiographical, one-woman show, aired nationally in 1997 on C-SPAN's Performance Series.

STEWART D. GOVIG, father to JAY, who is diagnosed with schizophrenia, wrote about his experience of Jay's schizophrenia in *Souls Are Made of Endurance: Surviving Mental Illness in the Family.* Govig, who was an ordained Lutheran minister and professor of religion at Pacific Lutheran University, published extensively on issues related to theology and ministry in light of disability in general and psychiatric disability in particular. Govig died in 2005.

SUSAN GREGG-SCHROEDER, after learning to live with depression, wrote a memoir about her experience: *In the Shadow of God's Wings: Grace in the Midst of Depression.* A United Methodist clergywoman, Gregg-Schroeder decided to devote herself to increasing the capacity of religious communities to respond sensitively and effectively to persons living with psychiatric disorders. As part of that effort she founded Mental Health Ministries.

DAN AND SUE HANSON are the parents of three adult children. Their youngest son, **J(OEL)**, is diagnosed with schizophrenia. J, who believes he is God, does not see himself as being ill and tends to resist treatment. In Dan's memoir, *Room for J: A Family Struggles with Schizophrenia,* Dan, Sue, and J's siblings discuss caring for a loved one who doesn't willingly accept help, a health care system that is often inadequate, and how their experience has affected their understanding of religion and of what it means to be human. Dan and Sue live on a small lake in Maple Grove, Minnesota.

In 1983, **DAVID HILFIKER** and his family left northern Minnesota, where David had a medical practice and moved to Washington, D.C., to live and work among the inner city poor. He first served as director of the Community of Hope Health Services, later became a staff member of Christ House, an infirmary for homeless men too ill to recuperate on the streets, and eventually helped found Joseph's House, a Washington residence for homeless men with AIDS. His books, *Not All of Us Are Saints* (1994) and *Urban Injustice: How Ghettos Happen* (2003), stem from his many years of work amid poverty. He has also written about his experience with depression.

ALBERT Y. HSU'S father committed suicide at the age of fifty-eight, three months after suffering a stroke. In *Grieving a Suicide: A Loved One's Search for Comfort, Answers, and Hope*, Albert struggles to come to terms, as a Christian, with the emotional and theological questions of being a suicide survivor. He is an editor at Intervarsity Press and lives with his family in the Chicago area.

WILLIAM (BILL) AND LUCY HULME authored several books alone and together; they tell the story of their battle with Bill's depression in *Wrestling with Depression: A Spiritual Guide to Reclaiming Life.* In "Our Daughter Need Not Have Died," Bill describes the circumstances surrounding the suicide of their daughter, who was suffering from prepartum depression. A Lutheran minister, Bill was professor of pastoral theology and ministry at Luther Seminary in St. Paul, Minnesota. Bill died in 1995, of leukemia.

KAY REDFIELD JAMISON reflects on her experience of mania and depression in *An Unquiet Mind.* With Frederick K. Goodwin, she has authored *Manic-Depressive Illness*, the classic textbook on bipolar disorder. The author of many other articles and books, she is a clinical psychologist on the faculty of the Department of Psychiatry at Johns Hopkins University School of Medicine.

NANCY MAIRS, who has written about her experience of depression, has published poetry, nonfiction, and autobiography. She earned a MFA in creative writing, holds a PhD in English literature, and has taught in both areas. She is the author of, among other titles, *Plaintext: Deciphering a Woman's Life, Remembering the Bone House, Ordinary Time: Cycles in Marriage, Faith, and Renewal, Waist-High in the World: A Life Among the Nondisabled,* and, most recently, *A Troubled Guest: Life and Death Stories.* She lives with her husband, George, in Tucson.

MARTHA MANNING is a clinical psychologist who has suffered from depression. In her books and other writings, which include a memoir entitled *Undercurrents: A Therapist's Reckoning with Her Own Depression,* Manning chronicles the legacy of depression in several generations of her family and describes her own suffering, treatment—including electroconvulsive therapy, or ECT, which became her last hope—and reemergence. She and her husband Brian Depenbrock, a licensed clinical social worker, are the parents of an adult daughter, Keara.

HENRI J. M. NOUWEN wrote often of his inner life. His many books on the spiritual life have become widely read sources of spiritual wisdom. Nouwen, a Catholic priest, taught at several universities and theological schools in the United States and in his home country of the Netherlands. But his writings convey that he found his true vocation as he lived and worked at L'Arche-Daybreak in Toronto, Canada, a community in service to developmentally disabled persons. A period of acute soul-suffering led eventually to *The Inner Voice of Love: A Journey through Anguish to Freedom.* Nouwen died in 1996.

SHARON O'BRIEN is the John Hope Caldwell Professor of American Cultures at Dickinson College in Carlisle, Pennsylvania. She has written a cultural history of depression by interweaving her experience with depression and the stories of several generations of her Irish Catholic family. Her memoir is *The Family Silver: A Memoir of Depression and Inheritance.* O'Brien is also an expert on the life and work of Willa Cather, about whom she has published two biographies and numerous articles.

PARKER J. PALMER is a well-known educator and author of several books. He published his essay recounting his struggle with depression in *Let Your Life Speak: Listening for the Voice of Vocation*. Palmer is senior associate of the American Association of Higher Education and senior advisor to the Fetzer Institute. In 1998, he was named one of the thirty most influential senior leaders in higher education. He is a member of the Religious Society of Friends (Quaker) and resides in Madison, Wisconsin.

LIZZIE SIMON developed bipolar disorder as a teenager. In her twenties, she took a break from being the creative producer of the Obie Award-winning Flea Theater in Manhattan to go on a road trip to interview other people her age with bipolar disorder. She interweaves the interviews with her own story in *Detour: My Bipolar Road Trip in 4-D*, which inspired the MTV special "True Life: I'm Bipolar," for which Simon was a consultant and field producer.

LAUREN SLATER worked as a clinical psychologist before becoming a full-time writer. She is the author of many essays and six books, including two in which she chronicles, among other things, her experience with emotional suffering and mental health treatment: *Welcome to My Country: A Therapist's Memoir of Madness* and *Prozac Diary*. She lives in the Boston area with her husband and daughter.

TRACY THOMPSON is a freelance journalist who has worked for the *Atlanta Constitution* and for the *Washington Post*, where, in 1992, she wrote a first-person article chronicling her decades-long battle with depression, including a suicide attempt and psychiatric hospitalization. The response was enormous and appreciative—"for many readers, the first news that their pain was, in fact, a medical problem and not a character weakness" —and the article later developed into her memoir, *The Beast: A Journey through Depression*. She lives in the Washington, D.C., area with her husband and two children.

DAN WEISBURD is an award-winning producer, writer, and director. He is also a mental health activist who has used his skill in media to heighten awareness of mental health issues. For many years he was the publisher and editor of *The Journal of the California Alliance for the Mentally Ill*. His firstborn son, David, is diagnosed with schizophrenia.

PROLOGUE

Much Madness Is Divinest Sense

Much Madness is divinest Sense—
To a discerning Eye—
Much Sense—the starkest Madness—
'Tis the Majority
In this, as All, prevail—
Assent—and you are sane—
Demur—you're straightway dangerous—
And handled with a Chain—

—Emily Dickinson, circa 1862[1]

We do not know exactly how the poet Emily Dickinson understood madness. But it is clear that she did not speak about it naïvely. She was sociable and fun-loving in her earliest years. But at the age of eighteen, after only a year at South Hadley Female Seminary, now Mount Holyoke College, she returned to her family home and became a virtual recluse. Over the course of the next thirty-eight years, except for one trip to Philadelphia and Washington, and several short trips to Boston to consult a doctor, she rarely left the house. Though she continued to cor-

---

1. Emily Dickinson, *The Poems of Emily Dickinson*, ed. by Thomas H. Johnson, 3 vols. (Cambridge, Mass.: Harvard University Press, Belknap Press, 1955), vol. 1, 337.

respond with a few friends by letter, for at least the last twenty years of her life, she refused to see most people, dressed only in white, and locked herself in her room for days at a time. She had a reputation for being—at the least—eccentric. Some scholars think she might have suffered from some form of psychiatric condition or what we today call brain disorders—bipolar disorder, possibly, or depression, or seasonal affective disorder, or agoraphobia. In her poetry, she wrote often and powerfully about her anguish, as in this example.

I felt a Cleaving in my Mind—
As if my Brain had split—
I tried to match it—Seam by Seam—
But could not make them fit.

The thought behind, I strove to join
Unto the thought before—
But Sequence ravelled out of Sound
Like Balls—upon a Floor.[2]

Given the consistency of her artistic ability and productivity, as well as her capacity to relate to others, however limited the form, perhaps Dickinson did not suffer from, as she put it, "the starkest Madness." Nonetheless, there is little doubt that when Emily Dickinson wrote of "madness," it was illuminated in some way by her inner life.

Yet "Much Madness" conveys that Dickinson experienced other forms of madness as well—those that are sociopolitical in nature. She wrote the poem in the opening years of the Civil War. The reference to being "handled with a Chain" by "the Majority" may reference the slavery perpetrated by whites in the colonial United States, and the ironic danger of being labeled mad if one dissented from such madness. She was exposed to the madness of war quite personally, through her correspondence with Thomas Wentworth Higginson, both while he was a soldier and after he was injured and hospitalized. But her exposure to sociopolitical dynamics in madness probably started earlier when, instead of assenting to majority beliefs, she demurred. As a young girl, she was

---

2. Dickinson, *Poems,* vol. 2, 682.

schooled at home by her father, who seems to have been maddeningly ambivalent about the strictures placed against girl children's development and aspirations. He simultaneously cultivated the curiosity of his vibrantly intelligent daughter and censored her education in hopes that she would accept without argument his Calvinist worldview.

Imagine how mad she must have been judged when Emily, the daughter of a prominent family, refused to affirm the Calvinism embedded in nineteenth-century New England society and instead aligned herself with the renegade American Transcendentalists. Emily later withdrew from public life and isolated herself within her father's home. But especially with so many women from New England providing leadership, she and her family could not have been sheltered from the emergence of the suffrage movement and its, for the time, mind-bending demands. We do not know exactly to which social dynamics of domination and subjugation she was referring in the poem. However, she is clearly saying that the madness of human society is sometimes projected on those who resist it and that the sickness of society sometimes causes or complicates the sickness of persons.

The first lines of the poem make a stunning claim—that "Much Madness is divinest Sense / To a discerning Eye." This claim is so arresting that we might be tempted to rush by the two qualifiers that flank the assertion. With her first word, Dickinson limits her own claim—*much* madness is divinest sense, she says, but *not all*. Dickinson seems to know that some people's lives are so dominated by the literal and spiritual meaninglessness of brain disorders and other forms of psychiatric illness that madness makes no sense at all, much less any divine sense. Also, she says, those who find some "divinest" sense in madness find it only with "a discerning Eye." *If* there is any divine sense in the harshness of madness within and without—*if*—it is discovered only through discernment, which, in its most developed form, is a spiritual practice. Such a radical claim—there is divinest sense in much madness—can be trustworthy only to the degree that it is made with the humility, discipline, and devotion that comprises the spiritual practice of discernment. Such a bold claim can be seen as wise only to the degree that it arises from a spiritual dedication to the ongoing process of differentiating that which is meaningless and without value from that which is of great worth and thus sacred.

With these qualifications, though, Dickinson *is* claiming that there is, sometimes, "divinest Sense" in madness. The poem offers no facile explanation of "divinest sense." Read in its entirety, however, the poem seems to argue for a particular form of divinest sense. It suggests that divinest sense is sometimes found at the stigmatized margins of society, in persons deemed "straightway dangerous" primarily because they are different from the norm. The poem also suggests that madness can be divinest sense when it tells us something of ultimate importance about "the Majority"—human experience in general. The American Transcendentalism that she embraced suggests at least two interpretations of what she might mean by "divinest." First, there can be divinest sense in madness because, as Transcendentalism argued, divinity can be immanent, human beings have the capacity to embody it, and human beings often must dissent from the majority in order to live out divine inspiration. Second, even more germane: there can be divinest sense in some madness because rationality—prized by the majority and seen as the hallmark of sanity—is not the only form of knowledge or reality. Rather, Transcendentalism says, matters of great value are comprehended not only empirically or by the senses but in spiritual truths realized through human intuition alone. The poem, then, calls attention to a particular form of divinest sense—human dissent that, though it seems or is mad, is valuable for revealing destructive social norms.

Emily Dickinson, "Much Madness," and the method of reflection in which we have just engaged serve as a microcosm of the study on which we are about to embark. There are thousands of people who, like Emily Dickinson, have experienced personally some form of madness and produced an account of it. Dickinson betrays no romanticism of madness, divinest sense, or the discernment of either—the poem is full of sober images, sharp words, and alienating tone. Similarly, neither the autobiographical accounts we will study nor our reflections on them will romanticize madness, any divine sense that might be in it, or the process of excavating that sense. If there is any value in the experience, the value does not exist and cannot be comprehended apart from the anguish in which it arose. As Dickinson did in her life, the autobiographical accounts we will study wrestle with "madness" comprised of many interlocking forms: emotional suffering that stops short of illness, as well as serious psychiatric disorders, both of which can be caused and complicated by the sometimes sick quality of human society.

In her poem, Dickinson captures in a few choice words the ambiguity, poignancy, and social criticism we will encounter in the memoirs we will study. As in the poem, other autobiographical accounts and this study state unequivocally from the start that a lot of madness makes no sense of any kind—brain disorders, especially, but also some other forms of emotional suffering wreak such unremitting havoc that they are nothing but chaos and pain. Indeed, much of the first half of our study will be challenging to read because it concentrates on the suffering associated with madness. It is also true that, as Emily Dickinson did, many persons who produce accounts of their struggle with madness, whether in themselves or in someone they love, assert on the basis of their experience that there is sometimes "divinest sense" in madness—something of ultimate value. As we have done with Dickinson's poem, we will respectfully engage that assertion, and seek to understand both—madness and the "divinest" sense it sometimes conveys.

PART ONE

MEMOIRS OF SOUL-SUFFERING

[Friends] reminded me that the books I had written since my period of anguish could not have been written without the experience I had gained by living through that time. They asked, "Why keep this away from those who have been nurtured by your spiritual insights? Isn't it important for your friends close by and far away to know the high cost of those insights? Wouldn't they find it a source of consolation to see that light and darkness, hope and despair, love and fear are never very far from each other, and that spiritual freedom often requires a fierce spiritual battle?"

—Henri J. M. Nouwen
The Inner Voice of Love

THIS BOOK IS A GATEWAY into the poignancy and power of the widespread struggle with madness and other forms of emotional anguish. Seeking to bring together and amplify the insights they convey, we will "listen in" on dozens of memoirs, broadly understood—autobiographical books and essays, but also newspaper articles and editorials, magazine stories, documentaries and other educational videos, television interviews, poetry, music, and visual art. The people you will encounter in these pages represent many others—there are thousands of such memoirs—who offer first-person descriptions and analyses of living with psychospiritual anguish from within the experience. Our relatively small sampling of memoirs will deal with psychic turmoil in several forms and from several perspectives. Some of the memoirs we will study are written by persons diagnosed with schizophrenia, bipolar disorder, or depression—three of the most common and serious psychiatric disorders. Others are written by family members of people with these severe psychiatric disorders: fathers, mothers, siblings, and partners write memoirs about the anguish they experience related to their loved ones' schizophrenia, bipolar disorder, or depression. A few of the memoirs we will study are written by persons who suffer emotional anguish that stops short of illness but is nonetheless agonizing. In all cases, people writing memoirs are also dealing with social sicknesses that at least complicate or perhaps even play a causative role in their inner anguish.

The writing itself can scarcely occur when psychic turmoil is at its height. Being within an episode of, for example, schizophrenia, or mania, or depression rarely allows for much reflection, much less experiencing any "divinest sense." So, whether they are primary sufferers—the persons initially afflicted—or family members, our memoirists usually communicate their stories between episodes, when the chaos abates a bit, or when there are periods of some healing. Four themes are commonly found in the memoirs they produce when these opportunities for reflection are found—identity, suffering, care that helps and harms and, if they experience any relief of their suffering, recovery and healing. Most important for this book, profound questions of ultimate meaning and value emerge explicitly and implicitly throughout their reflections.

Why Study Memoirs of Soul-Suffering?

I have been drawn to these accounts in part because I have personal and professional investments in this subject and engage in this work from two "sides" of the conversation. On one side, I am among the sufferers. I live with a low-grade, chronic depression, and I must make use of therapy, medication, spiritual practices, and exercise to cope with it. I also suffer alongside close relatives and friends who have struggled throughout their lives with psychiatric illnesses and other psychospiritual turmoil and used a variety of treatments, including hospitalization and electroconvulsive therapy (ECT). On the other side, I am also one among the caregivers. I am trained to provide pastoral care and psychotherapy and have done so in a variety of settings. Most relevant to this project, I have worked in public and private psychiatric facilities, as well as in several counseling centers. As a counseling professional, I have an investment in the mental health system, but my primary identity as a caregiver rests in my training as a religious professional to help care seekers sort through how religion and spirituality can harm and help.

Just as much, I have been drawn to these memoirs because they convey depth, resilience, insight, determination, and grace to a degree that is startling and educative—especially considering the negative connotations of madness and widespread prejudice against emotion. Through memoirs of soul-suffering, I have been drawn to a group of people who are endearing, articulate, rebellious, courageous, funny, inspiring. I have been drawn to these accounts also because their insights into suffering, caring, and healing are often intriguingly countercultural. First-hand accounts of living with emotional injury and illness are, of course, chronicles of pain that limits. Still, while many relationships break under too much strain, many of these memoirs are testaments of love that endures excruciating pain. While people with significant advantages often struggle to find purpose in their lives, these memoirs frequently tell of meaning honed amid severe and recurrent obstacles. While social forces tend to marginalize and have power to break the spirits of those who are different, these memoirs tell of discrimination and stigma challenged and sidelined.

Most fundamentally, though, I have been drawn to these accounts because they reveal spiritual wisdom worthy of our respect and study. Because of their enormous suffering, the majority of the memoirists we will study search for meaning, value, and wholeness with admirable integrity. Many of the memoirs convey a profundity of spiritual, theological, and religious inquiry, and do so with a complexity, rawness, and honesty that invites trust. The nature of emotional suffering brings many of them face to face with the mystery and ambiguity in and beyond our best understandings of that which is sacred, ultimate, and divine. They tend to attest to the possibility that authentic depth and integrity of spirit very often coexist with suffering and doubt, surely a humane assertion, given that reasons for demoralizing sorrow are rampant. They show how we might provide appropriate care for persons whom the world deems "least," but who are, from religious and spiritual points of view, sacred beings like all other humans. From their marginalized position, these narrators offer critical and theologically valuable perspectives on the sickness of human societies and the closely related evils rampant among us. In all these ways, they show that there is much futility in the anguish of psychiatric illness and other forms of emotional suffering, and that it also, sometimes, reveals that which matters most in lives well lived, what some religious traditions call G-d.[1] For all these reasons, memoirs of soul-suffering, though they have not been much studied, merit careful consideration.

As you may already have noticed, a certain fluidity and complexity of terminology is necessary to speak of the wisdom and the suffering that are the focus of our study. What is "divinest sense?" The previous pages have

---

1. It is my custom to use the formulation "G-d" to refer to divinity, rather than spelling the word in its entirety. Following its use in Judaism, this practice is a symbolic testimony to the incapacity of humans to fully know the divine. I use the full spelling when quoting memoirists who use it.

already alluded to many dimensions suggested by this curious expression, and its meaning will be teased out throughout the book. However, we will start with this: "Divinest sense" is, literally, sense that has a divine quality to it. We encounter "divinest sense" when we encounter experience or persons or understanding that help us glimpse divinity or that embody something sacred or holy. Of course, that which is sacred or holy is not easily perceived or expressed. However, for our purposes, we can say that "divinest sense" is that which is of ultimate or fundamental importance and value. It gives life meaning. "Divinest sense" is profundity, integrity, and wholeness. It gives life its fulsomeness and grace. "Divinest sense" is anything unfailingly trustworthy, resilient, and non-violent. "Divinest sense" is that which evokes the best in humanity, cultivates love in relationship and respect in community, and inspires hope where despair threatens to overwhelm us. Religious traditions' images and descriptions of the Divine, of G-d, are symbols of, and point toward, "divinest sense." As we saw in our study of what "divinest sense" meant to Emily Dickinson, it is not sentimental—"divinest sense" is often excavated amid suffering and marginalization. But that also means that "divinest sense" is not only transcendent but immanent—accessible not only to gods but also to humans. It is not only elegant and pleasing but also startling and challenging. It appears not only among the most powerful and highly regarded but also among the least powerful and shunned. "Divinest sense" comprises what we will call spiritual wisdom—not only the ultimate values themselves, or the human capacity to perceive them, but a quality of living that is founded on and embodies "divinest sense."

Similarly, the suffering we will encounter in these memoirs cannot be easily expressed in words. We will speak not only of soul-suffering but also of, for example, anguish, emotional suffering, psychic turmoil, social sickness, psychospiritual upheaval, emotional disability, illness. I use these characterizations interchangeably, for the most part. However, I use the term "soul-suffering" in the subtitle of the book and frequently in the text because it signifies and links two important emphases in our study. The reference to *soul*-suffering denotes our intent to focus on the most profound aspects of psychic life and on spiritual issues related to it—questions of ultimate meanings and values that psychic turmoil commonly precipitates. Where they are raised by our memoirists, we will touch on the beliefs and practices of a specific religious tradition. But our intent is not to study particular religious traditions but to track themes of spiritual importance that have potential to be significant for any human soul. The reference to soul-*suffering* denotes that we will be considering a range of emotional anguish not limited to psychiatric diagnoses themselves. Yes, psychiatric illnesses—and, in many cases, some recovery—have precipitated many of these accounts and, because they have spiritual significance, we will consider issues related to the stigma against "mental illness" and the strengths and limits of the mental health system. Still, our focus is not on the diagnoses or treatments themselves. Countless books and other resources are available that address specific diagnoses, treatment options, and additional forms of support, and the appendix offers information to guide you to those resources. Rather, the focus of this work is on the spiritual wisdom that can sometimes be discerned amid deep agony—wisdom that might illuminate more common, everyday anguish and thus speak to any of us.

Where they are accurate, psychiatric diagnoses helpfully delineate specific kinds of suffering and offer clarifying conceptualizations and treatment possibilities. However, diagnoses also tend to limit our understanding of soul-suffering to psychiatric conceptualizations. They tend to focus our attention exclusively on pathology, when the more wide-ranging distress secondary to the pathology and also the grace and resurrection sufferers sometimes experience are as important. Diagnoses can also tend to segregate "us" and "them" emotionally—exaggerating the differences between those deemed sane and those deemed insane, repudiating our commonalities, and denying us the benefit of each others' humanity. Soldiers are all fighting the same war, even if some are on the front lines and some are not. Similarly, not all of us are on the front lines of madness, but all human beings live with some degree of warring emotion. We also seek a similar peace. It is for these reasons that memoirs of psychiatric illness might speak to any of us about our soul-suffering.

As my mother used to say, rocking over the Shabbat candles, chanting Jewish prayers late, late into the night, "Hear, O Israel. The Lord our God, the Lord is one, *and so are we as a people.*"[2]

---

2. Lauren Slater, *Welcome to My Country: A Therapist's Memoir of Madness* (New York: Random House, 1996), 198–99. Italics added.

The texts provided by soul-sufferers would merit our study even if their experiences were rare. However, these texts are all the more important because they illuminate a condition of life that few of us manage to avoid completely and that, therefore, exists as an often unacknowledged bond among us. It may be the common denominator of soul-suffering that causes Lauren Slater, a psychologist who has suffered obsessive-compulsive disorder and depression, to reference the Shabbat prayer, which attests that, amid the things that divide us, there are some things that unite us. Few of us avoid moments when the madness of *life*—the nonsensical violence, fundamental unpredictability, rampant injustice—forces itself on our consciousness. Most of us have known at least one terrifying moment when we felt, or were treated by others, as if we were crazy. Human religiosity and the search for spiritual wisdom are incessant in large measure because most human beings have known psychic anguish that remains impervious to science or other human remedies. Even if we do not have an emotional disability, circumstances of everyday life—grief, war, poverty, bigotry, terror, deception, betrayal—can cause the sanest of humans to feel insane, behave madly, appear sick. And, ironically, sometimes our efforts to maintain a sense of humor or live with optimism in the midst of life's madness make us seem crazy to those made gloomy and cynical by their realism.

Most of the time, of course, all this is unconscious. For many of us what is especially hard to carry in full consciousness is how we bear, generation to generation, our maddening legacies—the many kinds of anguish known by our parents, our grandparents, our whole family tree, all our cultural ancestors—imprinted on us through oft-told stories and tattered belongings and the silence-that-speaks-louder-than-words. In part 2 we will consider essayist Jyl Felman's reflections on the connections between her social location and her depression. Maybe because she is Jewish, and because communities who have known genocide remember better than most the pain of past generations, she can articulate the denial even as she includes herself in it.

> We are in the midst of an inherited, historical crisis that includes the perpetual denial of psychic pain, offering up, instead, significant theories of abuse, dysfunction, deprivation, and abandonment that will contain the sorrow forever.[3]

---

3. Jyl Lynn Felman, "Nurturing the Soul," *Tikkun* vol. 11, no. 4 (July–August 1996): 50–51.

Except, of course, the theories do not contain it. So, many of us are among the so-called "worried well" and "walking wounded." We function effectively at most levels but our souls are, at the least, without buoyancy, weighed down by the conditions of life.

It has long been argued by experts and laypeople alike that the suffering of those with psychiatric disorders or in other acute emotional pain is different quantitatively but not qualitatively from the oft-hidden soul-sickness of the so-called healthy majority. This statement articulates two dimensions of our study—we will strive neither to minimize nor exaggerate emotional differences. We will not minimize the vast difference between the excruciating, incurable suffering faced by persons with brain disorders—schizophrenia, for example—and the existential or situational emotional anguish to which all of us are vulnerable. Indeed, it is the intention of this study to honor that difference by trying to learn from the people who deal with such extremity of suffering. At the same time, we will not exaggerate the differences, because to do so plays into the tendency to marginalize those in acute pain and act as if they have nothing to offer to those of us in less extreme pain but whose souls are sick or despairing nonetheless. Precisely because the need for what poet Emily Dickinson calls "divinest sense" is so pervasive and urgent, we will study with seriousness the soul-suffering that affects us all but is magnified in the lives of some. Therefore, we will read these memoirs with two intents: We will seek to better and more compassionately understand what many of us do not have to face—living with extreme and often disabling brain disorders and other anguish of soul. We will also explore what the experience of extreme psychic turmoil— and efforts to heal—reveal about how any of us might live with wisdom amid so many reasons to despair.

Even without such existential suffering in our own lives, it would be crucial to better and more compassionately understand those who live with psychospiritual anguish, because we interact with such people every day. Even if we don't consider all forms of soul-suffering but only diagnosed psychiatric illness, its prevalence means that it is inevitable that we encounter sufferers within our families and circles of friends, around our neighborhoods, through our workplaces, while volunteering in community service organizations, and among members of our religious communities. Psychiatric disorders affect persons of all ages, ethnicities, religions, incomes, and levels of education. According to the World Health Organization, approximately 450 million people worldwide are affected by psychiatric or neurological problems at any time and about 873,000 people die by suicide every year.[4] At any given time, one out of every four families is in the process of coping with a member who has a diagnosable psychiatric condition, and four out of five families have at least one member who has suffered at some time from a psychiatric illness.[5] Research suggests that at some time in their lives, half of the U.S. population will meet the criteria for a psychiatric condition.[6] The National Institute for Mental Health reports that, when all psychiatric disorders are considered, 22 percent of adults in the United States suffer from a diagnosable psychiatric disorder in a given year. Similar figures appear to apply to children.[7] Even the most disabling disorders are highly prevalent, affecting, in the United States alone, five to ten million adults and three to five million children (ages five to seventeen).[8]

Even if we are not aware of knowing someone with a psychiatric disorder, all of us are directly affected by the social costs. For example, psychiatric illnesses are the leading cause of disability in North America and Europe; if current trends continue, by 2020, Major Depressive Disorder is expected to be the leading cause of disability in the world for women and children.[9] Research shows that major depression, among the top three causes of lost productivity in the workplace, costs the U.S. economy

---

4. World Health Organization, "Mental Health," http://www.who.int/mental_health/en/ (accessed August 1, 2006).

5. National Alliance on Mental Illness, "About Mental Illness," http://www.nami.org /Content/NavigationMenu/Inform_Yourself/About_Mental_Illness/About_Mental_Illness .htm (accessed Dec. 20, 2005).

6. Laurie Barclay, "Half of Americans May Meet DSM-IV Criteria for a Mental Disorder During Their Lifetime," *Medscape*, http://www.medscape.com/viewarticle/506348_print (accessed June 24, 2006).

7. National Institute of Mental Health, "The Numbers Count: Mental Disorders in America," http://www.nimh.nih.gov/publicat/numbers.cfm (accessed Dec. 20, 2005).

8. National Alliance on Mental Illness, "About Mental Illness," http://www.nami.org/ Content/NavigationMenu/Inform_Yourself/About_Mental_Illness/About_Mental_Illness .htm (accessed Dec. 20, 2005).

9. National Alliance on Mental Illness, "About Mental Illness."

approximately $43.7 billion annually.[10] If undiagnosed or undiagnosable soul-suffering were included, those figures would be higher.

Soul-suffering is a sobering, even alarming, experience, no matter if we have a psychiatric disorder, encounter psychospiritual turmoil in others, or are typically healthy people swamped occasionally by our own depths. When "madness" surfaces, everyone is captive to fear, stereotypes, and stigma. Feminist essayist Kate Millett, diagnosed—wrongly, she says—with bipolar disorder, puts it bluntly:

> Mystical state, madness, how it frightens people. . . . How crazy craziness makes everyone, how irrationally afraid. The madness hidden in each of us, called to, identified, aroused like a lust. And against that the jaw sets. The more I fear my own insanity the more I must punish yours. . . .[11]

Sometimes, there are good reasons that fear and abhorrence characterize human reaction to madness and other forms of psychic turmoil. Though its frequency is exaggerated, it is true that those who suffer extreme psychic turmoil are occasionally violent against others, emotionally or physically. Any "divinest sense" we might find in psychic turmoil does not excuse or sidestep violence in it. Quite the opposite is true—that which is divine guides us directly into and through the harshest realities of madness and teaches us, in the midst of danger, how to reckon with death and contain violence, what it means to cultivate life. Mysteriously, precisely because sacrality is a powerful force among us, it is sometimes possible to find wisdom and other values even in the midst of destruction. Such wisdom and values never rationalize violence, but can redeem it.

Much more than it harms others, psychic turmoil is sometimes death-dealing to those who are ill. Use of any wisdom and value we might find in it to minimize or romanticize soul-suffering is misuse. Even those memoirists who wrest some wisdom from the experience

---

10. National Mental Health Association, "Depression in the Workplace," http://www.mcmha.org/facts/depression_and_workplace.pdf#search='DEPRESSION%20LOST%20PRODUCTIVITY%20WORKPLACE (accessed August 1, 2006).
11. Kate Millett, *The Loony-Bin Trip* (New York: Simon & Schuster, 1990), 67–68.

must also cope with what their suffering has cost them. Like those around them, many primary sufferers also experience their anguish as spiritual and physical violence. This is, in fact, another reason why their wisdom is worthy of our trust—they know the spiritual and physical violence of madness firsthand. They are learning compassionately to comprehend and set limits on the violence in madness, and can teach us to do the same.

But anguish of soul is sobering and alarming as well because those who suffer it provide evidence that violent madness almost always points beyond itself—to alarming violence and sickness in human society. They show us that acute emotional suffering is at least exacerbated, and is sometimes caused, by the physical violence and spiritual violence—for example, injustice, neglect, shallowness—that infect human societies. These memoirs, thus, by exploring the harsh realities of madness, warn us of social dangers posing threats of which we may be less aware. We will see that emotional illnesses and other forms of soul-suffering sometimes provide a kind of insulation against violent society, or serve as a form of protest or resistance against unjust society, or offer a window into profundity, numinosity, and sacredness in the midst of societies' shallowness. Then, as such, insanity has a certain kind of sanity about it. It may sometimes be just as congruent and appropriate a response to the ills of human society as the stability of the so-called healthy or normal. If we are honest about the extent of systemic violence around us, then soul-sickness is in some ways a reaction so very understandable as to make "divinest sense."

Mostly, the fear and abhorrence that characterize human reaction to psychic turmoil are unnecessary and deprive us of good things, such as insight, friends, and humor. We have much to gain from soul-sufferers—listening to their truths, learning from their pain and rage and humor and tenderness, being inspired by their grit. Lizzie Simon developed bipolar disorder in her late teens. By her early twenties, however, she found some healing and became the highly successful creative producer of the Obie Award–winning Flea Theater in Manhattan and developed a special on bipolar disorder for MTV. Simon knows well the drama of madness. As she puts it, though, "I know there's a lot of drama in people gone wrong, but there's so much magic in people gone right."[12] Speaking of a friend during one of his troubled times, she gives us an image for the magic: "he's like the potatoes we [cook] in the fire. They look like balls of charred matter, but inside there's still plenty of stuff, and if you add butter and salt, it's a dream to eat."[13]

As we will see, though there is not much about the soul-suffering itself that is funny, some of these memoirs surprise us by showing a sense of humor that helps keep perspective. Psychologist Martha Manning is one of the funniest of our memoirists, so it seems not accidental but symbolic that she chose as the very first words of her memoir about living and coping with her clinical depression a story that shows play, humor, and irony in the midst of soul-suffering. The memoir opens with Manning, unaware that she is on the verge of falling into a severe depression, on the floor of her office. She is playing the game "Sorry" with her nine-year-old patient, Stephanie, who is hooting over having beaten Dr. Manning for the third time. As time for the session runs out, Stephanie returns the game to the shelf, and Manning stands up.

> Without warning, my slip drops to the floor and lands on my shoes. We both stare at it, stunned. I stammer, "Oh, my goodness!"
>
> Stephanie, a rather solemn child, is seized with paroxysms of laughter, which become contagious. I step out of my slip and stuff it in my briefcase. Stephanie tries to catch her breath and exclaims, "My perfect Dr. Manning is coming apart!"
>
> She bursts into the crowded waiting room and graphically describes the scene to her parents. It is clear the whole waiting room enjoys this story. . . . My friend Ed passes me in the hall between our offices and asks casually, "That wouldn't be your Freudian slip, would it?"[14]

Understandably, the struggles of acute soul-pain are usually kept private, available only to dearest friends and family, support groups, therapists, or pastors. But, more and more individuals and families are com-

---

12. Lizzie Simon, *Detour: My Bipolar Road Trip in 4-D* (New York: Washington Square Press, 2002), 41.

13. Simon, *Detour*, 83.

14. Martha Manning, *Undercurrents: A Therapist's Reckoning with Her Own Depression* (San Francisco: HarperSanFrancisco, 1994), 2.

ing out of hiding, breaking silence, telling their stories publicly, inviting us to know better the world we share. They are rendering their views in support and advocacy groups, through political action, and in the range of autobiographical materials we are considering in this study. By listening to them we see more clearly ourselves, our fellow human beings, the beauty and cruelty of the societies we have built together and in which we are living, the qualities of well-being, and the requirements of holy, just living. You may find yourself thinking that the people you will meet in these pages are unusual, or not very sick, or especially privileged. The people to whom we are listening are statistically unusual, of course; there are millions of persons unable, for a variety of reasons, to articulate their emotional anguish, even privately. At the same time, because survivors of emotional suffering often say that the people who understand best are other survivors, there is good cause to think that the accounts we have probably give us a glimpse into the silence of others.

If you are struggling with psychic turmoil in yourself or in a loved one, I hope this book assures you of your innate dignity and affirms you in your efforts to struggle with integrity. If you think there might be some divinest sense in the madness around you, I hope the book inspires you to pursue it. If you find yourself unfamiliar with acute emotional suffering, with only stereotypes to inform you, I hope this book helps you to better and more compassionately understand and appreciate people whose soul-suffering startles and requires some response from you. If you are a mental health professional within or beyond religious communities, I hope this book nuances and nourishes your efforts to engage not only the spiritual challenges presented by emotional upheaval but also the spiritual capacities ready to be strengthened within almost every person and community dealing with soul-suffering. If you are a professional or lay member of a religious community, I hope this book increases your capacity to recognize, enjoy, and support all that is sacred within soul-suffering, your own and that of the sisters and brothers who cross your path. Of course, for all of us, I hope this book offers spiritual wisdom.

The remainder of this introduction to our study explores four questions. What makes the wisdom in the memoirs "spiritual?" Why do people create memoirs of their soul-suffering? How shall we deal with problems associated with the genre of memoir? What methods will we use to study these memoirs?

WHAT MAKES WISDOM IN MEMOIRS OF SOUL-SUFFERING "SPIRITUAL"?

When Dan Weisburd heard Jay Mahler say that he found his psychiatric disorder to be a spiritual journey, Weisburd was incensed. Dan was full of anguish for his son, David, who had been diagnosed with paranoid schizophrenia and found little relief in treatment. Dan tried to stay in the conversation. He respected Jay, who was living with a serious psychiatric disorder. In fact, Dan had appointed Jay to a state government task force on mental illness and felt Jay had provided invaluable service. But Dan found any association between spiritual matters and his son's disabling psychic anguish to be a diminishment of the tragedy and suffering.

> You must have something very different than what David has, Jay. Illness, disorder, disease, disability—all seem to define what he's got. But no way can I say that what is assaulting my son's ability to stay alive and function with some level of independence . . . could quantify as "a spiritual journey." My retort was loaded with disparaging intent, as I challenged him to explain, to my satisfaction, the justification for what he had just said.[15]

But Jay did not spiritualize his suffering, didn't use spiritual values to sidestep his suffering. Rather, he spoke of how spiritual questions and

---

15. Dan E. Weisburd, "Publisher's Note," *Journal of the California Alliance for the Mentally Ill* vol. 8, no. 4 (December 18, 1997), 1. Weisburd is providing an introduction to this issue of the *Journal*, which is dedicated in its entirety to the topic of spirituality.

values enlarged his life beyond the suffering. Spirituality "doesn't nullify" suffering, Dan remembers Jay responding. Jay explained his view:

> "The whole medical vocabulary to describe what has hit us brings with it a new set of conflicts and disturbances that they [medical professionals] don't address as they put us in the role of a 'labeled' diagnosed victim. *We* are the ones whom *they* must skillfully attempt to fix, according to them. But as they go though trial and error, looking to see if anything they have to offer works at all to control your symptoms, it doesn't take a genius to realize they haven't got the answers. No clue about cures! And oh boy, those side effects! I don't say medications can't help, or that treatments won't have value. But what I do say is that my being aware that I'm on a spiritual journey *empowers me* to deal with other enormous parts of the puzzle! The big, human 'spiritual' questions, Dan! Why is this happening to me? Will I ever be the same again? Is there a place for me in this world? Can my experience of life be made livable? If I can't be *cured* can I be *recovering* . . . even somewhat? Has my God abandoned me? Bottom line is, as victim of whatever the current docs call whatever it is *they see* that *we have*, we who have it have to wonder whether what remains constitutes a life worth living. That's my spiritual journey, Dan."[16]

Dan recalled that when as a nine-year-old he had disavowed God upon learning of the Holocaust, his grandfather gave him the only hug Dan remembers and said, "So many lessons in life, Daniel. Don't close doors." Dan recalled the words of Holocaust survivor and psychoanalyst Victor Frankl: "There is nothing in the world, I venture to say, that would so effectively help one to survive even the worst conditions as the knowledge that there is meaning in one's life." He remembered his son David saying, "I am more than the sum of my symptoms, Dad."[17] With these remembrances, Dan was brought to a point at which many of our memoirists arrive, where they determine that, however severe their psychospiritual suffering, they need to find meaning for their lives in and beyond it.

---

16. Weisburd, "Publisher's Note," 1. Quoting a personal conversation with Jay Mahler.
17. Weisburd, "Publisher's Note," 1, 2.

❦

"Mental" suffering is physical and emotional pain. It is also soul pain. Fortunately, psychology has heightened our respect for and understanding of emotions and the neurochemistry and brain function underlying them. However, for many people, there is a dimension of complex, holistic experience—in both joy and pain—that psychological language, or even language of "emotion" and "feeling," cannot adequately touch or express. This dimension is signaled by "spiritual" language, and psychology's distance from this dimension is one reason for the most recent surge of interest in spirituality. That physiology plays a significant, perhaps predominant, role in emotion and psychiatric illness is, thankfully, becoming clearer. At the same time, the growing emphasis on the neurology and chemistry of emotion, and on conceptualizing emotional illnesses as brain disorders, makes us no better able to attend to the depths of human experience, articulate the soul-pain caused by the disordered brain, or value the hard-won wisdom wrest from the battle to survive such suffering.

The relationship between experts in spirituality and religion and in psychology, and between the powers of their respective fields of expertise, is extremely complex and complicates our task. Psychology has far eclipsed religion in common discourse as an explanatory framework for human experience, and psychological explanations for soul-suffering have come to almost completely dominate religious ones. In recent years, psychologists are showing more interest in spirituality, but most mental health professionals lack expertise to address it. With the guidance of scholars in spirituality and religion mostly relegated to the margins of both academic and public forums, average citizens have little help to discern what might be the spiritual dimension in their psychic anguish, and its costs and benefits, much less to know what care religious professionals might be able to offer. Thus, amid the dominance of psychology and the marginalization of spirituality and religion, many sufferers assume that psychological explanations are the only expert advice available, and they are left largely on their own to find appropriate help in the spirituality marketplace.

We will refuse to bifurcate human experience into psychology, religion, or spirituality. This book assumes that in the case of most forms of soul-suffering, the languages of spirituality, religion, and psychology are all necessary and valuable in our efforts to articulate the complexity of human experience. It is appropriate that in so doing we will embody a point of view articulated by Anton Boisen, famous for inventing Clinical Pastoral Education (CPE), which remains one of the most significant approaches to education for spiritual care. From 1920 to 1922, Rev. Boisen suffered several psychotic breaks and psychiatric hospitalizations. Even during his recovery, he refused to turn his back on the possible significance of his suffering, and, throughout his career, he courageously made his suffering the subject of his own research. Boisen's moderate position serves our project well.

> Certain forms of mental disorder and certain forms of religious experience are closely interrelated. Mental disorder is, I hold, the price humanity has to pay for having the power of choice and the capacity for growth, and in some of its forms it is a manifestation of healing power analogous to fever or inflammation in the body.[18]

We will assume that to speak of psyche and soul, or of emotion and spirit or, for that matter, brain and mind, is to speak of the same complex organism—human being—with different languages, all potentially illuminating. Our method will be interdisciplinary, open to engaging all relevant fields of human expertise—psychology, psychopharmacology, physiology, sociology, religion, theology, spirituality, among others—as lenses in our effort to see the spiritual wisdom we seek.

Spiritual wisdom gained from struggling through emotional dis/ease tends to be both remarkably unpretentious and distinctly unsentimental, especially when viewed against current popular conceptualizations and marketing of spirituality. The complexity of the function of spirituality for persons suffering psychiatric symptoms is in contrast to the typically polarized characterizations of it in scholarly arguments and research data. On the one hand, there is the long-standing argument that religious belief and spiritual practices not infrequently are symptomatic of emotional immaturity or illness. On the other hand, research reports that spirituality helps people who are experiencing acute emotional suffering. For example, a report on interviews with fifty-four persons with psychi-

---

18. Anton T. Boisen, *Out of the Depths: An Autobiographical Study of Mental Disorder and Religious Experience* (New York: Harper & Brothers, 1960), 9.

atric diagnoses identifies three potential benefits of spirituality: providing a buffer from stress, linking sufferers to sources of social support, and lending a sense of coherence to a life fragmented by illness.[19]

But for our memoirists, the harmful and helpful aspects of spirituality are often more interwoven. Consider the first two benefits just reported. As we will see, some memoirists report that spirituality increases their distress, at least in the short run. Similarly, memoirists routinely report that religious and other spiritual communities rarely seek actively to provide social support to them, and not infrequently fail to provide spiritual sanctuary as well. But also, persons suffering acute psychospiritual distress often speak with unusual candor and complexity about the layers of significance spirituality imparts to *both* suffering and healing. For many people in acute emotional distress, the search for meaning-making and soul-sustenance that characterizes spirituality yields very complex purposes, values, and dangers. Arguably the most demanding aspect of these accounts is their portrayal of spirituality as profoundly ambiguous: spirituality can be simultaneously a maze of dread and grandiosity, terrifying and empowering, to be pursued and avoided, challenging and yet compelling. For example, noted writer and educator Parker Palmer writes that healing required him to image his depression as having a "befriending impulse" and that when he was "finally able to . . . [ask of the friend], 'What do you want?' the answer was clear: I want you to embrace this descent into hell as a journey toward selfhood—and a journey toward God."[20]

Many religious and psychological value systems identify the ability to thrive in the midst of ambiguity and paradox as a sign of human maturity.[21] In religious experience, the richness of possibility and meaning inherent in ambiguity and paradox can not only lead us toward knowing that which is holy, it can be argued to be a quality of numinosity itself. That which is holy may well require ambiguity and paradox in order to

---

19. W. Patrick Sullivan, "Recoiling, Regrouping, and Recovering: First-Person Accounts of the Role of Spirituality in the Course of Serious Mental Illness," in *Spirituality and Religion in Recovery from Mental Illness*, ed. Roger D. Fallott (New York: Jossey-Bass, 1998), 25–33.

20. Parker J. Palmer, *Let Your Life Speak: Listening for the Voice of Vocation* (San Francisco: Jossey-Bass, 2000), 68, 69.

21. I discuss these ideas at more length in *Reckoning with Aggression: Theology, Violence, and Vitality* (Louisville: Westminster John Knox Press, 1997), 15–20.

be manifest. Psychoanalyst Carl Gustav Jung, who had a period of psychic turmoil that nearly broke him, put it this way:

> The paradox is one of our greatest spiritual possessions, . . . because only the paradox comes anywhere near to comprehending the fullness of life. Non-ambiguity and non-contradiction are one-sided and thus unsuited to express the incomprehensible.[22]

Only in the context of ambiguity and paradox can any spiritual value in the experience of psychic turmoil be affirmed, and then only gingerly, always weighing the cost as well as the benefit of the turmoil. We will return to this theme in the epilogue. For now, the words of the seventeen-year-old artist who painted the cover image for this book are representative. She articulates that, paradoxically, the self and the experiences of soul-suffering can be all at once dark/light and colorless/colorful, sadness/goodness: "The tree is me. It lacks color and has a sense of anger, sadness, and regret. The tree like me is dark, but still gives off life and energy. It is strong, highlighted with color and goodness."[23]

Another profound level of challenge posed by the spirituality portrayed in these accounts is that it functions not only as an aid to navigate the ambiguous phenomenology of madness but also as a doorway to comprehend the politics that swirl around the social construction of sanity and insanity. In this function, spirituality shows that qualities deemed to characterize sanity and health are elevated not necessarily because of their inherent value but sometimes simply because they describe the majority. Often, "normal" turns out to be equated with what most people do. As Emily Dickinson's poem conveys, the "divinest sense [in] much madness" sometimes produces dangerous minority positions—sociopolitically and theologically—that assert sacred values challenging to personal and social sanity. Certainly, persons in emotional distress sometimes pose a danger to themselves or others. But they also pose a danger to fundamental assumptions and practices within social systems. These accounts can be interpreted to claim that

---

22. Carl Gustav Jung, *Psychology and Alchemy,* vol. 12 of *The Collected works of C.G. Jung,* ed. Herbert Read, Michael Fordham, and Gerhard Adler, trans. R. F. C. Hull (New York: Pantheon Books, 1953), 15, para. 18.
23. Anonymous, *Childhood Revealed: Art Expressing Pain, Discovery, and Hope,* ed. Harold S. Koplewicz and Robin F. Goodman (New York: Harry N. Abrams, 1999), 6.

mature spirituality is, to a degree, a combination of that which religion and society distinguishes as sanity and insanity.

❀

In summary, as we study memoirs of soul-suffering, we will be alert to specific topics and qualities that in any human discourse suggest a "spiritual" significance. These include topics such as ultimate meanings, values, and purposes; moral and ethical issues in social and personal life; characteristics and development of wellness, wholeness, or maturity; religious and theological questions. Qualities that suggest spiritual significance include ultimacy; unpretentiousness and lack of sentimentality; holism and integrity; and ambiguity and paradox.

Why Produce Memoirs of Soul-Suffering?

S tudy of memoirs of soul-suffering shows that spiritual values are revealed in memoirists' motivations. Several common motivations emerge, each of which has relevance to spiritual values and practices. First, much like the reflective writing done in spiritual practices of journaling, many memoirists compose their stories as an exercise in the maturing processes of self-naming and self-reflection. The constructive power of self-naming is widely recognized. When we speak for ourselves about our most profound experience, we access and enhance our own depths but also speak to the soul of our communities. In some religious traditions, choosing a name for oneself is the culminating moment of a young person's pathway to adulthood. Having been tested and thereby coming to the mature self-knowing that allows one to take a responsible role in community, self-naming in such situations is not narcissistic but rather an act that signals one's readiness for contributing to the common good.

Also, providing help to persons in need is a core value in most spiritual and religious traditions, and it is a preeminent motivation among our memoirists. With near unanimity, the authors of the accounts I have studied affirm that the primary reason for making their stories available to others is their hope that the path they have hewn through the suffering might bring solace to other sufferers. As essayist and journalist Andrew Solomon puts it, "empathy" is the "first goal" of his memoir.[24]

---

24. Andrew Solomon, *The Noonday Demon: An Atlas of Depression* (New York: Scribner, 2001), 12.

The writers share both information and emotion, hoping to break through the isolation so common to suffering shrouded in shame and stigma. This help that they give to others is significantly altruistic—they sacrifice their privacy, expose themselves to the stigma associated with mental illness, and stir up their own pain. The poet Jane Kenyon suffered from bipolar disorder and wrote an account of her soul-suffering in "Having it Out with Melancholy," a poem frequently referenced by other sufferers. Her husband, Donald Hall, later wrote:

> It pained her to write this poem. It pained her to expose herself. But writing the poem also helped to set her depression out, as she knew it—depression and its joyful tentative departure. She wanted the poem to help others who were afflicted. The first time she read it aloud . . . she paused during her reading, resisting tears. When she ended, a line of people waited to talk with her: depressives, people from the families of depressives.[25]

Taking action on behalf of the common good is another practice urged by most religious and spiritual value systems. Many memoirists are motivated by this value, and they tell their stories in order to contribute to social change of two types. Some are pressed by a sense of duty to alert others to dangerous weaknesses in the health care system and play a part in its reform. William Hulme is reluctant to tell the story of his daughter's illness and death: "Family sorrows are private matters, not something one writes about for public information. One feels repugnance against any activity that might exploit the deceased." But because, largely due to inadequate medical care, his pregnant daughter hanged herself while hospitalized for delusional prepartum psychosis, Rev. Dr. Hulme quells his reluctance.

> One has obligations . . . to the larger family—the community, the society one belongs to. Our daughter's death could have been prevented. It was a tragic example of what can happen when specific acts of carelessness reflecting weaknesses in the current state of health care come one upon another. That is why

---

25. Donald Hall, "Ghost in the House," in *Unholy Ghost: Writers on Depression,* ed. Nell Casey (New York: Harper Perennial, 2002), 168.

I undertake the difficult task of telling the story of how our daughter died.[26]

Other memoirists expose themselves to the stigma associated with mental illness in order to combat the stereotypes, stigma, and discrimination. Many of them tell their stories in the hopes that it will inform the public, increase social compassion, and stimulate more generous and effective public services. They want to increase awareness of—and increase the will to share—what Professor David Karp calls "the burden of sympathy."[27] One of the first accounts to capture the imagination and outrage of the public was published in 1908. Clifford Beers—born to a privileged New England family, a graduate of Yale University—daringly related his experience of psychiatric illness and recovery. But he also provided readers a rare look into the dehumanizing and horrific conditions inflicted on the mentally ill through his detailed descriptions of the treatment given him during years in sanitariums. The attention and support of psychologist William James and others propelled Beers' autobiography to national attention and assisted his efforts to start a mental health and educational and reform movement in the United States. His organization survives today as the National Mental Health Association.[28] The capacity of self-revelation to educate the public about psychic upheaval and ease stigma is documented in recent decades by the constructive response given to public figures who reveal their experiences with psychiatric illness, for example, actress Patty Duke's 1987 biography describing her manic episodes and writer William Styron's 1990 account of his melancholy.[29]

Finally, honesty and integrity are widely understood to be good for the soul, and many of our memoirists convey that they risk social approbation for exactly these values. They are tired of hiding, they say, because

26. William E. Hulme, "Our Daughter Need Not Have Died," *Christian Century* vol. 91 (December 4, 1974): 1144–6.
27. David A. Karp. *The Burden of Sympathy: How Families Cope with Mental Illness* (Oxford: Oxford University Press, 2001).
28. Clifford W. Beers, *A Mind That Found Itself: An Autobiography*, 5th ed. rev. (Garden City, N.Y.: Doubleday, Doran & Co., 1944). For more information about the National Mental Health Association: http://www.nmha.org/about/index.cfm.
29. Patty Duke and Kenneth Turan, *Call Me Anna: The Autobiography of Patty Duke* (New York: Bantam, 1987). See also Patty Duke and Gloria Hochman, *A Brilliant Madness: Living with Manic-Depressive Illness* (New York: Bantam, 1992). William Styron, *Darkness Visible: A Memoir of Madness* (New York: Random House, 1990).

of its costs both to self-respect and to relationship with others, and because of its wastefulness. Among the memoirists we will consider are several mental health professionals who suffer from psychiatric disorders, and this reason for writing takes on special significance for them. Psychologist Lauren Slater, who has a history of in-patient as well as outpatient psychiatric treatment, finds herself assigned to care for a young woman who has been admitted to the same hospital in which, at about the same age as her patient, and with the same diagnosis, Dr. Slater was once a patient. Unnerved, trying to avoid being stigmatized, she makes a concerted effort not to reveal to the staff her familiarity with the place.

> The funny thing is, I'm supposedly in a profession that values honesty and self-revelation. . . . But at the same time, another, more subtle yet powerful message gets transmitted to practitioners. . . . *Admit your pain, but only to a point.* Keep it clean. . . . . Along these same lines, practitioners are allowed to admit their *countertransference* but not the *pain pain pain the patient brings me back to, memories of when I was five. . . .* No. To speak in such a way would make the rift disappear, and practitioners might sink into something overwhelming. We—I—hang on to the jargon that at once describes suffering and hoists us above it.[30]

Eventually, Slater could not bear the rift and has reflected on the relationship between her emotional suffering and her work in several autobiographical publications that have received wide circulation. One of the first persons to be treated with the antidepressant drug Prozac, Slater says that she told her story also because she felt a responsibility to weigh in and complexify the controversy swirling around a drug that "irrevocably altered" a generation.[31]

Kay Redfield Jamison, who knows manic depressive illness as a sufferer and as a professional, tells of starting speeches quoting "a patient with manic-depressive illness," and then reading it "as if it had been written by someone else, although it was my own experience."[32] Later, Dr. Jamison revealed her experience with the illness in a now famous mem-

---

30. Slater, *Welcome to My Country*, 188–89.
31. Lauren Slater, *Prozac Diary* (New York: Random House, 1998), 25.
32. Kay Redfield Jamison, *An Unquiet Mind* (New York: Random House, 1995), 104.

oir. In the prologue she notes that she has no way to judge the long-term effects of her revelation on her career as a mental health professional, but

> whatever the consequences, they are bound to be better than continuing to be silent. I am tired of hiding, tired of misspent and knotted energies, tired of the hypocrisy, and tired of acting as though I have something to hide. One is what one is, and the dishonesty of hiding behind a degree, or a title, or any manner and collection of words, is still exactly that: dishonest. Necessary perhaps, but dishonest. . . . One of the advantages of having had manic-depressive illness for more than thirty years is that very little seems insurmountably difficult.[33]

---

33. Jamison, *An Unquiet Mind*, 7–8.

Problems with Memoirs of Soul-Suffering

As it has become increasingly popular with writers and readers, the genre of autobiography has come under increasing scrutiny. Some of this criticism comes from beyond those who write autobiographically, but questions are also raised by the authors we will be considering. Whatever the positive reasons for telling their stories, most persons who reveal their experiences with psychospiritual suffering have reservations about "marketplace confessions," as Slater dryly calls them (including her own) and are analytical about the genre.[34]

First, outsiders and insiders alike note that memoirs might actually have the opposite of their most desired effect—perhaps telling their stories will cause more hurt to others, rather than less. Fortunately, though she is able to articulate the risk, Dr. Ruth Sullivan had the opposite experience. Founder of Autism Services Center in West Virginia[35] and the mother of Joseph, who has autism, in March of 1988 Sullivan met Dustin Hoffman through Gail Mutrux, associate producer for the film *Rain Man*. Looking for materials for Hoffman to study in preparation for the role of Raymond, a high-functioning autistic much like Joseph, Mutrux had located the film *Portrait of an Autistic Young Man*, in which Joseph is featured. Joseph became one of two models for the character Hoffman developed, and later, they all met on the set of *Rain Man*. Dr. Sullivan

---

34. Slater, *Welcome to My Country*, 178f.
35. For more information, see http://www.autismservicescenter.org/ (accessed August 21, 2006).

was deeply moved by the respect and skill Hoffman brought to the role of Raymond, because

> You put information about your loved one in the hands of reporters, editors, and other media people with widely varying sensibilities and interests in the subject. You hope they will be accurate and kind in their telling of your story. The cost of going public is the risk that the media will distort, demean, misrepresent, or even hurt the very one(s) you are trying to help.[36]

In light of this risk, many memoirists take steps to protect the privacy of their loved ones. Similarly, Parker Palmer worries that "someone may take the wrong counsel" from what he publishes about his struggle with depression. Though this misuse cannot be prevented, many memoirists address the problem by emphasizing the personal and unique aspects of their stories. Palmer implies the same by differentiating his communication from that of a doctor's: "I am not writing a prescription."[37] These sufferers know from personal experience that what helps some people usually doesn't help all people.

Second, memoirists are sometimes criticized for being self-revelatory to the point of self-destructiveness. Most of our authors know well the cost of revealing one's emotional suffering and do not undertake such risk naïvely. Typically, they are quite consciously balancing possible gains with what their revelations will cost them by way of stigma and other dangers of self-exposure. This is especially a concern for those who already suffer marginalization of some kind. In part 2, when we consider identity, we will explore the added risks of self-revelation to women, people of color and, especially, women of color, because their identities and their stories of soul-suffering are complicated by sexism and racism. It is also a concern for professionals like Jamison, whose careers can be negatively affected by stigma's subtle effects: she worries that students might hold back, her work might be seen as biased—"a personal ax to grind"—and thus sidelined, colleagues might question her clinical privileges and ability to treat patients.[38] But she also speaks for another worry

---

36. Ruth C. Sullivan, "Rain Man and Joseph," in *High-Functioning Individuals with Autism,* ed. Eric Schopler and Gary B. Mesibov (New York: Plenum Press, 1992), 246.
37. Palmer, *Let Your Life Speak,* 57, 58.
38. Jamison, *An Unquiet Mind,* 203.

of our memoirists: they are protective of the authenticity and depth of these profound experiences and live in the tension of wanting to help others but perhaps causing more hurt to themselves by telling their stories. "I am deeply wary that by speaking publicly or writing about such intensely private aspects of my life, I will return to them one day and find them bleached of meaning and feeling."[39]

A third criticism is that the genre of memoir is of questionable value because the writing can be narcissistic or at least undertaken for questionable and idiosyncratic therapeutic purposes. Such concern is voiced within the community of memoirists as well. Journalist Tracy Thompson, who has written a memoir about her depression, is at the same time wary of the genre and critical of some of its implications.

> The stigma of depression is sometimes unwittingly perpetrated by those of us who write about it, who subscribe to the notion that having a mood disorder makes one "special." Many first-person accounts of depression contain a hopelessly compromised message: it is wrong, those writers say, to attach a stigma to an illness which is a medical problem like any other . . . except that it *is* different, since only artists suffer. This is an elitist view. Grocery store clerks and bus drivers also suffer, but lack the leisure to write about it. And it is a view which ignores some unattractive truths, including the fact that depression tends to foster an array of personality traits which can remain as its permanent legacy: manipulative behavior, passivity, unremitting self-absorption.[40]

Though some writings may arguably be characterized by such qualities, stigma and shame attached to the admission of emotional turmoil are more potent deterrents than such charges admit. This is especially the case when the self-revelation requires the sustained and reflective activity of writing a manuscript as compared, for example, to the fleeting and unconsidered activity of confessing to a TV or radio doctor. Further, though the end product brings most writers some sense of accomplishment and

---

39. Jamison, *An Unquiet Mind*, 202.
40. Tracy Thompson, *The Beast: A Journey through Depression* (New York: Penguin; Plume, 1995), 11–12.

contribution, it is notable that the writings rarely convey explicitly or implicitly that the writing or the revelation is only restorative. As noted above with Kenyon and her writing of "Having it Out with Melancholy," the writing is often painful, rarely adds insight beyond that already gained by the living of the experience, and is humbling much more often than it is self-congratulatory. Dr. Dan Hanson had earlier written a book about his experience with cancer and found that writing therapeutic, but he did not find such solace in writing about his experience with J and schizophrenia. "One day I write out of feelings of compassion [for J] while the next day all I feel is fear, frustration, and anger."[41]

Arguably the most common criticism of memoir is that its reliance on memory and its partiality radically undermine memoir's reliability and value. In the case of memoirs of soul-suffering, most authors are painfully and personally aware of the limits of their memories and wrestle intentionally with the questions raised thereby. Indeed, for more than a few people who have endured severe psychospiritual suffering, the pain of memory loss is at the center of the work. Playing off the title of one of the most widely admired memoirs of soul-suffering—William Styron's *Darkness Visible*—Susan Alloway calls her essay "Darkness Invisible," precisely because the memory loss she experienced as a result of ECT treatments of her depression and an unexplained blood clot in her brain was at the center of her suffering.[42] While most memoirs of emotional turmoil argue for the validity of their perceptions, it is a rare narrative that claims to be the only truth.

Reflecting on the limits of their own genre, our memoirists wrestle with several other inherent limitations. As a whole, the literature of first-person accounts of soul-suffering contains important gaps in representation of the population of sufferers: there are soul-sufferers who surely have wisdom of value for us all but who, in various ways, are too marginalized to be able to produce their stories. For example, some soul-sufferers are too marginalized socially: working-class, immigrant, homeless, impoverished, or illiterate persons rarely publish memoirs for many reasons, insufficient social capital and leisure chief among them. We will explore further in part 2 why the persons who get their work produced

---

41. Daniel S. Hanson, *Room for J: A Family Struggles with Schizophrenia* (Edina, Minn.: Beaver's Pond Press, 2005), 5.
42. Susan Alloway, "Darkness Invisible," *Pastoral Psychology* vol. 42, no. 2 (1993): 73–79.

tend to be white, middle-class, at least, and well-educated. Also, some are too marginalized by their soul-suffering to produce their stories. For example, people who die by suicide tend never to have been well enough to write memoirs, and so the genre does not represent well those whose illnesses have been fatal. And some people produce accounts of their psychospiritual experience, but they are considered too bizarre to merit publication. J—who is diagnosed with schizophrenia in part because he believes that he is God—has written about his experience. But his writings have been published only because his father included some of them in his own book. After ten years, Dan has come to see much spiritual wisdom in what others dismiss as Joel's psychotic delusions. Dan struggles with the painful invisibility and inequity forced on sufferers like J.

> Some who are diagnosed with severe mental illness learn to adapt to a world where they do not easily fit. They are the success stories we read about in best selling books or watch on movie screens, Hollywood style. But there are a number of people like J who are not able to accept their illness even with medication. . . . We prefer that these misfits be kept away from the rest of us, out of sight and out of mind.[43]

The accounts we will consider do not describe unrelentingly positive trajectories. Though most convey at least modest accomplishment, not utter failure, they are also remarkable for their frank assessment of the author's past failures, present limitations, and future uncertainties. Still, Hanson's point stands. First-person accounts of soul-suffering are rarely published if they do not reflect some norms of rationality and composure.

Some memoirists, too, are concerned that their inability to write from within their most acute experience, or even to capture it in words, means that their memoirs inadequately represent their experience. They recognize that their ability to write about their experience is usually dependent to some degree on progress toward recovery, which, ironically, puts them at some distance from the suffering that is their purpose for writing. Lucy Hulme—wife of William, whom we met earlier, and mother of the pregnant daughter who committed suicide while hospitalized—wrote a memoir with William about his recovery from a suicidal

---

43. Hanson, *Room for J*, 90.

depression. However, she notes at the start of her story that, "Had it had a different outcome, I do not know whether I could or not."[44] Physician David Hilfiker, who suffers from depression, addresses this problem.

> It is, of course, both easy and clean to write all this from a safe emotional distance. The path that we are asked to walk, whether with the mentally ill or with our own mental illness, feels in the experience so much less clean and crisp than what I've written here. It's so much dirtier, so much messier, so much more vague and unclear.[45]

However, even if sufferers could write from within their most excruciating moments, we would still need to remember, as we must with all the memoirs we will consider, that we do not and cannot know another's experience. We can empathize, but we cannot get inside another's skin, cannot walk in their shoes. Our comprehension is empathic only if we know its partiality. In fact, a risk of memoir is that reading a manuscript or watching a documentary may blunt our awareness of the enormous difference between hearing about a life and living it, day in and day out. Joshua Wolf Shenk, who himself has studied a life—Shenk authored an award-winning biography of Abraham Lincoln, focusing on Lincoln's melancholy—puts it succinctly: "these words are too thin to contain a life."[46] When it functions well, our reading of memoir—and our writing of it—makes us both better informed and still humble, tentative, mindful of the gap between the fulsomeness of life and its symbolic representation in word or image. When we misuse memoir, we forget about the difference between our comprehension of part of a person's story and comprehending a whole person. Jamison tells of being asked, when she was an undergraduate, to tutor a UCLA student living with blindness. Over the course of their semester's work together, she tried to learn as much as possible about what his life was like.

---

44. William Hulme and Lucy Hulme, *Wrestling with Depression: A Spiritual Guide to Reclaiming Life* (Minneapolis: Augsburg Books, 1995), 14.

45. David Hilfiker, "When Mental Illness Blocks the Spirit," *The Other Side* (May and June 2002), 15.

46. Joshua Wolf Shenk, "A Melancholy of Mine Own," in *Unholy Ghost*, 250. Shenk is the author of *Lincoln's Melancholy: How Depression Challenged a President and Fueled His Greatness* (Boston: Houghton Mifflin, 2005).

I was very affected by working with him, seeing how difficult it was for him to do the things I so much took for granted. . . . After several months, I had deluded myself that I had at least some notion, however small, of what life was like for him. Then one day he asked me if I would mind meeting him for his tutorial session in the blind reading room of the undergraduate library, rather than in my office.

I tracked down the reading room with some difficulty and started to go in. I stopped suddenly when I realized with horror that the room was almost totally dark. It was dead silent, no lights were on, and yet there were half a dozen students bending over their books or listening to the audiotapes of the professors' lectures that they had recorded. A total chill went down my spine at the eeriness of the scene. My student heard me come in, got up, walked over to the light switch, and turned on the lights for me. It was one of those still, clear moments when you realize that you haven't understood anything at all, that you have no real comprehension of the other person's world.[47]

Noting the problems and limitations of the genre, then, we will treat memoirs of soul-suffering as valuable for the *emotional* truth they convey. Obviously, the memoir is subject, like all our utterances, to the vagaries of memory and the bias of self-reference. Memory is always incomplete, and autobiography is constructed more intentionally and explicitly of the subjectivity that affects all human productions. Though altruistic purposes serve as a principal motivation for the persons telling these stories, and they are notably self-reflective and self-critical, neither do they avoid being self-serving. Arguably, it is impossible for any of us to tell our stories picked clean of personal benefit. Though truth is always relative, it is especially so when we tell our version of events that happened as well to others, who almost certainly would tell the story somewhat differently. Of course, since the reliability of emotional truth depends on integrity in storytelling, in any case where a memoirist deliberately falsifies her story, she has undermined the capacity of the story to contribute to lasting transformation in herself or her readers.

---

47. Jamison, *An Unquiet Mind*, 167–68.

The limitations of reliability imposed by the subjectivity of any narrator are real and must be taken into account methodologically. Finally, however, morality requires us to care as much for idiosyncratic psychic reality and common themes as for verifiable fact. For this reason, first-person accounts cannot be justifiably omitted from research. Rather, in order to take into account the partial nature of the data, we will work according to the principle that analytically considered anecdotal human experience has heuristic value through the revelation of particular and thematic insights that thoughtful readers neither disregard nor universalize. Also, for the purpose of seeking spiritual wisdom, uniqueness and unpredictability in the data cannot be discarded for quite another reason: it might suggest the extraordinary presence of the holy.

Thus, despite their limits, to the degree that we learn from the example of others how to live more meaningfully, memoirs are valuable textbooks. A beloved storyteller observes that "facts bring us to knowledge, but stories lead to wisdom."[48] I embarked on this study not because these narratives are factual but because they are wise. There are many facts in these stories, and we will reflect on some of them. But our focus will not be on the facts—most of which can be found via other sources—but on the spiritual wisdom these memoirs convey but that is not generally emphasized. Wisdom, too, is relative, but it is marked by its capacity to awaken us, challenge us to grow, and give us hope. To the degree that in first-person accounts there is emotional truth that increases our wisdom and motivates us to mature, these testimonies are indeed reliable and worthy of our attention.

---

46. Rachel Naomi Remen, *Kitchen Table Wisdom: Stories That Heal* (New York: Riverhead Books, 1996), xxx.

Studying Memoirs of Soul-Suffering

ersons in emotional pain—let alone those with symptoms of psychiatric illness—are frequently disregarded and usually suspect. Whether in public policy debates about mental health care, classroom sessions on abnormal psychology, therapeutic consultations on particular "cases," theological debates on suffering "faithfully," or the countless popular workshops on attaining spiritual wisdom, the voices of those experiencing most immediately the soul's tumult—and its resilience—are often missing or inadequately regarded. If we do listen to those in psychic turmoil, usually it is because they are celebrities or public figures of some kind—acclaimed novelist William Styron, for example—or because the drudgery of their suffering and healing can be ameliorated by emphasizing their artistry—Zelda Fitzgerald, for example.

Sometimes the emotional distress necessitates the lack of consultation with those in psychospiritual anguish—the primary sufferers may be rendered mute, or without energy to participate in decision making, or with cognition so distorted they cannot make safe assessments of their needs. But too often those in psychospiritual turmoil, and their families, are unnecessarily excluded from discussion and decision making. Among the general public, stereotypes are substituted for talking with and trying to understand real people in pain. Diagnoses and treatments are discussed in the presence of, but not with, the listening sufferer. Even families who provide the bulk of day-to-day care for the primary sufferer may not be informed, much less consulted, when professionals make decisions about their loved one's treatment. Clinicians write case studies instead of studying the writings published by clients. Psychiatrists regularly spend mere minutes with their patients when adjusting medications, even though the prescribing of psychiatric medications is widely admitted to be as much art as science. Sometimes, when we are in such turmoil personally, the soul-suffering and the prejudice against it cause us to silence ourselves.

For these reasons, our focus is on insights about soul-suffering that come from those who communicate from within the experience, rather than on insights of those who write about it from a distance. Because others so often speak for people in emotional distress, because their voices are so often not heard, I have taken great pains to make this book a study only of autobiographical communications by people living with soul-suffering. The only sources used for this project are produced by the affected people themselves—not therapists writing about their patients, not reporters writing about interviewees, not sufferers writing about the experience of others, not researchers reporting on research interviews, not theorists writing in general—only sufferers or their loved ones writing about their own lives. The expertise of those most directly affected merits our undivided attention.

There are thousands of memoirs of soul-suffering, and the numbers continue to grow. More and more, probably due to the synergism between sufferers' growing refusal of marginalization and stigma's gradual decline, memoirs and other first-person materials exploring psychic turmoil are being produced at a rate that defies exhaustive tracking. As I noted earlier, these narratives come in a variety of forms: the majority of sources used as data for this study are printed narratives, though video, poetry, and music lyrics are also included. I am regularly asked if I conducted interviews for this study. It would be valuable to conduct ethnographic research on this topic; early in my research I conducted one very moving interview with a woman whose story was not otherwise available. I discontinued this approach, however, for two reasons. I determined that those who have taken the initiative to make their first-person accounts available have already provided a voluminous amount of material in need of study. Also, a study of already produced materials can be less affected by researcher bias than materials evoked secondary to the researcher's agenda and subject to the vagaries of interviewing conditions.

Given their large and growing number, we are able to touch on only a fraction of the available sources. A few principles have guided my selection of texts for study and reference. I have intentionally sought to build a body of texts in which the authors are as diverse as possible with regard to race, ethnicity, gender, class, and religion. Also, while we will study texts offered by famous people, I have sought to give at least equal weight to the voices of "average" people whose experiences are not already familiar to the public and more likely to be everyday and common. Because mental health standards and treatment are so historically contextualized, I have focused on texts written within the last few decades. Because the diagnoses of schizophrenia, bipolar disorder, and depression are among the most common and most serious psychiatric disorders, most of the memoirs I have chosen for our study describe psychic turmoil from within those experiences. Given our interest in spiritual wisdom, I have chosen some texts because they address spiritual, religious, or theological issues explicitly. Not all our memoirists characterize themselves as religious or their work as having spiritual meaning; we will seek to draw out from their memoirs any spiritual wisdom we might derive from their memoirs, while remaining aware that the authors may not share our views. Within these parameters, my choice of texts has been relatively random.

No work occurs in a vacuum of values, and two biases need to be identified relative to this project. First, this study has an intentional positive bias. Many textual studies have a positive bias—students usually do not spend time studying a text unless they are seeking and expect to find something of value. But the positive bias of this study goes further. The criticism that tends to be part of "objective" analytical studies is intentionally relegated to a minor role. I have chosen this approach because, at this point, the criticism levied against the communications of people in emotional distress still outweighs genuine inquiry into their value, to the extent that a counterweight is merited. My stated goal is to excavate the wisdom in these accounts, which requires analytical readings of the text in order to discern the integrity that marks such wisdom, but makes other aspects of criticism less central. At the same time, it is true and important to acknowledge that even the wisest people can be very difficult to deal with in person. This project is not hagiographical—people in emotional distress are not saints and their views are not unquestionable.

Indeed, some of the authors we will consider recognize and openly admit that they can be very difficult to live with—"high maintenance," as we say. Those relational difficulties are crucial to address, but they are not the subject of this work.

This study also has a personal bias. I mentioned earlier that I have both personal and professional investments in this subject. This double identity—sufferer and caregiver—means that I am at risk of being too prejudiced either to hear or tell any of these stories fairly. It also means that I have twice the investment in speaking truthfully and listening carefully. I work diligently at assuring that the latter outweighs the former. Ruth Sullivan's words, quoted earlier, provide me both standard and caution—my goal is to be both "accurate and kind" in my telling of others' stories, while knowing my words still might "distort, demean, misrepresent, or even hurt the very one(s) [I am] trying to help."

This is a project in pastoral theology. The methods of pastoral theology, which will fundamentally shape our study of the memoirs, will result in an analysis that, in short,

- Holds care to be a core value and the area of its special expertise, seeking always to clarify standards for excellence in care, especially soul-care, and to embody such care
- Studies human experience and relationality as its primary text
- Gives particular attention to a pastoral interpretation of spiritual, theological, and religious claims, whether implicitly or explicitly stated
- Identifies within the human text, in its social as well as personal dimensions, insights relative to meaning, ethics, values, and their implications for care
- Engages in professional and personal actions that increase care socially, interpersonally, and intrapersonally.

This project is an expression of pastoral theology's role in justice work and social change. Its method is quite akin to that undertaken in liberation theology, where theology is written on the basis of listening and helping to give voice to the theological perspectives of those most directly affected by oppression and injustice. It is similar as well to narrative theologies, which attempt to construct theological insight from what can be identified as "true to life" within fiction, or human life stories of any form. Also, I quote at length from these texts because it is my conviction that one role of pastoral theologians is to find ways to assist the suffering to speak for themselves. Enabling these persons to speak to you in a substantial way is one means for me to use what power I have to bring to greater public awareness the pain and courage of socially marginalized communities.

Following these principles, which serve to both amplify and coordinate the disparate voices in these texts, I have sought to identify both common themes and intriguing distinctions that suggest wisdom for all of us relative to soul-suffering and spiritual growth. The autobiographical texts that are our data reveal wisdom constellated around these major themes, each of which serve as the core of the book's remaining sections:

> Part 2: Constructing identity in the face of fear, prejudice, and stigma
>
> Part 3: Naming and analyzing suffering, in the face of assumptions, exaggerations, caricatures, and minimalizations
>
> Part 4: Communicating what kind of care hurts and what kind helps
>
> Part 5: In the absence of a cure, working to heal

The epilogue analyzes insights from parts 2 through 5 in search of spiritual wisdom that might illuminate anguish and liberation for us all.

One final issue: we have already mentioned the fluidity in language used to refer to the experience that is the focus of our study. Hoping to keep our conceptualization of the suffering and the sufferers free of too limiting categorizations, I use a wide variety of terms to refer to those affected, the pain they suffer, and the pathways they carve out in their coping. This is intentional and is in part a strategy to try to break open the pigeon-holes of language that mask the complexity and universality of profound soul-pain. But also, it reflects a stand in the politics of language relative to our subject. Kay Redfield Jamison—who, remember, suffers from and is also an expert on manic-depressive illness (now known as bipolar disorder)—relates that the most vitriolic letter she ever received was from a woman who blasted her for using the word "madness" in the title of a lecture.

I was, she wrote, insensitive and crass and very clearly had no idea at all what it was like to suffer from something as awful as manic-depressive illness. I was just one more doctor who was climbing my way up the academic ranks by walking over the bodies of the mentally ill.[49]

The letter-writer—in both the content and strength of her opinion—represents a controversy about how to speak of emotional experience, given the stigma against "mental illness." Some advocates are adamant that any language that is antiquated or that has been used disrespectfully—mad, crazy, mental, loony, and the like—be banned from use. These activists are trying to reform the ways we think by reforming the ways we talk: for example, the term "mental" illness is in declining use, in favor of "psychiatric disorders," "brain disorders" or, even, "no-fault brain disorders."

Other advocates wrestling with the issue of stigma agree that it is important to deal with the ignorance and hurt that language can perpetuate. But they also argue that we must protect the right of sufferers to speak of their experience as they see fit. Some sufferers, like Jamison, find some of the debatable language truthful and some of the new and improved language no improvement. For example, about the updated nomenclature for her own illness, Jamison says, interestingly, that

as a person and patient, . . . I find the word "bipolar" strangely and powerfully offensive: it seems to me to obscure and minimize the illness it is supposed to represent. The description "manic-depressive," on the other hand, seems to capture both the nature and the seriousness of the disease I have, rather than attempting to paper over the reality of the condition.[50]

These activists argue that the destigmatization of mental illness—or, we can add, any emotional experience outside the status quo—will require much more aggressive and wide-ranging efforts than change of language—efforts like successful treatment, advocacy, and legislation.[51] I agree, and I also think that destigmatization is furthered by showing the

---

49. Jamison, *An Unquiet Mind*, 179.
50. Jamison, *An Unquiet Mind*, 181–82.
51. Jamison, *An Unquiet Mind*, 183.

variety of ways people most directly affected by the stigma use language to speak of their experience and their stigmatization. This book materializes the position on "correct" language taken by Stewart Govig who, as the father of a son diagnosed with schizophrenia, experiences with little relief the harshness of the suffering and the stigma: "Ignoring social reality is a hollow answer to social rejection. To assault prejudice, I prefer another strategy: let people who know tell what it is like."[52]

Through the memoirs we will be studying, soul-sufferers *will* tell it like it is, and it will often be hard to bear. Reading the first half of this book, especially, might be draining, because we will be persistently focused on trying to grasp the varieties of suffering involved and the limitations of the care they receive. But we can be heartened by one of the things soul-sufferers insist upon when they tell us like it is: "we are more than our suffering," they remind us, and they ask us to relate to them as whole people who—just like us—laugh, work, love, play, give service, and seek meaning. So, we start by bearing the suffering, just as they must. But midway, our study will turn to the power of caregiving not only to bind wounds but also to create hope and joy. We will explore inspiring stories of people who refuse to be captive to suffering and instead construct meaning, recovery, and healing for their lives.

This book represents my effort to bring a discerning eye to madness—as Emily Dickinson put it—in order to show that wisdom and other things of value can be found in the midst of psychospiritual turmoil and illness. I do not make this claim naïvely or exclusively. Psychiatric illnesses or other forms of psychic turmoil are always difficult and too often devastating. I know this first-hand—from my own emotional suffering, from the devastating soul-sicknesses of my loved ones, and from years of pastoral-clinical work alongside persons seeking care and healing for their aching souls. I am not saying there is divinest sense in all madness: some madness is so destructive that it is senseless. I am not saying that where there is divinest sense, there is no madness: divinest sense and madness can co-exist, exemplifying the ambiguity and multiplicity of

---

52. Stewart D. Govig, *Strong at the Broken Places: Persons with Disabilities and the Church* (Louisville: Westminster John Knox Press, 1989), 2.

sacredness. I am saying, however, that there is in *some* madness *some* divinest sense. This is providential. Precisely because of the hardship it brings, those of us who try to cope with the madness within and beyond ourselves need desperately to avail ourselves of any holiness in it.

Parker Palmer has commented that "when suffering becomes intense, we are forced to examine the deeper dimensions of our condition and to consider sources of insight that may have seemed uncouth when we and our world were humming with power and success."[53] The stories that follow are sometimes uncouth, but they resonate with integrity and have much to teach us about navigating the mysteries of life, especially when power and success fail to shield us and our world from heartache.

---

53. Parker J. Palmer, *To Know as We Are Known: Education as a Spiritual Journey* (San Francisco: HarperSanFrancisco, 1983), x.

PART TWO

IDENTITY

Look at us.

Look hard.

We're not who you thought we were.

And we're everywhere.

> **— Lizzie Simon**
> **Detour: My Bipolar**
> **Road Trip in 4-D**

Real healing comes from realizing that
your own particular pain is a share in
humanity's pain.

> **— Henri J. M. Nouwen**
> **The Inner Voice of Love**

IN THE SPRING OF 1996, a frightened woman wandered the streets of Los Angeles, telling people that she was the target of a conspiracy. Her hair hacked off and wearing worn and dirty clothes, she appeared to be just one more homeless person. She came to public attention only because a resident of an L.A. suburb called police to report someone sleeping in a leaf pile on her property, and reporters learned that the woman was the actor Margot Kidder, suffering an acute episode of bipolar disorder. The media exploded with stories about the incident, her illness, and the tantalizing drama of a film star gone mad. Best known, ironically, for having played Lois Lane to Christopher Reeves' secret Superman, and unwilling to let the media dictate her identity, Kidder started to tell her own story. While continuing her acting career, she now speaks publicly about her illness and its stabilization, has become a spokesperson for public education about bipolar disorder, and, importantly, portrays herself as more than her illness. In so doing, her identity is shaped not simply by what others say about her but by what she says about herself.

Many persons living in emotional pain are voluntarily taking the step that Kidder had to take under duress. In the autobiographical accounts that are the focus of our attention, persons who live with emotional illnesses and other kinds of soul-suffering participate in the shaping of their identity—and the identity of the class of persons designated "crazy." By claiming their voices and conveying their version of their experience, their first-person accounts vie with stereotypes and reach across social barriers separating those deemed sane and those deemed insane. In part 2, we will examine who it is that writes memoirs of soul-suffering. What are the overall life circumstances of these memoirists? What are their personal and social locations? In part 3 we will narrow our focus to their suffering, in its most personal and psychospiritual manifestations. We begin, however, with a wider-ranging and more representative angle of vision of their suffering, but also of their personhood.

Significantly, our inquiry into the life locations of these memoirists will not take us far from our own. A persistent theme in the memoirs is that, on the one hand, their lives are quite average, not unlike yours and mine. On the other hand, they are sickened, at least in part, by circumstances that are sickening us all, or could, or should. It is a fortunate few humans, indeed, who are never touched by tragedy and violence. As we noted in part 1, the quantitative difference between acute and common soul-suffering must not be overlooked. But to different degrees, we are all soul-sufferers, or most of us are. From this perspective, the material in this part of the book promises to illuminate us all, call us to a more holistic view of psychic turmoil, and testify to pain that we share, amid our differences. We met Jyl Felman in part 1, a Jewish woman who suffers from depression and has written a meditation on the mixed blessing that the antidepressant Prozac is for her. She sees the kinship in many passing faces:

> I feel like handing out white and green [Prozac] capsules to everyone I meet on the street. It's in their eyes: all that accumulated grief. How do we, as human beings, coalesce against the torrents of our fear?[1]

Thus, we will shortly reflect on these memoirists' social locations, psychosocial contexts in the United States that commonly are at play in the lives of persons in acute psychospiritual distress and that have the capacity to bring any of us low. We will begin, though, locally and personally. We noted in part 1 that persons driven to produce these narratives are often motivated by a commitment to help others by illuminating an illness or other kind of anguish, and paths of recovery, if they find any. But in their memoirs many also seek to convey that their lives are much more than the pain and labels that so often function to circumscribe their lives. Not satisfied with being characterized by others or with being told by others how to understand themselves, they are telling us, in their own words, who they are. They do this to remind themselves, to chip away at our stereotypes of them and, should any readers be feeling overshadowed by soul-suffering, to testify that the shadow is just that, shadow and not self.

---

1. Jyl Lynn Felman, "Nurturing the Soul," *Tikkun* vol. 11, no. 4 (July–August 1996): 51.

Personal Contexts, Particular Suffering

I am a Jewish lesbian vegetarian chicken writer; attorney at law, performance artist, silky smooth dancer, high femme, soft butch, adjunct gender-bender Brandeis professor, racquetball player, *vilde chaye* wild beast, grilled salmon lover, portobello mushroom gorger; loving friend, would-be rabbi, cultural worker, post modern Zionist, deconstruction activist, five-mile-a-day jogger, U Conn women's basketball *aficionado*, French food connoisseur; Scrabble fanatic, budding Rollerblader; hot bath soaker, snorkeler supreme, and coalition-builder between Blacks and whites; Jews and Gentiles; gays and straights; men and women; nuclear families and non.

I am unsolidly middle class, upwardly mobile, highly educated, politically astute, and intellectually gifted. And I have been severely depressed, hospitalized, aspirin overdosed, stomach excruciatingly pumped, and therapized since my Bat Mitzvah in Dayton, Ohio, thirty years ago.[2]

People are far more than their suffering. Not all people who have known psychic distress could or would want to describe their lives as colorfully as does Jyl Felman. But the complexity and humor of her self-portrait ought to warn us that stereotypes we might have about people who suffer disabling episodes of emotional turmoil are likely to be laughably naïve. Even when their suffering is severe and chronic, people in psychic distress are multifaceted, sometimes more

2. Felman, "Nurturing the Soul," 50.

than even they can comprehend, especially when in the grip of a crisis. Persons who write memoirs of soul-suffering are so diverse as to defy any sweeping generalizations.

This diversity is due in part to the sheer numbers of persons who live with some kind of psychic suffering. As previously mentioned, the literature of memoirs written by persons about psychiatric illness and other forms of psychic anguish is enormous and still growing. Though the current popularity of the genre of memoirs brings public attention to a few, those are but the tip of the proverbial iceberg. Similarly, the vast majority of soul-sufferers is invisible to us and may thus seem few in number. It may appear that persons in severe psychic distress are rare, or in the minority, but such appearances betray reality. Our practices of stereotyping and marginalization make it difficult for us to see all the sufferers in their diversity, or sufferers may choose to hide themselves out of fear of stigma. However, the statistics provided in part 1 make clear that their numbers are staggering, approximately 44.3 million people, at any given time, and this counts only those with a condition diagnosable within psychiatric categories.[3] One reason the personal contexts of soul-sufferers differ so significantly is simply that there are so many.

This diversity also results from the spiritually significant reality that psychic turmoil, especially in the form of psychiatric illness, occurs with remarkable impartiality. Suffering may feel unfair, but *"mental illness does not discriminate."* This sentence, or one like it, is found in the majority of first-person accounts of emotional suffering. *People* discriminate and try thereby to separate themselves from soul-suffering, especially those illnesses recognized as "mental," but psychic turmoil is found in every context, country, community, class, and clan. Disabling psychospiritual suffering transcends culture. Nothing in the circumstances of our lives is failsafe protection from this kind of suffering—not education, wealth, physical health, religion, therapy, or any other mechanism of human self-improvement. People in acute psychiatric turmoil are found in all walks of life: all income levels, disciplined and undisciplined, socially powerful and socially marginalized, professional and working class, religious and nonreligious. Emotional suffering strikes every age

---

3. National Institute of Mental Health, "The Numbers Count: Mental Disorders in America," http://www.nimh.nih.gov/publicat/numbers.cfm (accessed Dec. 20, 2005).

group, persons of every ethnicity, nationality, and language, and with no regard for our relational and family status or sexual orientation. Psychiatric illness happens to infamous people and to famous people.[4] But mostly it happens to everyday people like you and me. Paradoxically, then, soul-sufferers are both unique and average.

UNDERREPRESENTED DIVERSITY

It is expectable that the memoirs we will study can represent the diversity of sufferers only to a limited degree. However, it is important to note three particular limits that stand out. First, lesbian, gay, bisexual, and transgendered people tend not to write about their experiences with psychiatric disorders, probably because they still have not fully escaped from being labeled mentally ill simply because of their sexual or gender identity; our sample of memoirs does not adequately represent their experience. Second, only English-language research materials are used in this study, and most of those texts are written by persons living in the United States; international and multilingual perspectives on the issues we are considering are a valuable area for further research. Third, diversity in race and ethnicity is barely represented in the memoirs. Meri Danquah's memoir provides a rare exception to that absence. A Ghanaian immigrant, she discovered this problem when she sought the voices of other blacks engaged, as she was, in a struggle with depression.

> At first, I had a hard time figuring out why there were no glossy magazine articles or literary books about depression by black people. . . . Surely there were other black women suffering from depression, questioning their sanity, searching for an affirmation, if not an answer. Why were they not coming forward or writing about it like their white counterparts?[5]

---

4. In the effort to fight stigma, lists of respected public figures rumored or known to have suffered emotional illness are made widely available. See, for example: Stamp Out Stigma, "Famous People with Mental Illness," http://www.stampoutstigma.org/famous.html (accessed March 22, 2006); National Alliance on Mental Illness, "People with Mental Illness Enrich Our Lives," http://www.nami.org/Template.cfm?Section=Helpline1&template=/ContentManagement/ContentDisplay.cfm&ContentID=4858; http://www.schizophrenia.com/family/Famous.html (accessed March 22, 2006).
5. Meri Nana-Ama Danquah, "Writing the Wrongs of Identity," in *Unholy Ghost: Writers on Depression*, ed. Nell Casey (New York: Harper Perennial, 2002), 175.

There are critical sociocultural reasons for the dominance of European American voices in this genre, and we will reflect on those in the next section. Here it is important to add that in addition to a few persons of African descent, I located autobiographical work by persons of Taiwanese and Chinese descent.

Doubtless there is ethnic diversity among the European American memoirists but, as is common with white writers, most reflect very little on the significance of their race or ethnicity. We will encounter a comment or two about how the particularities of Anglo-Saxon Protestantism appear to produce a particular synergism of restrained affect, reserved relationship, and disdainful attitudes toward soul-suffering. Otherwise, historian Sharon O'Brien's exploration of the relationship between her depression and her Irish Catholic heritage provides a remarkable, though singular, exception. When O'Brien's depression "did not disappear as the Prozac ads promised" but proved to be treatment-resistant, and she began to reflect on the prevalence of depression in her family, the question of the family's history and culture came to the fore. Her research illuminated many things, including the familial and cultural history embedded in the event to which Sharon traced her depression: her mother throwing Sharon's sister Maureen out of the family for getting married rather than going to graduate school. First, Sharon learned that her mother had been traumatized when her mother's sister was thrown out of the family for getting married. Then, she realized the larger meaning.

> "Eviction is in the racial memory of the Irish," an Irish friend once told me. "In every family there's a forgotten image of furniture and belongings in the street, right outside the house they couldn't enter anymore." Even safe in America, far away from the British landlords who evicted starving tenants in the nineteenth century, my family has passed along homelessness and abandonment as part of its legacy. . . . .
>
> Given that my Irish ancestors lost their homes because of poverty and starvation and oppression, not individual choice, I find it absurdly sad that my mother and her family could choose to abandon any of their kin. I've always remembered the line from "The Death of the Hired Man," "Home is the place where,

when you have to go there, / They have to take you in," and I've wanted to say back to Robert Frost, *haven't you known any Irish?*[6]

Even this one example demonstrates the crucial role played by cultural history in both our experience and understanding of soul-suffering.

DEMOGRAPHIC DIVERSITY

Our memoirists *are* diverse in other ways. Though the majority of the authors appear to be middle-class at the time of their writing, they have traveled diverse paths to whatever economic security they have. Some of our authors have known wealth, but many more have lived in poverty or cope with ongoing economic vulnerability, in part because insurance provides so little coverage for mental health care. Also, though the majority of our authors are well-educated, there is significant diversity of personal and social location within that broad generalization. Education is neither protection from the many ways soul-suffering can devastate a life, nor any substantial advantage in efforts to heal: as we have already seen, among the primary sufferers and their families we will find literary notables, mental health professionals, religious leaders, educators, and persons from many other walks of working life. Our authors are also diverse in terms of age, relational status, and sexual identity.

Of special relevance to our interest in the spiritual wisdom of these narratives, the collection of memoirs represents a variety of perspectives relative to religion and spirituality. A few do not reference religion or spirituality at all. In those texts where authors identify themselves as religious, the majority is affiliated with Christianity, though we will be studying the memoirs of a few persons who identify themselves as Jewish. Within the numerous accounts that reference Christianity, a range of perspectives from traditional to progressive are represented. Some of our memoirists are active religiously. Others, though apparently inactive, reference their religious upbringing or use religious concepts and language, primarily from Judaism, Christianity, and Buddhism. Not infrequently, our authors are alienated from institutional religion, in

---

6. Sharon O'Brien, *The Family Silver: A Memoir of Depression and Inheritance* (Chicago: University of Chicago Press, 2004), 35.

some cases because their soul-suffering was caused or worsened by religious persons or teachings. Still others are interested in spiritual issues and practices that, for them, are not connected to institutional religion.

DIVERSITY IN SUFFERING AND HEALING

Just as important as the demographic categories we normally associate with diversity are diversities of personal location relative to suffering and healing. First, the personal context of soul-suffering includes not only those we have been calling the primary sufferers, the persons initially affected, but all the lives that person touches. Most immediately and profoundly touched, of course, are loved ones—most memoirs are written by parents, siblings, partners, or children of the primary sufferer; yet, cousins, grandparents, aunts, uncles, and friends are significantly affected, too. The primary sufferer and loved ones affect, and are affected by, friends and neighbors, people at school or work, relationships through social or religious groups. Because soul-suffering puts enormous strain on relational dynamics, a few sufferers have few personal connections—maybe one or two stalwart family members, maybe one or two friends, maybe none of these.

There is also diversity in coping among the primary sufferers and their loved ones. Some families, from the moment an illness emerges, keep the ill one at arm's length or refuse to relate at all. These families, obviously, do not write memoirs about their experiences. Some families try to stay together but are torn apart—even families that had been strong. Kay Redfield Jamison, for example, writes tenderly of her first husband: their marriage did not survive her illness, though their appreciation for each other did. Most families do endure, but take differing amounts of time and space in order to cope with the often-excruciating struggle. Dan and Sue Hanson, for example, write movingly of their love for J and of their exhaustion from trying to cope with his refusal of treatment. In their memoir they share with other families what they do to get an occasional break from the strain. This is especially crucial in those families where, because of genetics, shared social conditions, or simple chance, there is more than one person in a family with a serious emotional disability. Whatever their particular reaction, however, the experiences of loved ones who try to stay close to the suffering at some point seem to bear out Dan Hanson's characterization:

Mental illness is a family affair.... The illness impacts each member of the family in one way or another. We can try to run away from it, and believe me, we all have at times. But we cannot hide from it....

When one part is broken, the rest of the family doesn't work well. Our world is not the same anymore....

I suspect that it is this way for most families that deal with illness. When one person is ill, we are all ill. It is a family illness, yet it is unique to each member of the family.[7]

Ultimately, the most influential diversity lies in the kind of soul-suffering at issue and, if they seek it, the quality of care the sufferers receive. As noted in part 1, soul-suffering that yields spiritual wisdom is not limited to those with diagnosable or diagnosed psychiatric disorders. However, among those whose soul-suffering does arguably fit those criteria—which is the case for the majority of our memoirists—it matters enormously what kind of illness and care are experienced. In parts 3 and 4, we will explore in detail the soul-suffering experienced relative to the emergence of illness and the seeking of care. Here it will suffice to sketch a picture of three typical situations that characterize the diverse personal contexts of our memoirists.

Denial of Illness, Refusal of Care

Psychiatric illnesses are now frequently referred to as brain disorders for good reason: these brain disorders tend to inhibit insight, rational thinking, or both. In many cases, to have a psychiatric illness is to be unable easily to understand that you have a psychiatric illness. The memoirists we are considering have been diagnosed with a variety of psychiatric disorders, but the majority have experience related to one of three diagnostic categories—major depression, bipolar disorder, and schizophrenia—all of which, at least when untreated, interfere with rational thought and insight. Thus, one typical situation is that the primary sufferer disputes that he or she is ill and refuses to seek professional treatment or other care. In this situation, the primary sufferers and their loved ones are often in tension. Relationships are stressed to the breaking point as families wait for the primary sufferer to develop insight and openness to

---

7. Daniel S. Hanson, *Room for J: A Family Struggles with Schizophrenia* (Edina, Minn.: Beaver's Pond Press, 2005), 57.

treatment. In some cases, insight and openness never come. Without professionals involved, families typically make significant sacrifices to be caregivers, even as the illnesses leave the primary sufferer indifferent or even threatening to loved ones. If a person with a psychiatric condition does come to see his or her suffering as an illness in need of treatment—always a hard-won understanding—more challenge immediately looms: accept not only that you have an illness, but that you have an illness that is stigmatized, and for which there is no cure or even surefire treatment.

As we will see, this is very much the situation in which the Hansons find themselves. J Hanson has the symptoms of what psychiatry calls schizophrenia, in part because of J's belief that he is God, which the doctors assess as delusional. J disputes that this belief is delusional, but neither does he exercise sufficient judgment to keep himself out of life-threatening situations. (For example, he goes outside without warm clothing during Minnesota's winter weather.) Sue Hanson perceives that J refuses the diagnosis and treatment in part because he knows it to be a stigmatized illness. Because J won't seek the help of professionals, Dan and Sue Hanson must keep watch over J's safety. They try to respect J's right to choose, until he puts his life at risk. Then they have him involuntarily hospitalized and medicated. This act of care causes alienation between them and their son. When under medication his judgment returns and he can be safely discharged, the cycle starts again.

Acknowledgment of Illness, Disillusionment with Treatment

A second common situation that shapes a distinctive personal context emerges when primary sufferers acknowledge that they have an illness and go in search of treatment. Finding professionals who can provide effective care eases the pain of the primary sufferer and eases the burden on loved ones. However, it is not uncommon for it to take *years* to find effective treatment and, once found, for treatment to provide only limited relief. In parts 3 and 4 we will detail problems encountered in mental health care and how they sometimes worsen the suffering. Here it is sufficient to say that when families and the primary sufferers make the decision to seek help, they typically think, like the general public, that medications and other treatments are increasingly available and effective. Instead, what most families find is that the mental health system and its treatments are complicated at the least, harmful for some, and in the best circumstances are only slowly tailored to each family's need. Dedicated professionals do their best, most families and primary sufferers get some help, and their relationships may be less tense as a result. But for most, the realization slowly dawns that recovery, if it is found, is a lifelong effort for most primary sufferers and their closest family members. Mental health treatment is in its infancy, the system of resources is not sufficient to meet needs, and care is offered only to a limited extent through most insurance policies. They cannot simply submit themselves to care, as is usually sufficient when seeking treatment for a medical condition. Rather, the families—and the primary sufferers, if able—often must become coaches, sleuths, advocates, and critics on their own behalf.

These practices do eventually pay off for many families and primary sufferers, and they find some form of recovery or at least a significantly improved means of coping with ongoing illness. Psychologist Martha Manning's situation illustrates this context. She sought treatment fairly promptly, but then she, her husband, and her teenage daughter endured months in which Manning tried different medications, only to find that none adequately treated her depression. Accepting ECT as her last resort, she finally found relief, though not a cure.

> Each time I feel myself slowing down, losing vitality and strength, I am terrified that I will be drawn like a magnet back down those dark stairs and long halls to that awful time and place and self. I am still having smaller depressions that typically respond to simple alterations in medication. I have good days and bad days.[8]

Resistance to the System; Activism for Reform

Mental health treatment alienates, betrays, and fails many more people than the public realizes. So a smaller but significant number of families and primary sufferers exist in a third kind of situation and personal context, in which their relationship to the mental health system is largely one of different degrees and kinds of resistance and/or critique. As noted previously, some primary sufferers start and stay here: they never agree with the psychiatric system's view of sickness and health, and they never submit themselves for treatment. After disillusionment or even mistreatment by the mental health system, other primary sufferers and their loved ones

---

8. Martha Manning, *Undercurrents: A Therapist's Reckoning with Her Own Depression* (San Francisco: HarperSanFrancisco, 1994), 183.

may stay involved but consistently voice criticism and seek alternatives. Disillusionment and mistreatment fire up a remarkable number of primary sufferers and their families to become vociferous critics, not only for themselves, but for others. This position may soften later, if help is ever found; they may return to being proactive and wary consumers, though the system rarely again has these consumers' trust. Still others are activists for reform, arguing for and in some cases offering a different way of conceptualizing and treating psychic turmoil. Some of these activists, interestingly, are psychiatrists who decry the easy and extensive prescription of drugs—the "alternative psychiatry movement" has, for example, shown success in treating first episodes of schizophrenia with intensive residential programs along with or even instead of drugs.

Before her death in 2001, Rae Unzicker epitomized persons in this context. An internationally recognized civil rights advocate for persons with psychiatric disabilities, she was appointed by President Clinton to the National Council on Disability. Her insights were born from decades of seeking treatment and receiving the worst the mental health system has to offer. Her friend, Pat, told her about some graffiti she had seen on the wall at a state psychiatric facility, which she relates and builds on.

> "You can run to the bridge and count the bodies floating under it, OR, you can go to the bank and pull out those you can reach (at some peril to yourself) OR you can go upstream and stop the person throwing them in."
>
> As a caring society, we must stop throwing people into the mental health system, to drown in the murky waters of drugs, labels, and hopelessness. It should be the primary objective of the system to put itself out of business, and we should never settle for less. To support programs that promote chronicity is unconscionable. To support real people with real problems, one at a time, is the very least we can do.[9]

That these three contexts are fluid is reflected in memoirists' choices of self-designation relative to their suffering and the care they receive.

---

9. Rae Unzicker, "On My Own: A Personal Journey through Madness and Re-Emergence," *Psychosocial Rehabilitation Journal* vol. 13, no. 1 (July 1989): 76.

Sometimes sufferers call themselves "patients"—when they judge themselves to be ill, acknowledge or even accept the diagnosis given to their illness, when they have a paradoxically hopeful resignation relative to treatment, and when they are inclined to defer to mental health professionals. Other times persons dealing with psychic distress refer to themselves as "clients" or "consumers (of mental health services)"—especially when they are emphasizing their agency relative to diagnosis and treatment. "Clients" and "consumers"—and families of primary sufferers also sometimes claim this designation—tend to educate themselves about their options, formulate their experience according to their own opinions, question their caregivers, and exercise judicious choice with regard to any decisions that need to be made. At still other times, in protest, sufferers and their loved ones call themselves "psychiatric survivors"—survivors of psychiatric illness and/or survivors of psychiatric treatment. Many "survivors" are resisting the position of victim often conferred by serious illness. But some name themselves "psychiatric survivors" in order to protest the whole mental health paradigm. These persons tend not to feel that they are ill, yet most of them have been labeled with diagnoses and forced into treatments they deplore. For them the designation "survivor" signals that they have survived traumas imposed by the mental health system.[10]

Most persons coping with psychic distress come to know all these positions. At least at the start, most persons avoid pathologizing their own emotional suffering or that of a loved one for as long as they can, determined to be "survivors" of pain and hardship by their own will and effort. For many, a day comes when—not infrequently because the suffering has become life-threatening—they become "patients," dependent on someone else's ability to provide access to the mental health care that they can only hope will provide some safety and relief. But another day, when the mental health system fails them—and it almost always does, because of its underdeveloped and difficult-to-access condition—they must become advocates for themselves. Even if they are still patients, to be patient with the mental health system is too often to lose ground, and so they or their loved ones must find the strength to start acting like "clients" and "consumers" in search of needed services. Finally, for too many, their search for help in the mental health system is thwarted, and the search itself be-

---

10. I use all these ways of naming; when referring to a particular person, I try to use whatever nomenclature they choose for themselves.

comes something they survive or, after too many lost rounds, something to which they succumb. After their son J's first episode of psychosis in 1995, Dan and Sue Hanson struggled to find appropriate care for J and, by extension, for themselves. During that time, it was terrifying to see human examples of the downward spiral that results for too many.

> Many people who are diagnosed with a severe mental illness struggle to live in a world that refuses to accept them. For a while their families try to care for them. But eventually their behavior wears down even those who love them. They end up in a system that recycles them from psychiatric wards to county or state hospitals to group homes to halfway houses to subsidized housing, only to spiral through it all once again. This scenario goes on until they finally learn to live in society or surrender to "those who know better." We have watched worn-out and defeated victims of the system sitting in the lounges of psychiatric wards and group homes, smoking cigarettes, vacantly watching television. When they no longer find refuge in the system, some of them end up on the streets or locked tight in a prison cell. Many don't survive.[11]

Dan Hanson's terse summary makes plain another point common to almost every first-person account: while personal circumstances of soul-sufferers matter enormously, what matters at least as much are troubling existential realities and social dynamics that emerge starkly in relation to soul-suffering. The personal contexts of soul-suffering make clear that persons dealing with emotional turmoil are not monolithic in their experience or opinions. But they all agree that psychic turmoil has "external" aspects as well as "internal" ones. Their personal soul-sickness is inextricably linked to existential circumstances, sociocultural values, and historical contexts. Mental illness is a family affair, but it has for too long been seen, misleadingly, as a private matter. Instead, psychiatric disorder and other forms of psychic turmoil are a communal affair. In the next section, we will first explore some broad dynamics of communal psychic turmoil. Then we will turn to three specific aspects of our collective sicknesses and suffering that our memoirs suggest are insufficiently understood to be inextricably linked with personal psychic turmoil: relational and existential violences, social "progress," and bigotry.

---

11. Hanson, *Room for J*, 2–3.

SOCIAL SICKNESSES, COLLECTIVE SUFFERING

"Surely oppression drives the wise into madness." (Eccl. 7:7a, ESV)

E
very time I opened the front door, the world was warped." The camera shows Karen Wong, dark hair and eyes defining her against the white sofa on which she sits and the red-hued painting behind her, telling her story in staccato-like bursts. The double entendre in her statement would be lost on many of us who, if we took note of her at all, would likely privatize her statement and assume that delusions warped her world. Heard in its entirety, however, Karen's narrative conveys as much or more the other meaning of the statement—every time she ventured outside her home she found that the world was *actually* sick. Racism from her elementary schoolmates and their mothers because of her Chinese heritage, police suppression of demonstrations in support of China during her college years, expulsion from her community when her psychiatric illness struck in early adulthood—the world she found outside her home was no less distorted than her inner world. Ultimately, she lost her life to sickness beyond herself; a short time after making her story of suffering and healing available on film, an intruder broke into her apartment and murdered her.[12]

---

12. Allie Light and Irving Saraf, prod., Allie Light, dir., *Dialogues with Madwomen*, 90 mins, 1993. Interview with Karen Wong.

Observers see people in emotional turmoil primarily as abnormal individuals. But many of the sufferers know themselves first and foremost contextually, as persons caught in conditions that are sick or at least sickness-inducing—the "precipitants" every competent mental health professional is trained to ask about. Even in those circumstances where a person can be said to have a psychiatric disorder caused by chemical or structural irregularities in the brain, these seemingly personal conditions are predispositions provoked into illness, usually by contextual conditions. Persons in turmoil are overcome by existential and sociocultural realities as much as, or more than, by their personal character, emotions, brain functioning, or illnesses. Their stories are accounts of life in shared, public realities just as much as they are accounts of private life. Memoirs of soul-suffering confront us with disordered social values as much as they illuminate disordered inner lives.

CULTURAL CONDITIONS

When our memoirists are deemed ill, it is according to values that are seldom universal or objective. Definitions of illness and wellness are constructed—and regularly reconstructed—within cultural value systems that are subjective, contextual, fluid, and temporal. Temperament and behaviors prized in one cultural context are avoided or even pathologized in another. For example, in most westernized contexts, a person who does not make immediate and sustained eye contact when greeting others is quite quickly assessed to be psychologically and socially underdeveloped. In many other cultural contexts, lowered eyes convey respect for others, mature humility, and appropriate social deference. Similarly, in some cultures we are considered healthy if we seem autonomous and productive, in other cultures these qualities are assessed to be shallow and antisocial.

Not all social expectations are disordered, of course, even when they prove overwhelming to persons made already vulnerable by soul-suffering. Emotional suffering may be worsened by relatively benign cultural rules and expectations; for example, psychic turmoil may render a person unable to conform to nuanced social expectations about emotion and behavior. *New York Times* television critic Virginia Heffernan describes this dimension of social repression: "I had betrayed something by getting depressed—whatever informal government supervises the tone of interactions in offices and social life, the one that frowns on euphoria but also mandates a measure of happiness."[13]

But social expectations that are benignly constraining in some situations and for some people can become malignant cultural conditions in other situations, and are enforced on some people through social domination. Many of the memoirists find that the definition and burden of their "illness"—and the likelihood of recovery—is significantly shaped by questionable collective values held by the so-called "healthy"—fear of difference, desire to control others, effort to protect a status quo that serves questionable values. Our memoirists are deemed ill by "healthy" and socially powerful subjects who have articulated culture-specific standards of mental health—relatively arbitrary standards of "appropriate" personality, temperament, behavior, attitude, and productivity—and have the power to impose them. Reflecting on her six-month hospitalization in her teenage years, author Nancy Mairs came to see herself as "a cultural prisoner"—in her case, 1960s gender politics formed the standard of health against which her illness was articulated.

> I do not believe that I was not "sick" at the time I was locked up.
> . . . I was sick, all right, but what I see now is that sickness forms
> only in relation to some standard of health which does not exist
> of itself in some fictional objective other world but which is cre-
> ated from the observations, responses, values, and beliefs of those
> "healthy" subjects who seek to articulate it.[14]

Imprisoning cultural conditions increase risk of death. Realizing she was in danger, Tracy Thompson—at the time a staff writer for the *Washington Post*—says

> I dreamed of confessing to someone, anyone, that I was getting
> preoccupied with thoughts of suicide. . . .
> In real life, though, confession was unthinkable. . . . In white
> Southern culture, women held their emotions in check. Intensity
> of feeling could get you labeled crazy, like the pathetic Blanche
> DuBois—even though the constant effort to suppress emotion

---

13. Virginia Heffernan, "A Delicious Placebo," in *Unholy Ghost*, 11.

14. Nancy Mairs, *Plaintext: Essays by Nancy Mairs* (Tucson: University of Arizona Press, 1986), 140–41.

gave many Southern women that shrill, slightly hysterical tone which was the basis of the ditsy Southern belle caricature.[15]

Gender politics reveal sick or sickness-inducing cultural conditions, as do racial politics. Ethnic-racial differences in standards of illness and wellness, and the capacity of the white majority to enforce its standards on others, go a long way toward explaining why our memoirs are not very representative of the racial-ethnic diversity in the United States. Emotional transparency is a mark of emotional health in many European American cultural contexts, and revealing one's personal and familial pain is becoming increasingly acceptable—even fashionable, in some circles. But more politically significant, such self-revelation is a reasonable social risk for European Americans, because white skin offsets the stigma against mental illness. In nondominant racial-ethnic cultures, such revelation of personal and familial pain is less often seen as a sign of maturity. But the political ramifications are at least as important: given the stigma associated with emotional illness and the vulnerability created by emotional expression, psychospiritual revelation poses too great a risk to families and groups already affected by racism and other forms of bigotry and marginalization.

In a similar way, emotional politics figure in the cultural conditions that define and shape psychospiritual illness and health. In the experience of many of our memoirists, cultural standards of illness and health serve the needs of the "healthy" to distance themselves from people who embody emotional difference, vulnerability, and need. Resistance to some emotions and behaviors arises not because there is anything inherently dangerous about them, but simply because there is no social space for unexpected patterns of behavior, and because such unpredictability is a frightening reminder that all of us are vulnerable and need the support of others to survive. As Dan Hanson puts it, "By labeling them ['mentally ill'], we excuse ourselves from their world . . . [and] keep them from disrupting our well ordered and 'in control' world"[16]—though disruption is never fully held at bay, of course. More than one memoirist notes that the illness would be less hard on all of us if social life were more spacious and

---

15. Tracy Thompson, *The Beast: A Journey through Depression* (New York: Penguin; Plume, 1995), 49.
16. Hanson, *Room for J*, 100.

not so dominated by the majority's fear of its own susceptibility. This sensibility is so strong for Dan Hanson that he chose for the title of his memoir the poignant desire that there be room for J. Dan Hanson feels it is a betrayal of his son, but he presses J to take medication—despite J's protests and the terrible side effects. Dan does this because without it, J believes himself to be God, and there is no room in most societies for anyone who asserts such a thing.

> I hate forcing J to take his medication. If only there were a better way. I wish there were a place were J could go and just be who he believes himself to be—a safe place where he could be manic for awhile and preach his messages if he wants to. Maybe if we lived in a faraway tribal community things could be different. It wouldn't matter if J were a shaman, a prophet, or a clown. But I know of no village like that, certainly not here in Minnesota.[17]

Whether the sickness at issue is a personal condition or a cultural condition, psychic turmoil also has a historical location. Many memoirists come to see that their suffering is contexualized not only in contemporary cultural conditions, but also in the suffering of generations—persons and societies—long gone. Not infrequently, the emergence of one family member's anguish causes conversations that reveal an historical accumulation of contextually provoked suffering. After six months in therapy, Martha Manning realizes that

> My family is haunted by depression. My mother can trace it back in her family at least six generations and it's in my father's family, too. . . . The melancholies, nerves and breakdowns of my ancestors landed them in sanitariums, rest homes or in upstairs rooms from which they never emerged.[18]

But it is also important to see that the evolution of genetic inheritance within family lines happens in the context of specific cultural histories. Perhaps predispositions toward an illness are inherited not just from blood family but from a cultural history of hardship and/or discrimina-

---

17. Hanson, *Room for J*, 50.
18. Martha Manning, "The Legacy," *Family Therapy Networker* (January–February 1997): 34.

tion, and the temperament that evolves from it. We noted earlier that Professor Sharon O'Brien used her training as a historian as one means to analyze and cope with her depression. She describes her insight into the historical environment in which the genetics of her family evolved.

> As I began to think of my parents as children, themselves shaped by history, culture, and the lives that had come before them, the question of . . . depression's origins broadened. Helped by my training as a teacher and scholar in American studies, I began to see that my family inheritance—of which depression was only a part—had been shaped by Irish history and American culture, forces much larger than the family. . . .
>
> I felt as if I were casting a net out into the vast ocean of lost years. I kept throwing the net farther and farther back in time, back to the stories of my grandparents, growing up in the 1880s in Elmira, New York, and Lowell, Massachusetts, in communities of other Irish immigrants and exiles; then going farther back—to the Famine, the devastation that brought my great-grandparents to America in the 1840s and early 1850s.[19]

The historical research she did became a major portion of her memoir of her own soul-suffering.

It is not just that cultural conditions that are sick, or sickness-inducing, or sickness-ascribing, can trigger psychospiritual turmoil among persons or families predisposed to it. The memoirists consistently point out that any of us can be made mad by social conditions, even the persons we think most healthy or spiritually mature. During the entirety of a fifty-minute interview about the spiritual effects of war on the soldiers he serves, the voice of Iraq veteran and chaplain Major John Morris communicates someone strikingly compassionate, steady, even hallowed. Then, toward the end of the interview he speaks personally.

> I came to the abyss of hate in Fallujah. The body parts of four Americans, charred and hanging off a bridge over the Euphrates, brought me to a point where I could truly sense myself going

---

19. O'Brien, *The Family Silver*, xiii.

down a vortex of hate, that in a city people were harbored who were that debased. So at that point I felt that I was crossing a line to say, "Yes, these people's time on the planet is over, they need to leave. There's no second chance, there's no other form of justice. They have forfeited all rights to humanness." That was a chilling, chilling moment for me, because I knew I was entering a new territory. And once you cross this line, there's no coming back. When do I become like them?[20]

The interview is not intended as a memoir of madness—indeed, it is mostly a testament to surviving the soul-sickening effects of war. Yet, Chaplain Morris foreshadows his own experience when he says early in the interview that war "drives some soldiers mad. But, for all of them, it bruises their spirit." It shows, as our memoirs often do, that sickening "external" conditions—especially violence—inevitably touch all of us within. What fells the most vulnerable among us can infect any of us— a military chaplain enraged, a rape victim shattered, a police officer embittered, a parent of a starving or dying child desperate. Meri Danquah had her personal resistances to taking Prozac in treatment of her depression, but its widespread use also gave her pause: "There is something that seems really wrong with the fact that Prozac is one of the most prescribed drugs in this country. Maybe I just don't want to accept the reality that so many of us are in pain."[21]

The attunement of these memoirists to suffering pushes to still another dimension: it is not only that the world in which we live brings us down one at a time—one soldier here, one abused child there. Sickening social conditions bring us down collectively, whole communities or nations or continents brought low by bloodshed or famine or meaninglessness. Jyl Felman's essay about her experience with major depression and the isolation it brought into her life is just as much a meditation on a larger human breakdown she intuits, a slow and widespread draining away of energy and connection. "I have come to read my sheer despera-

20. Krista Tippett, prod. and host, "The Soul of War," *Speaking of Faith,* American Public Media, prod., May 25, 2006. Transcript available at http://speakingoffaith.publicradio.org/programs/soulofwar/transcript.shtml (accessed May 25, 2006).
21. Meri Nana-Ama Danquah, *Willow Weep for Me: A Black Woman's Journey through Depression—A Memoir* (New York: W.W. Norton, 1998), 258.

tion as a symptom of a greater ailment, a societal malaise left untreated for decades . . ."[22] "The depletion is collective. While the panic about economic survival grows larger day by day, and global ethnic cleansing is commonplace, the communal need boils over, scalding everyone in sight."[23] Too many of our "communities" have this experience she seems to feel: when the soul needs nurture, a pill—Prozac, in her case—is more readily available and effective than human relationship.

These broad dynamics in our collective sicknesses and social needs take three specific shapes—relational and existential violences, social "progress," and bigotry and discrimination—that, in the view of our memoirists, pose insufficiently noted and extraordinary complications in personal soul-suffering.

RELATIONAL AND EXISTENTIAL VIOLENCES

Genetic inheritance is an existential circumstance especially important in psychic suffering. For some people, emotional turmoil is a legacy, handed down through DNA shaped by generations of suffering. But this does not mean that the rest of us can breathe a sigh of relief. The prevalence of psychic suffering in every generation means that it is an inheritance, but not one limited to unlucky families with weak genes. Martha Manning's family can trace depression through at least six generations, but when she was exasperated about not finding an explanation that could excise her suffering, she demanded of her therapist, "'Why are there so many problems in my family?' He shrugged and replied calmly, 'Because there are so many people in it.'"[24] His refusal to settle for a too simplistic understanding honors the reality that the life challenges that cause our souls to suffer strike widely. There are many other markers for soul-suffering besides genetic markers. It is not always the case that psychic upheaval is precipitated by some other crisis—it does seem, occasionally, to come out of the blue. But most acute psychospiritual suffering has existential and relational bases any of us might encounter. In

---

22. Felman, "Nurturing the Soul," 50.
23. Felman, "Nurturing the Soul," 52.
24. Manning, "The Legacy," 36.

almost all circumstances, violence in its many forms is the common denominator among different forms of soul-suffering.

The psychospiritual violence of losing loved ones precipitates much
soul-suffering. Henri Nouwen's six months of soul-sickness was sparked
by an excruciating estrangement in a precious friendship.[25] Clifford
Beers' hospitalization happened not long after the death of a beloved
brother.[26] At about the same time as David Weisburd began exhibiting
symptoms of schizophrenia, four members of his extended family died.[27]
The psychic break that led to the institutionalization of novelist Maxine
Hong Kingston's aunt began when Moon Orchid was persuaded to come
to the United States to see the husband who had left her and their daughter in China years earlier, ostensibly to make them a better life, only to
find that he had married another woman.[28] When Maureen O'Brien was
abandoned by her mother for choosing marriage instead of graduate
school, Sharon O'Brien lost more than contact with her sister; she lost
more innocence about love's limits: "to shun someone, placing her in a
circle of silence, is to cut her off from the family's and the culture's
lifeblood. It's the cruelest thing you can do."[29]

Physical violence is inextricably linked with psychospiritual anguish:
Stewart Govig's son Jay suffered extensive head injuries in three motor
vehicle accidents prior to the emergence of his symptoms of schizophrenia; in her fourteenth year, Tracy Thompson endured first the emergence of her suicidal depression, which was immediately complicated by
a horrific accident that left her with multiple injuries, followed by multiple surgeries, including plastic surgeries on her damaged face.

Some of our memoirists know all the forms of violence—physical,
psychospiritual, intrapersonal, interpersonal, social. Natural disasters are
not often referenced in the memoirs, but we need only look at the post-
Katrina mental health statistics to see the capacity for all the forms of

---

25. Henri J. M. Nouwen, *The Inner Voice of Love: A Journey through Anguish to Freedom*
(New York: Doubleday, Image Books, 1996), xv.

26. Clifford W. Beers, *A Mind That Found Itself: An Autobiography,* 5th ed. rev. (Garden City,
N.Y.: Doubleday, Doran & Co., 1944), 7.

27. Dan E. Weisburd, "Planning a Community-Based Mental Health System: Perspective of
a Family Member," *American Psychologist* vol. 45 (November 1990): 1246.

28. Maxine Hong Kingston, *The Woman Warrior: Memoirs of a Girlhood among Ghosts* (New
York: Random House, 1989), 113–60. Originally published in 1976.

29. O'Brien, *The Family Silver,* 34.

violence to interlock. Before she was an adult, Meri Danquah had lived through the multiple forms of violence inherent in immigration, the racist cruelty of other children, rape, abortion, sexual abuse, and mortally wounding accidents in the lives of two friends. Rev. Susan Gregg-Schroeder's depression emerged in conjunction with a week of events that brought violent impact: the day after she articulated for the first time that she had been abused during childhood by her mother, her birth father, with whom she had been trying to reestablish relationship, died; a week later, a firestorm raging through the Oakland/Berkeley hills destroyed her birth home and the neighborhood in which she had grown up.

The existential "precipitants" recounted in memoirs of soul-suffering are situations any of us could encounter. Soul-sufferers emphasize that their distress is related as much to the hardships of life that might befall any of us as to discrete psychiatric disorders. When a diagnosable illness strikes, it rarely comes out of the blue but is rather the logical outcome of the difficulties of life. And, as Meri Danquah notes, techniques to deal with emotions and stress weren't foolproof: "They did not shield me from the outside world, where I could encounter any number of events that might set off a disastrous reaction . . . like hidden land mines."[30] Our memoirists may be more sensitive than average, or more unlucky than average, but the circumstances that precipitate their crises are often quite average. The novelist Susanna Kaysen's words summarize:

> I think depression and despair are reasonable reactions to the nature of life. Life has its ups and downs. It is unreliable and conditional and provisional. It can be, as we used to say in my youth, a real bummer. Failure, disease, death: standard life events. Is it any surprise if some of the time, some of us feel like hell?[31]

SOCIAL "PROGRESS"

William Hulme—we met him in part 1 through his comments about his pregnant daughter's suicide while hospitalized—explores in his memoir the cost to our souls of social emphases on competitiveness, extroversion, and intelligence, as compared to Christianity's gospel of grace, which asserts that our worth is a gift to us from our beginning. Memoirs of soul-

---

30. Danquah, *Willow Weep for Me*, 255–256.
31. Susanna Kaysen, "One Cheer for Melancholy," in *Unholy Ghost*, 42–43.

suffering are full of stories suggesting the soul-costs secondary to social progress. Consider the ecological devastation we have been willing to allow for the sake of industrial development, for example. The number of children diagnosed with autism has ballooned in recent years.[32] The first explanations for this increase blamed parents for being too impatient with children's normally disruptive behavior and too willing to medicate their children to relieve the parents' own distress. Evidence now strongly suggests that toxins from industrial waste ingested by children through contaminated air, water, and food are negatively affecting children's development and may account for at least some of the increase of autism.

Some toxins we ingest are not material, and the negative effects not always so widely recognized to account for soul-suffering. For example, a number of our memoirists comment on the relationship between economics and the state of our souls. Soul-suffering is aggravated by—or sometimes the result of—pressure in industrialized countries to work exhaustively in order to accumulate wealth and goods or, sometimes, simply to survive. Ironically, the very pressure to work can increase the inability to work. Meri Danquah's memoir describes a typical vicious circle: as the sole support for her daughter, constantly under the pressure to work; as a writer constantly struggling to make money, much less art; as a mother and writer, constantly fighting her depression in order to be able to mother and to write. Danquah was young at the time that her parents immigrated to the United States from Ghana and, though she does not comment much on the effects of immigration on her, her story is a reminder of millions more who immigrate to escape poverty or other oppression, only to find that their progress comes at an enormous psychospiritual cost to them and their families. In industrialized countries, citizens' value is based on their capacity to work, produce, and achieve. It is also based on their capacity for individualism and autonomy—not

---

32. The U.S. Department of Education's "Twenty-First Annual Report to Congress on the Implementation of the Individuals with Disabilities Education Act" (1999) reports the following comparison of growth rates during the 1990s: while the U.S. population increased 13 percent, and disabilities increased 16 percent, autism increased 172 percent. For more information on increasing rates of autism diagnoses, see: FightingAutism, "Fighting Autism: Research, Education, Treatment," http://www.fightingautism.org/idea/autism.php (accessed August 23, 2006).

needing help, or more exactly, not appearing to need help. The sickness of those unable to cooperate in such a system reveals the inhumanity of the system. Jyl Felman:

> I tried to understand what my responsibility was to care for myself. Only I couldn't understand. Anything. This was my dilemma. In capitalistic terms, the means of production had broken down, ceased to produce, and the worker could not fix the machinery alone. The worker needed help.[33]

In the 1940s, Sharon O'Brien's father, employed in radio advertising, moved his family to Boston to take a job with a new station. In less than a year he was fired, probably, O'Brien reflects, because his temperament did not fit the increasingly competitive and profit-driven economic expansion happening in radio advertising. The firing precipitated a two-year period of clinical depression and unemployment. O'Brien puts her family's experience in a broader historical and economic context.

> I must have been one of the few American children growing up in the fifties who heard about her father's depression long before she learned about the Great Depression. On the day my eighth grade history teacher began to speak about the Great Depression, I was shocked—how could this stranger know about my father? It didn't occur to me until much later that there might be a reason why my country's economic collapse and my father's personal collapse had the same name. Both were affronts to capitalism—in the national case, the economy fell apart and there was no work, in my father's case, he was unable to work. (Sometimes I wonder if depression is, in part, an unconscious form of resistance to the work ethic . . .)[34]

Poverty obviously can have negative effects on mental health but, in different ways, prosperity has its own soul-costs. Some of our memoirists have experienced this rarely acknowledged reality. As a child, Lauren Slater's suffering was increased by the unhappiness of her mother who, though wealthy enough to have household help, still did not use her free-

---

33. Felman, "Nurturing the Soul," 52.
34. O'Brien, *The Family Silver,* 160.

dom to create a meaningful life for herself. Sharon O'Brien's comments, after several more decades of U.S. economic growth, about the coincidence of depression and prosperity, put Slater's mother's situation in a broader context.

> Sometimes an illness seems to embody the spirit of the age, and it had seemed strange to me that during the 1980s and 1990s when the American economy was flourishing and the cold war was finishing, depression seemed more and more the illness that signified our time. I might have been suffering in private, but I was, it seemed, part of a mass movement.[35]

Susanna Kaysen seconds this observation and adds another dimension: "decades of prosperity [in the United States] have given the middle classes more time to ruminate on whether we feel good or bad."[36] Unfortunately, time to ruminate has not yet motivated us to seek any remission of the pressures and costs of materialism or its attendant meaninglessness.

Another aspect of social progress bringing with it significant soul-costs is especially relevant to the situation of our memoirists: the near-total deference we give to science and technology. This deference is evidenced by giving to science nearly sole authority for the conceptualization and treatment of soul-suffering, which costs us, among other things, an appreciation for the religious and spiritual dynamics in psychic upheaval. Our unquestioned trust of science also fuels our love affair with technology and drives us into the multitasking that it purports to make possible. While a few people thrive on it and actually are made more productive, the effect on most people living at the furious pace of overdeveloped countries is information overload, ruined focus, undermined productivity, and increased dysfunction. This frenetic way of living may also be distancing us from religious and spiritual values. One Sunday morning Martha Manning's family oversleeps, and races to church with bed-head.

> We are late for choir practice and grab pieces of coffee cake on the way in. . . . Between songs I surreptitiously devour pieces of coffee cake and wonder whether I'll have time after practice to

35. O'Brien, *The Family Silver*, 267.
36. Kaysen, "One Cheer for Melancholy," in *Unholy Ghost*, 41.

find a soda machine so I can get in my two hits of Diet Coke before mass begins.

    I know I'm forgetting something. I see Maria, the liturgy coor-
dinator, in the hall and she checks in to make sure I have written
the litany of prayers that comes after the sermon. I try to look like
I wrote them weeks ago. . . . I rummage around in my backpack for
paper and pencil. . . . The best piece of paper I can find is a grocery
store receipt. Luckily it was for over two hundred dollars, so I have
some space. . . . We are a quarter of the way through the service and
I have yet to register a word of what is going on in the mass. When
I finish with the prayers I realize that I have to plan my Sunday
school class, which meets immediately afterward.[37]

Reflecting later on this event, Manning comments: "Whoever said that
the Sabbath was a day of rest was a fool. . . . It is Sunday afternoon and
I'm exhausted. I'm becoming an overachiever at church."

    A more subtle sign of our devotion to science than our love affair with
technology is our idolization of health and pathologization of normal difficulties. As Susanna Kaysen says, "things that used to be adjectives"—
depressing, hyperactive—"are now diseases."[38] Our confidence in human
ingenuity has led us to treat normal human difficulties as problems that
can be solved.

    Extraordinary leaps in medicine have raised extraordinary ex-
    pectations for the cure (or at least mitigation) of ailments that
    have plagued people for millennia. . . . A lot of people [are] clam-
    oring to label themselves diseased in the hope that they can be
    cured. This faith in science is ill-advised. Despite Prozac and her
    daughters, there's no cure for sadness.[39]

Because we operate under the collective delusion that science will find the
solution for mental health problems, we fail to attend adequately to finding alternatives. Thus, proactive help for the most vulnerable is neglected
and whole societies suffer the costs of insufficient health care, shelters,
and food programs. Expediency is demanded in the marketplace, while

---

37. Manning, *Undercurrents*, 15–16.
38. Kaysen, "One Cheer for Melancholy," in *Unholy Ghost*, 41.
39. Kaysen, "One Cheer for Melancholy," in *Unholy Ghost*, 41.

inaccessibility is tolerated in human services. "Convenience. Everything is open twenty-four hours but the human spirit," observes Jyl Felman.[40]

BIGOTRY AND DISCRIMINATION

Another collective sickness affecting soul-sufferers is bigotry and discrimination. Psychic turmoil is sometimes caused, but always complicated, by prejudice and marginalization. We will first reflect on how and why those deemed sane carry out their prejudice and stigmatization of psychiatric illnesses and other kinds of emotional difference. We will then explore how stigma against emotional difference is complicated when additional bigotries are also involved and focus on racism and sexism as cases in point.

"Mentalism"

Because of stigma's prevalence and life-threatening effect, all memoirs of soul-suffering engage in what Susanna Kaysen calls "stigmatography," the charting and describing of the stigma associated with being thought mentally ill.[41] Stewart Govig says that human society (and the mental health system is not immune to this sickness) is infected with "mentalisms," prejudices akin to racism, sexism, and classism.[42] While the "healthy" tend to assume and zero in on the "illness" of those in psychic distress, the memoirs are absolutely consistent on one point: soul-sufferers make plain that they are stigmatized so severely that the stigma is as hard to bear as, and sometimes harder than, the psychic turmoil itself. For example, stigma forces people into hiding, as it did Margot Kidder.

> The hiding is the killer. . . . I hid by taking drugs, I hid by getting drunk, I hid by literally hiding in my house and not going out and not picking up the phone. I hid by all manner of deceit. . . . The hiding has taken such an *extraordinary* toll, as much as the illness itself. . . . Mental illness is the last taboo, the one that scares everyone to death . . .[43]

40. Felman, "Nurturing the Soul," 52.

41. Susanna Kaysen, *Girl, Interrupted* (New York: Random House, 1993), 123–25.

42. Govig, *Souls Are Made of Endurance*, 89. Citing William Anthony, Mikhal Cohen, and Marianne Farkas, *Psychiatric Rehabilitation* (Boston: Center for Psychiatric Rehabilitation, 1990), 18–36.

43. Barbara Walters, "Interview of Margot Kidder," *20/20*, American Broadcasting Company, September 6, 1996.

This is not to say that stigma always has the last word. Those stigmatized do not always give in to it; in part 5, where we reflect on healing, we will explore the honorable ways some resist. Also, there are individuals, families, and organizations devoted to practicing respectful care for those whose emotional expression is outside the mainstream and to reforming the social service systems on which they rely for support. The efforts of these primary sufferers and their advocates to fight stigma are increasingly effective. However, those efforts are still far overshadowed by the widespread disrespect and hostility shown in popular discourse and opinion and in everyday interactions toward people in psychic distress. Even having one's work included in this book risks stigmatization, so I have been careful in my discussion of the memoirs to distinguish between those who identify themselves as persons with psychiatric illness and those who are reflecting on other kinds of soul-sickness.

The effects of stigma are often worse than the suffering itself. This is a remarkable charge. While those who are not ill have focused on the tragedy and terror of emotional crises, those afflicted are telling us that the illnesses and other emotional crises are hard, yes, but the way they, as persons, are treated is often worse. This speaks, of course, to the extreme means and extent of stigmatization. However inclusive of particularity and difference we may be on other counts, few individuals or societies deliberately make space for people who are emotionally different. Those who do not hide their emotional distress are seen as senseless, frightening, without much value to the common good, even repellent. Consequently, they are grossly marginalized. But that's not the end of stigma's devastation. Another reason that the stigma is often more destructive than the disease is because, in the psychological dynamics of oppression, it is nearly impossible for those who are stigmatized as mentally ill not to internalize their own oppression, not to stigmatize themselves, not to feel immense self-hatred and shame. We will reflect in part 3 on how internalized stigma increases soul-suffering.

There have been many liberation movements, but the liberation of people who are emotionally different is barely visible on the horizon. Indeed, some argue that, as Kidder puts it, mental illness is the last taboo and that stigmatization of those who are emotionally different is more socially acceptable than any other kind of bigotry. For example, while consciousness is being raised about the impropriety of using racist, sexist, xenophobic, and even heterosexist language, it is still socially acceptable to use prejudiced language about emotional difference: crazy, weirdo, psycho, lunatic, loony, etc. While other bigoted jokes are still made, we do not tolerate them to the extent we will tolerate jokes about emotional difference. It is socially acceptable in almost all cultural settings for "healthy" people to make jokes about craziness or about people with psychiatric illnesses, and it is done by people who would never make such public jokes about race or gender. Gross stereotypes appear regularly in media, caricaturing people in emotional turmoil as either violent or idiotic; rooting out racism or sexism in the media has become more challenging because it has become somewhat more subtle, but no such challenge exists where bigotry toward the emotionally disturbed is concerned. A particularly poignant bit of evidence that emotional difference is the least acceptable form of difference is that research has revealed a "scale of acceptability" within disabilities. Stewart Govig, who has a physical disability himself, as well as a son diagnosed with schizophrenia, summarizes the findings.

> Most acceptable are individuals with obvious physical disabilities (using wheelchairs, for example). Then come sensory impairments involving sight and hearing. Developmentally disabled people and alcoholics are listed next. Those with mental illness are the least accepted.[44]

The most concrete evidence that stigmatization of those who are emotionally different is more socially acceptable than any other kind of bigotry is blatant discrimination in the health care system and insurance industries. Despite its far greater statistical prevalence, medical knowledge about psychiatric disorder lags far beyond expertise regarding other kinds of medical illnesses. Money for research and treatment is far less than that available for other illnesses. When his son developed symptoms of schizophrenia, Stewart Govig learned about the vast differential between heath-care delivery systems for psychiatric conditions and that of all other conditions. "One wonders what the public response

---

44. Govig, *Souls Are Made of Endurance*, 10. Source of original citation unknown.

would be to heart disease treatment if it were delivered in the same way [as mental health services]."

> First, a politicized and fragmented system of national "cardiac health centers" would require those with [cardiac] disease to present just cause (difficult to obtain!) for hospitalization if a "cardiac breakdown" had occurred. A cardiac episode that required hospitalization would mean "stabilization" and discharge in five to ten days unless the patient was ruled a criminal (having somehow wound up in jail overnight along the way) or had been admitted for "involuntary commitment." Meanwhile, at the "state cardiac hospitals" authentic criminal patients would be housed on the same grounds as everyone else. And the hospital itself might be on an accreditation probationary status for understaffing or other inadequacies. After release from the hospital, patients would see a doctor at a center for perhaps fifteen minutes a month for "medication." It would be up to the patient to get to a center, even if that meant walking for miles.
>
> Americans would respond to such health care for heart disease with a public outcry. Investigations, local and congressional, would boost the rocket of change. . . . Funding would appear. Citizens across the land would no longer tolerate such a national disgrace.[45]

Similarly, unique levels of discrimination are rampant in health insurance. Parity between coverage for mental health care and for all other health conditions is nearly nonexistent. Health plans will pay adequately for visits to psychiatrists for the medications they prescribe but, otherwise, most insurance policies set low and arbitrary limits on outpatient care and hospitalization, even when such care is ordered by a physician. Chronic and expensive medical conditions receive long-term insurance coverage, except in the case of psychiatric conditions, where their chronicity and its associated expense are used as rationalization for providing only short-term care. Like other psychiatric conditions, "depression is frequently not a short-term problem," notes history professor Robert Dawidoff, adding, wryly, that while his friends are investing in mortgages, he is paying his

---

45. Stewart D. Govig, *Strong at the Broken Places: Persons with Disabilities and the Church* (Louisville: Westminster John Knox Press, 1989), 60–61.

therapy and medication bills.[46] Insufficient medical insurance can impoverish anyone, but those in need of psychiatric care will get less help than people with other medical conditions. Even where there is coverage, Kathleen Norris learned that symptoms of a psychiatric illness covered in your policy can cause the company to cancel it.

> My husband once went into a depression so severe that he had to be hospitalized for several weeks. I was stunned to learn that we had no medical insurance—in his descent into despair he had cancelled it. . . . I discovered a catch-22 in medical insurance: when mental illness causes a person to stop paying insurance premiums, Blue Cross can drop you even though the illness is covered in the policy.[47]

Whether or not it is true that the stigma against emotional difference is of the worst kind, it is serious. The manifestations of "mentalism"— prejudiced attitudes and behaviors toward emotional difference—are countless. There is the tendency to disregard people in psychic turmoil. "Some of you refer to me as crazy or insane. The real fact is most of you don't refer to me at all,"[48] says Ed Cooper, who is diagnosed with bipolar disorder and has written about and done advocacy work regarding psychiatric illnesses. When they are noticed, they tend to be accorded little or no credibility—they are treated like children or as if emotional distress causes a loss of intelligence. With too much regularity, sufferers report being ill-treated—"put down by some (stigmatization) and put up with (patronized) by others"[49]—even by some medical and mental health professionals; condescension is only a more genteel form of prejudice. People suffering from physical illnesses might be considered uninformed *about* their condition, but those in psychic distress tend to be considered unfit to comment *by virtue of* their condition. Kate Millett, the most vocal critic of the mental health system among our memoirists, sounds re-

46. Robert Dawidoff, "His Depression Is 'Real,' All Right," *Los Angeles Times* (July 5, 1999), B5.
47. Kathleen Norris, *Amazing Grace: A Vocabulary of Faith* (New York: Riverhead Books, 1998), 33, 35.
48. Ed Cooper, "To Touch the Untouchable," *Mental Illness Awareness Worship Resources* (St. Louis: Pathways to Promise).
49. Govig, *Strong at the Broken Places*, 21.

signed when she comments on it: "How little weight my own perceptions seem to have. I am the discussed; what do I know . . . ?"[50] Such dismissiveness toward sufferers is self-serving for those who want to silence
disagreement and critique. In her memoir, Kate Millett argues that her
hospitalization was an "incarceration" that resulted from her refusal to
agree with her family and doctors that her mania required medication.

> Patients with my opinions on psychiatry are treated as hard cases.
> . . . Disbelief makes those in charge hostile. . . . All those author-
> itarian elements, whose tone and fabric contract when defied,
> grow rigid, and the jail reveals itself.[51]

Mentalism and stigma also reveal themselves when people with emotional illnesses do commit crimes and are denied any compassion. People
charged with crimes can use the so-called insanity defense in a court of
law but, even if they have a documented history of psychiatric disorder,
in the courts of public opinion they will be judged by many as simply
dodging responsibility. These kinds of moments reveal another level of
mentalism and stigma—the extent to which, despite the fact that they
cross paths every day with people in emotional distress, "healthy" persons
feel no obligation to avail themselves of information about the progress
being made in understanding and treating brain disorders and other
forms of psychic turmoil: as Tracy Thompson puts it, despite an "avalanche of information, the stigma remains."[52] Such ignorance is de-
plorable anywhere, but especially damaging in religious communities.
Norma Swetnam was reluctant to have anyone in the congregation
where her husband was pastor know about her depression because, as
she puts it, "since many believed mental illness is a lack of belief in God,
it was especially embarrassing for a minister's wife to have such a problem."[53] In religious communities and elsewhere, ignorance about emotional anguish is a threat to employment and drives sufferers into hiding.
Drs. Slater and Jamison earlier described the risk for psychologists when
they are honest about having a psychiatric diagnosis, and similar expec-

---

50. Kate Millett, *The Loony-Bin Trip* (New York: Simon & Schuster, 1990), 72.
51. Millett, *The Loony-Bin Trip*, 65.
52. Thompson, *The Beast*, 10.
53. Norma G. Swetnam, "My Journey through Hell," in *Presbyterians Today Online* (August 1998): http://www.pcusa.org/today/archive/features/feat9808d.htm (accessed August 1, 2006): 1.

tations and costs threaten clergy's employment. When Rev. Susan Gregg-Schroeder asked to be put on the denomination's clergy prayer chain, asking for prayers for her depression, the response from colleagues was not only "overwhelming" but surprising: "Ministers whom I thought had it all together revealed to me their own experiences with depression." Perhaps they had stayed hidden because of what happened to Gregg-Schroeder—the church hierarchy held meetings to reconsider her fitness for ministry.[54]

Why so much prejudice and stigma against emotional difference? Arguably, the stigma is most fundamentally driven by fear, of at least three things. First, there is fear of the nonconformity of those who are "emotionally different." Sufferers' pain is anarchic; their lives often mirror values opposite to those prized by the dominant culture and cause alarm and judgmentalism in so-called normals. In an era bent on accumulation, psychiatric disorder signals both psychological and social loss. In an era that prizes self-sufficiency and high individual achievement, those laid low by emotional anguish are almost always reliant on others for assistance.[55] In an era that prizes control, or at least the appearance of it, psychic turmoil "thoroughly smashes the cultural icon of individual control over our own lives."[56] In an era that prizes social amenities and the small talk that goes with it, sufferers' pain is isolating and, as Virginia Heffernan put it earlier, causes betrayal of the social rule that "frowns on euphoria but also mandates a measure of happiness." In an era when the ability to be verbal and articulate is prized, soul-sufferers' pain is often indescribable. Martha Manning captures the wariness conveyed toward such nonconformity, which she experienced as she signed herself into a psychiatric unit.

> The assistant head nurse gives me a tour [of the unit] and asks how I have gotten so depressed. I stare at her blankly and can't find the words. . . . I tell her that I am mostly depressed about

54. Susan Gregg-Schroeder, "I Am Susan, and I Am Depressed," *The Christian Ministry* (November–December, 1995), 29.
55. Govig, *Souls Are Made of Endurance*, 10.
56. David Hilfiker, "When Mental Illness Blocks the Spirit," *The Other Side* (May and June 2002), 15.

being depressed. Her expression informs me that this clearly is not the correct answer. I imagine the opening statement in my chart: "Patient demonstrates limited insight into her current problems." She says dubiously, "Dr. Samuel said you are a psychologist," as if somehow that should make me more articulate about my pain.[57]

Soul-sufferers' pain, too, is nonconformist. Being articulate about pain is desired in part because it makes the suffering less, well, painful, to on-lookers. As Stewart Govig observes, in an era that widely expects cheer-fulness, we have little tolerance for people in temporary pain, much less chronic pain.[58] The inner torment of soul-suffering, however, is too-often inescapable and unmasked. The editor of a national magazine called for a second photo session with William Styron, because the editor found the pictures from the first session, even the ones with smiles, "too full of an-guish."[59] Perhaps most nonconformist and threatening of all, in a society that can see in psychic distress nothing but tragedy and terror, sufferers sometimes strive to find humor in their situations, as we have already ex-perienced. Martha Manning tells this story about her encounter with a student nurse who is learning to take vital signs.

> The student handles me like I'm made of porcelain and has diffi-culty finding my pulse. Trying to diffuse her anxiety, I make a stab at a joke, suggesting that maybe I'm so depressed that I don't have one anymore. She looks alarmed and pats my shoulder, saying, "Oh no. Don't worry. I'm sure we can find it." She gropes around the contours of my wrist until she randomly falls upon it. She looks puzzled and protests, "But it's not where it's supposed to be."
>
> I shrug and answer, "That's okay, neither am I." She is not amused.[60]

There is a second fear undergirding stigma, paradoxical to the first: fear that there is not so much difference after all between the sane and the insane. In many soul-sufferers' opinions, this fear is grounded in fact. Susanna Kaysen describes her illness as existence in a universe parallel to,

---

57. Manning, *Undercurrents*, 111.
58. Govig, *Strong at the Broken Places*, 15.
59. William Styron, *Darkness Visible: A Memoir of Madness* (New York: Vintage Books, 1990), 58.
60. Manning, *Undercurrents*, 127–28.

and not so much different from, that of the "normal." Rather, it is more that proportion has been lost. Everything is exaggerated or minimized. There is too much meaning or too little. Susanna Kaysen describes perception as having the extreme qualities of either viscosity or velocity.[61] Sometimes the world of the "sane" embodies the very nonconformity and danger it tends to associate with the world of the "insane." Kaysen watched Vietnam War protests on the television while hospitalized and describes their appearance from the perspective of a psychiatric unit.

> People were doing the kinds of things we had fantasies of doing: taking over universities and abolishing classes; making houses out of cardboard boxes and putting them in people's way; sticking their tongues out at policemen.
>
> We'd cheer them on. . . . We thought eventually they'd get around to "liberating" us, too. . . .
>
> So it went on, month after month of battles and riots and marches. These were easy times for the staff. We didn't "act out"; it was all acted out for us.[62]

Speaking of his experience in the hospital nearly thirty years later, Styron says, "the place I found refuge was a kinder, gentler madhouse than the one I'd left."[63]

Arguably the basest fear undergirding stigma is a third one: fear of emotion itself. It is very difficult for the majority to remain unconscious of the susceptibility of their emotional life to be upset, though we try. Emotional expression is judged to be excessive at exactly the point where the fear of strong affect is evoked in onlookers. The loss of control might be catching, madness could strike close to home, it could happen to me. This sameness and fear of contagion causes "normal" people to sense a palpable hazard in "abnormal" people: "There is coming to be a kind of danger around you," Kate Millett explains to other stigmatized ones.[64] Therefore, in order to assuage that fear, stigma is applied, in Kaysen's words, as a "general taint,"[65] used to distinguish not only clearly but com-

---

61. Kaysen, *Girl, Interrupted*, 75–78.
62. Kaysen, *Girl, Interrupted*, 92–93.
63. Styron, *Darkness Visible*, 73.
64. Millett, *The Loony-Bin Trip*, 34.
65. Kaysen, *Girl, Interrupted*, 124.

pletely and perpetually between the ones who are "sick" and the ones who are "sane." For those given a psychiatric diagnosis, stigma causes all aspects of their soul-suffering to pass over from being a partial or passing condition to a lasting, latent state, never to be left behind. Even healing is suspect, where psychic turmoil is concerned. Dan Hanson contrasts public attitudes toward his battle with cancer with those toward psychiatric disorders: "With other incurable diseases, there is a measure of dignity in fighting the illness even when the battle is lost. With mental illness there is little dignity. Even when the symptoms are gone the stigma remains."[66] Martha Manning speaks from inside the experience.

> As the admitting secretary types out the forms, I think to myself, "This is going to become part of my *permanent record*." . . . When I was arrested for shoplifting with my friends at the age of fifteen, the policeman warned us that if we "kept our noses clean" for a year, our slates would be wiped clean and it would not become part of our "permanent record." There is no such reprieve here. Like losing your virginity, hospitalization for a psychiatric disorder involves crossing over a line that can never be erased.[67]

Mentalism, and More: Adding Racism and Sexism

Some oppressed people manage to ward off psychic anguish in the face of oppression. But it is no wonder when oppression does make otherwise well persons sick at heart. And if persons already contending with psychic anguish and the bigotry against it must also bear other oppressions, the weight of the soul-suffering increases exponentially. In this section we will consider what our memoirists have to say about living in the crucible of more than one stigmatized reality. We will use racism and sexism to focus our discussion, but these dynamics are at play in any context where oppression happens—class, religion, nationality, sexual identity, and all others. Reflection on these dynamics reminds us and again illustrates for us that soul-suffering has both a sociocultural and a historical location. We will not understand the capacity of bigotry and discrimination to cause and complicate soul-suffering if we do not comprehend or will not accept the capacity of soul-suffering to accumulate over cen-

---

66. Hanson, *Room for J*, 27.
67. Manning, *Undercurrents*, 114.

turies. Sharon O'Brien discovered this characteristic of suffering—and is still trying to grasp it—by studying her own family.

> Some people believe that the untold stories of your ancestors get passed down in your blood and bones, generation after generation, without your even knowing it. You can feel your great-great-grandfather's sorrow, you can dream your great-grand-mother's dreams. . . .
>
> I am one of these believers: I think that we inherit our ancestors' emotional histories, particularly their unexpressed stories of suffering, exile, and yearning. It's only recently that the Irish and Irish Americans have begun to name the Famine as a holocaust-like devastation, to construct memorials, and to begin to remember. . . . I'm a great-grandchild of famine immigrants, so the sources of loss and exile seem very far away. How could any of this far-off Irish suffering or yearning for home ever have been passed on to my generation? And yet I think it has been.[68]

Our understanding of soul-suffering is incomplete until we learn how to comprehend that the political is personal and is carried generation to generation.

Asked to contribute to a book of essays about depression, Meri Danquah ends up describing how the notion of race and the experience of racism compound depression's ways of diminishing her.

> In deciding exactly what it was that I wanted to share in this essay about my experiences with clinical depression, I realized that mental illness and race are topics that can not be divorced from one another. Not easily. Not for me. You see, the mask of depression is not all that different from the mask of race. So much of clinical depression has to do with identity, with images, with how those of us who suffer from the disease perceive ourselves and how, based on these oftentimes grossly distorted perceptions, we interact with others. So much of racism has to do with the same. It, too, barrages its prey with groundless images; it concerns itself more with the fiction of a prescribed identity

---

68. O'Brien, *The Family Silver*, 80–81.

than with the notion of any true individuality. It, too, seeks to blur a person's vision of herself, and her place in the world. Racism is also an illness. Perhaps not in the same way as depression, but an illness nonetheless. To contend with either one is bad enough. To grapple with both at the same time . . . that's enough to drive a person—pardon the expression—"crazy."[69]

Even as racism and depression combine to weaken her, she is forced to contend as well with the complications of racism's sexism, which places on her the fiction—the falsehood—of an opposite stereotype: the indefatigable black woman.

In these lies black women are strong. Strong enough to work two jobs while single-handedly raising twice as many children. Black women can cook, they can clean, they can sew, they can type, they can sweep, they can scrub, they can mop, and they can pray.[70]

"The societal images of black female wellness, as evidenced (still) in present-day popular culture, have nothing at all to do with being well. Far from it."[71] That which is purported to be strength and health is actually a product of racism and sexism. From this perspective, we can understand why Danquah makes what would otherwise be a confusing statement: "As a black woman struggling with depression, I don't know which I fear more: the identity of illness or the identity of wellness."[72]

Neither did Danquah easily find refuge in the black community to deal honestly with her depression. Simply trying to open a conversation often did not go well.

I have had conversations about my depression with black people—both men and women. . . . I've frequently been told things like: "Girl, you've been hanging out with too many white folk"; "What do you have to be depressed about? If our people could make it through slavery, we can make it through anything"; "Take your troubles to Jesus, not no damn psychiatrist."[73]

69. Danquah, "Writing the Wrongs of Identity," in *Unholy Ghost*, 175.
70. Danquah, "Writing the Wrongs of Identity," in *Unholy Ghost*, 176.
71. Danquah, "Writing the Wrongs of Identity," in *Unholy Ghost*, 175–76.
72. Danquah, "Writing the Wrongs of Identity," in *Unholy Ghost*, 175.
73. Danquah, *Willow Weep for Me*, 21.

Danquah is troubled by—but not without understanding of—such responses.

> When there aren't dismissive questions, patronizing statements, or ludicrous suggestions, there is silence. As if there are no acceptable ways, no appropriate words to begin a dialogue about this illness. And, given the oppressive nature of the existing language surrounding depression, perhaps for black people there really aren't any.[74]

Psychotherapist Julia Boyd, writing to black women about depression in her own life and in the lives of other black women, articulates the rub. "In reality, the symptoms [of depression] often do mirror the stereotypes that have been projected onto Black women for years."[75] But refusing acknowledgment of soul-suffering in order to avoid racist stereotypes and the stigma of psychiatric illness has another set of costs, as Boyd describes.

> Our fears about craziness, laziness, of being a failure or weak keep us from accepting what is true. Our fear of wearing yet another "label" attached to our ethnicity and gender as Black women has locked many of us into a state of helpless and sometimes hopeless confusion concerning our emotional well-being.[76]

These are life and death issues. As Boyd sees it, it is true that psychiatry has been tainted by racism, and yet that problem is compounded by the rate of suicide in the black community.

> As a sister I can . . . respect and understand our need for caution when it comes to accepting the word as gospel when it's presented by a field of science that has not always respected our needs. However as both a Black woman and a mental health professional I can't ignore the disturbing facts that as sisters we're hurting in large numbers, and the magnitude of that pain has been strong enough to cause some of us to take the most precious gift we've been given . . . our lives.[77]

74. Danquah, *Willow Weep for Me*, 21.
75. Julia A. Boyd, *Can I Get a Witness?: For Sisters When the Blues Is More Than a Song* (New York: Penguin, Dutton, 1998), 8.
76. Boyd, *Can I Get A Witness?*, 6.
77. Boyd, *Can I Get A Witness?*, 10.

Meri Danquah and Julia Boyd help us see how bigotry and discrimination confuse the differences between well-being and sickness, whether we are in psychic turmoil or not. Other memoirists also make clear that bigotry and discrimination can—often do—actually *make* us sick, or make our suffering worse. Several of our women memoirists identify connections between sexism, gender proscriptions, and their anguish. For Lauren Slater, it started in childhood, even before depression emerged full force. "Illness was a temporary respite, a release from the demands of an alienating world."

> In my world, women had hair as hard as crash helmets. In my world, girls did not play. They practiced: the piano, the flute, French, manners so refined they made all speech stiff. Illness was not stiff. You went kaput. . . . Getting better was a grief. . . . You looked across your orange carpet and saw your black patent dancing shoes, your child-sized golf clubs. You saw your French and Hebrew workbooks, with all those verbs you would have to conjugate before dinner tonight. You wanted to weep.[78]

Nancy Mairs advances the chronology, speaks to how she knew in her young adulthood that she had to escape—even by way of illness—from the gender proscriptions ready to knead her into the right size and shape.

> My life became troubled . . . when I emerged from the long undifferentiated dream of my female-supported childhood into the Real/Male World, an environment defined and dominated by the masculine principles of effectiveness, power, and success, an environment containing a ready-made niche for me which happened to be the wrong size and shape. . . . I believe now that my depression was—and still is—my response to the struggle not to go under, not to go down for the last time, sinking into acceptance of that space which crabbed and cramped me. . . . I will die first. For this reason I call it the saving of me.[79]

Mairs writes that she found out what was wrong with her "size and shape" years later, when her therapist said she was not aberrant, only in-

---

78. Lauren Slater, *Prozac Diary* (New York: Random House, 1998), 22.
79. Mairs, *Plaintext*, 141–42.

troverted. But gender socialization had taught Mairs early that her introversion would keep her off the road to happiness. At least in a world of gendered expectations, she did not value adequately

> the paving stone of a womanly existence: to create and elaborate the social bonds that sustain community. Church fairs. Choir picnics. PTA. Summer playground programs. Covered-dish suppers. Christmas pageants. The men may leave the community regularly . . . but they leave their women behind . . .[80]

And so, for many years to come, she tried to make herself into the kind of wife and mother gender socialization said she was not and ought to be. As part of that effort, she suppressed her passion—writing—and "almost died of sorrow."[81]

Soul-sufferers stand as reminders to the so-called sane that none of us should simply adjust to the violence, and "progress," and bigotry among us, but we should protest it. If soul-suffering is in some sense a protest against injustice, then the stigmatization of the psychiatrically ill is evidence of the social pressure levied against all of us not to protest but to adjust, to acquiesce to the din of social violence with our silence or appropriateness or sanity. From this point of view, ironically, psychic anguish may in some cases be a more appropriate response than the numbness, denial, and adaptation that so-called healthy persons manage to maintain in the face of our society's sicknesses.

---

80. Mairs, *Plaintext*, 143.
81. Mairs, *Plaintext*, 145.

SICK FROM SEEING TOO MUCH

H er story is a paradigmatic example of how soul-sickness can be a knot of personal and social madness that is impossible to unravel. Beautifully poised, draped in a shawl of earth colors, R.B. sits on a sofa and speaks of her experience with psychic anguish. She was a student at Stanford Law School. She was the first in her family to study law. She was one of only a few African American students at the law school. She recalls being appalled by the entitled attitudes and behaviors of students—especially the male students—from privileged backgrounds. Law school is a lot of pressure for everyone, of course, and, given R.B.'s personal and social locations, the pressure was even greater for her. When things got, as she put it, "too intense" for her, she did something that probably caused a lot of people at Stanford to think she was crazy: she went into the stairwells and sang spirituals—"Way down in Egypt land, tell old Pharaoh, let my people go . . ." "My experiences there were challenging," she says, so she decided to take a leave of absence and join an intentional community for some respite. While there, in what was supposed to be safe space, she was sexually assaulted by an acquaintance who, just before he attacked her, called her "goddess." "I said to Life, 'if this is what I can expect of my species, *I need another reason to stay here,'*" and then describes having an experience not uncommon after sexual violence: "After him, I left my body, I *left my*

body.... It was as if all my boundaries had melted away." She danced and slept in forests. She wandered the streets of the city, carrying a harp and a bag with a few belongings. She spent the night in airport bathrooms. Only later, in the midst of a suicidal crisis, was she able to find her way to the healing that made it possible for her to tell her story.[82]

We find in R.B.'s suffering the tangle of personal contexts and social sicknesses on which we have been reflecting. There is some personal vulnerability in her story, certainly. Even amid racism and sexual violence, not all persons suffer madness and homelessness. But R.B.'s eventual disintegration into a state resembling dissociative identity disorder is complexly and cumulatively only a part of a larger social madness, what she calls "the matrix of miseducation"—racism, sexism, poverty, physical violence. This articulate African American woman's narrative is a river of troubled waters: the history of slavery, contemporary race-based marginalization, sexual assault at the hands of someone she thought she could trust, and society's inability to shelter its wounded.

Are psychiatric disorders overdiagnosed, as many think? Or is the prevalence of diagnosable suffering a measure of how crazy life can—and often should—make any and all of us? There are social values that, from any point of view, are sick and affect us all. They can make even the healthiest among us sick at heart. But as Sharon O'Brien says, "we prefer to offer individual solutions to what are social and economic problems. (That way nothing really has to change.)"[83]

But we also resist bringing a social analysis to bear on emotional turmoil because, if we did, it would be harder to deny our own vulnerability. For this reason, even feminist Gloria Steinem had trouble bringing a feminist social analysis to bear on the psychospiritual suffering her mother experienced:

> I still don't understand why so many, many years passed . . . before I understood that many of the forces in [my mother's] life were patterns women share. Like a lot of daughters, I couldn't afford to admit that what had happened to my mother was not

---

82. Allie Light and Irving Saraf, prod., Allie Light, dir., *Dialogues with Madwomen*, 90 mins, 1993. Interview with R.B.
83. O'Brien, *The Family Silver*, 268.

all personal or accidental. It would have meant admitting it could happen to me.[84]

For different reasons, many people cannot choose what Steinem could—to not see the social patterns and their costs to us. One final dynamic in mentalism needs to be addressed. People in psychic turmoil are often treated like invalids and as if what they perceive is, as well, invalid. Those whose perceptions are different from the status quo are caricatured as "out of it," not "with it": assumed to be diminished in their capacity to perceive, understand, and assess reality—material or spiritual. But in many cases the opposite seems to be true—that people become psychospiritually ill at least in part because they see too much, because they lack the screens and filters most of us have to distance ourselves from extremes of pain and evil—joy, too. Perhaps the intensity of soul-sufferers' stories, the searing pain they experience, and the wisdom they have to convey comes from being immersed "in it"—near drowning in life, in sensitized awareness not only to the pain and evil but also to core spiritual values like responsiveness and justice. Perhaps we can be functional according to the standards of health only when we do not allow ourselves acute sensitivity to the world, are able to go numb, avoid seeing or feeling not only that which is terrifying and enraging but also the exquisitely beautiful and joyful enticements of our world. If so, in a very real sense, then, it is the so-called healthy who are "out of it," and those marginalized because of their psychiatric disorders or other soul-anguish who often demonstrate the capacity for spiritual integrity and religious searching for which many in contemporary times say they are yearning.

Having attuned ourselves to the multifaceted identity of our memoirists—they are more than their suffering, they are unique individuals, and they struggle with social sicknesses in which we are all immersed— we turn our attention to their descriptions of their suffering.

---

84. Gloria Steinem, *Outrageous Acts and Everyday Rebellions*, 2nd ed. (New York: Henry Holt, 1995), 155.

PART THREE

SUFFERING

Time is fluid, and so are the boundaries

between human beings, the border separat-

ing helper from the one who hurts always

blurry. Wounds, I think, are never confined

to a single skin but reach out to rasp us all.

When you die, there's that much less breath

to the world, and across continents someone

supposedly separate gasps for air.

—Lauren Slater
Welcome to My Country

BUILDING ON OUR REFLECTIONS that people are more than their illnesses and that social sicknesses complicate personal experience, we will now delve more deeply into how the suffering affects primary sufferers and their loved ones personally in the context of their day-to-day lives. Even when we want to understand soul-suffering, however, we are immediately confronted by the difficulty of doing so. First, nearly every memoir testifies to the indescribability of the suffering. Soul-sufferers are often overlooked and not listened to and then are frustrated to find that when someone is listening, it is hard to put the story into words. In part, this is because words are inadequate. But the indescribability is also because the suffering (and the healing, if any) is embedded in a whole life narrative that is difficult to convey in a book, impossible to convey in an essay or a conversation. We are cautioned not to mistake the descriptions of moments for a lifetime of experience.

> It is inevitable that we abbreviate and simplify. (It is apparent even in this essay that I see no way around the words "depression" and "melancholy.") But it is one thing to use shorthand while straining against the limits of language. It is quite another to mistake such brevities for the face of suffering. . . . When we discuss suffering in simple terms of broken and fixed, mad and sane, depressed and "treated successfully," we choke the long streams of breath needed to tell of a life in whole.[1]

Also, in this part of the book we will emphasize suffering's most negative aspects, thus making it more difficult to remember that, as we will address in part 5, soul-suffering is often paradoxical, and some people find some healing. Most of us are inclined anyway to think that suffering is to be avoided and illness is completely negative. When we comprehend our memoirists, however, it will be easier to remember that what is experienced as pain and society labels as disorder sometimes also has value. Also, those experienced in emotional anguish convey with remarkable frequency that their efforts to avoid their suffering brought greater heartache, while their

---

1. Joshua Wolf Shenk, "A Melancholy of Mine Own," in *Unholy Ghost: Writers on Depression,* ed. Nell Casey (New York: Harper Perennial, 2002), 246, 247.

willingness to confront their suffering increased their well-being. Thus, they caution us: in describing the severity of their suffering they are not necessarily wishing it away, condemning it as pointless, or implying that health and happiness are entitlements. For some, at least in retrospect, the suffering can even be seen to have conveyed important meanings. Previously we considered Susanna Kaysen's candid description of depression's suffering—"some of the time, some of us feel like hell"—but she presses on.

> I think melancholy is useful. In its aspect of pensive reflection or contemplation, it's the source of many books (even those complaining about it) and paintings, much scientific insight, the resolution of many fights between couples and friends, and the process known as becoming mature. . . .
>
> Those feelings are unpleasant, but they spur change. What would we be without self-doubt and despair? . . .
>
> If the price of being happier is an occluded worldview, I don't want to pay it. I'd rather see things clearly.[2]

So we begin by reflecting on the initial and most acute aspects of the suffering. Given the chronic nature of much soul-suffering and all psychiatric conditions, we will then explore longer-term dynamics of the anguish. In the third section, we consider the special anguish of suicidality. The anguish is remarkably similar for the primary sufferer and for her or his loved ones, but there are some burdens particular to friends and, especially, family, and we turn to those to conclude this part of the book. Because of its relentless focus on the suffering, this part of the book has been difficult to write, and you may find it difficult to read. It is important to remember that in this part of the book we bracket the more positive and healing functions of soul-suffering for the sake of comprehending a depth of suffering that is hard—intellectually and emotionally—to grasp. Do hold in mind, however, that the lives of soul-sufferers are far more than their suffering, and in life positive experiences more integrated with the pain. Our adequate comprehension of their lives cannot be gained by looking at this one facet but depends also on what we will address as we proceed—care, healing, and wisdom.

---

2. Susanna Kaysen, "One Cheer for Melancholy," in *Unholy Ghost*, 38, 39, 40.

ACUTE ANGUISH

ITS EMERGENCE

Remarkably, the emergence of soul-suffering may be invisible to everyone but the sufferer. Suffering is more than meets the eye—we can be in the presence of psychic turmoil and never know it. Sometimes this is because people in emotional anguish can remain unexpectedly productive. Although Professor Howard Stone was depressed for months, he notes that "my melancholy never reached the point of incapacitation; I functioned in my job, gave service to the community, visited friends, stayed married."[3] Sometimes the suffering is invisible to onlookers because they cannot see the gap between productivity and potential: writing of her breakdown, Charlotte Perkins Gilman sounds exasperated when describing people's insistence on her giftedness and refusal to believe in suffering they cannot see.

> Friends gibber amiably, "I wish I had your mind!" I wish they had, for a while, as a punishment for doubting my word. What confuses them is the visible work I have been able to accomplish. . . . They do not see blank months of idleness; nor can they see what the work would have been if the powerful mind I had to begin with had not broken . . . [4]

---

3. Howard W. Stone, *Depression and Hope: New Insights for Pastoral Counseling* (Minneapolis: Fortress Press, 1998), 1.
4. Charlotte Perkins Gilman, *The Living of Charlotte Perkins Gilman: An Autobiography* (New York: D. Appleton-Century, 1935), 98.

Of course, sometimes, because of stigma and the shame it breeds, sufferers hide their suffering until they can't anymore: "I have kept the severity of my depression hidden from everyone I know until twelve weeks ago, when I reached zero. Completely depleted, I collapsed," writes Jyl Felman.[5] Some people are able to hide their suffering for a long time. For two years, Rev. Susan Gregg-Schroeder did not reveal to her congregation that she was suffering depression and undergoing several hospitalizations.[6]

Whether obvious to all or known only to themselves, however, it is important to almost all memoirists to comment on when and how their suffering emerged—the day or the age is important to identify, a reader senses, because it marks a turning point in their lives beyond their wildest imaginings. There is great variation, but some patterns in emergence can be identified. For example, numerous memoirists relay stories of soul-suffering that emerges dangerously in childhood and teenage years, even though the general public tends to think that children are spared soul-suffering. For some of our memoirists, their psychic turmoil is a presence from their earliest memories.

Meri Danquah: There are times when I feel like I've known depression longer than I have known myself.[7]

Kay Redfield Jamison: For as long as I can remember I was frighteningly, although often wonderfully, beholden to moods. Intensely emotional as a child, mercurial as a young girl, first severely depressed as an adolescent . . .[8]

Nancy Mairs: Two days after my fifteenth birthday I wrote, "For the 1st time in my life I asked God to take my life & meant it." I soon made this prayer an almost daily habit.[9]

---

5. Jyl Lynn Felman, "Nurturing the Soul," *Tikkun* vol. 11, no. 4 (July–August 1996): 50.

6. Susan Gregg-Schroeder, "The Face of Depression," *Circuit Rider* vol. 27, no. 1 (January–February, 2003): 5.

7. Meri Nana-Ama Danquah, "Writing the Wrongs of Identity," in *Unholy Ghost*, 174.

8. Kay Redfield Jamison, *An Unquiet Mind* (New York: Random House, Vintage Books, 1995), 4–5.

9. Nancy Mairs, *Plaintext: Essays by Nancy Mairs* (Tucson: University of Arizona Press, 1986), 132.

Sharon O'Brien: When I got depressed for the first time I had no idea what was happening, and no words for the experience.

It was the summer after tenth grade.[10]

These and other female memoirists, as we noted in part 1, reflect in their memoirs on the effect of gender socialization and racial dynamics on emotional experience; it is probable that the dawning awareness of sexism and racism that affects most schoolgirls is one of several factors affecting the emergence of psychic turmoil in girl children.

Tracy Thompson remembers feelings and behaviors that suggest she was depressed in grammar school. She also remembers the day in her fourteenth year that she began a private journal and wrote that she had two reasons for trying this experiment. One was, endearingly, to practice her writing. The other purpose, she wrote in the journal, was "to put down the cause of my depressions and to see if I can help myself that way. . . . It sounds horrible, and it is, but a couple of times I have thought how nice it would be to kill myself!!!"[11] Lizzie Simon's experience crystallizes that of others whose anguish surfaces as they embark on college or other transitions into young adulthood—the emergence of her anguish came in the form of an abrupt psychotic episode.

It all started the day after I had been accepted for early admission to Columbia College.

December 19, 1993.

I was seventeen years old. . . .

And everything was perfect. For just a moment, a few hours really, a morning. And then I went insane.[12]

These examples remind us that emotional illness strikes at a young age and that children and teenagers struggle, too often with very few resources, to understand what is happening to them.

---

10. Sharon O'Brien, *The Family Silver: A Memoir of Depression and Inheritance* (Chicago: University of Chicago Press, 2004), 45.

11. Tracy Thompson, *The Beast: A Journey through Depression* (New York: Penguin; Plume, 1995), 5.

12. Lizzie Simon, *Detour: My Bipolar Road Trip in 4-D* (New York: Washington Square Press, 2002), 1, 11.

We tend to assume that persons who reach midlife or old age without previous psychic turmoil will live out all their days in a similar way. However, the memoirs tell of devastating psychic suffering that occurs in persons who had previously known psychic well-being. Not infrequently, this new aspect of a person's life is interwoven with losses associated with aging. Until his retirement, James Farmer was one of the dynamic "Big Four" of the civil rights movement, working tirelessly alongside Martin Luther King Jr., Whitney Young, and Roy Wilkins in the mid-1950s and '60s. However, in the final pages of his autobiography, he recounts that late in life, due to grief over the death of his wife and a dramatic decline in his eyesight, he fell into depression.[13] Given our exploration in part 2 of the ways in which racial politics can complicate depression in people of color, we need also to consider that perhaps the grief and blindness finally precipitated depression in a man who had long borne the trauma of racism and the fight against it. Albert Hsu's father committed suicide at age fifty-eight, three months after suffering a stroke that left him physically impaired; although others saw his physical abilities returning, Hsu's depression, perhaps an effect of the stroke and not only a reaction to loss of ability, did not relent. For William Hulme, the factor of his age at the first emergence of depression was so significant that he begins his memoir with these sentences: "Had I died shortly before my seventieth birthday, I would never have known a depression. It was the last thing that I anticipated."[14]

Stereotypes of mental illness tend to portray its emergence as a sudden, unmistakable eruption. This is sometimes the case—there can be a moment remembered that changed everything forever. Not infrequently, schizophrenia's onset happens this way: in a matter of hours or days, a family is drawn into the vortex of illness, as was true for the Hansons. Dan recalls: "Parents live in fear of the dreaded phone call, the one with the message that their child is ill, hurt, or otherwise in trouble. . . . I remember our phone call as if it were yesterday. . . . Sue was on the phone frantically explaining that J was missing."[15] Betty Holder remembers

---

13. James Farmer, *Lay Bare the Heart: An Autobiography of the Civil Rights Movement* (New York: Arbor House, 1985), 350–351.

14. William Hulme and Lucy Hulme, *Wrestling with Depression: A Spiritual Guide to Reclaiming Life* (Minneapolis: Augsburg Books, 1995), 7.

15. Daniel S. Hanson, *Room for J: A Family Struggles with Schizophrenia* (Edina, Minn.: Beaver's Pond Press, 2005), 19.

when the reality of her son's illness broke into her consciousness: "One January afternoon in 1970 . . . my husband, a physician, said to me in a voice choked with grief, 'Alan is schizophrenic.'"[16] For others, it *feels* out of the blue: "overnight, it seemed," Virginia Heffernan recalls, "I'd gone from a twenty-eight-year-old optimist, the type advertisers and politicians take into account, who might find a career and start a family, to a person who is unreliable and preoccupied, a person other people find themselves trying to avoid."[17]

However, our memoirists also struggle with soul-suffering that insinuates itself slowly, in ways that are hard to understand or sometimes even to notice. Even in adulthood, people may not be informed enough about soul-suffering to recognize it and tend it. Or, persons already marginalized may think they cannot "afford" emotional illness. As Meri Danquah puts it, "Clinical depression simply did not exist within the realm of . . . possibilities for any of the black women in my world." In such situations, it can sneak up and, untended, erode a life, as Danquah recounts.

> My relationship with depression began long before I noticed it. . . . Out of nowhere and for no apparent reason—or so it seemed—I started feeling strong sensations of grief. . . . My life disintegrated; first, into a strange and terrifying space of sadness, and then, into a cobweb of fatigue. I gradually lost my ability to function. It would take me hours to get up out of bed, get bathed, put clothes on.[18]

As Kay Redfield Jamison learned, however, education about psychic turmoil does not guarantee that one will recognize it when it emerges closer to home. Even as she was being trained to recognize in other people the symptoms she exhibited herself, she made no connection between her problems and what her textbooks then called manic-depressive illness.

> In a strange reversal of medical-students syndrome, where students become convinced that they have whatever disease it is they

---

16. Betty Holder, "Living on the Edge: Experiences of Family Members," in *New Directions in the Psychological Treatment of Serious Mental Illness*, ed. Diane T. Marsh (Westport, Conn.: Praeger, 1994), 151–52.

17. Virginia Heffernan, "A Delicious Placebo," in *Unholy Ghost*, 9.

18. Meri Nana-Ama Danquah, *Willow Weep for Me: A Black Woman's Journey through Depression—A Memoir* (New York: W.W. Norton, 1998), 18–19, 27.

are studying, I blithely went on with my clinical training and never put my mood swings into any medical context whatsoever. When I look back on it, my denial and ignorance seem virtually incomprehensible.[19]

When persons in emotional distress are perceived to be in denial of their illness or other soul-suffering, they are often judged, disdainfully—and, often, inaccurately—for what is seen as willful recalcitrance or denial. But this impatience on the part of the well is directed at an effect of illness, the cognitive impairment that accompanies many acute psychic disturbances. In Clifford Beers' response to such situations, the pain that is secondary to being judged for one's unrecognized suffering in an episode of mania is barely hidden.

When one possessed of the power of recognizing his own errors continues to hold an unreasonable belief—that is stubbornness. But for a man bereft of reason to adhere to an idea which to him seems absolutely correct and true because he has been deprived of the means of detecting his error—that is not stubbornness. It is a symptom of his disease, and merits the indulgence of forbearance, if not genuine sympathy.[20]

Similarly, people being drawn into an episode of melancholia are often judged for not seeing that they need to get help, but as Tracy Thompson points out, "a person who is slipping into depression cannot know the changes going on in his brain. It is impossible to understand that you are getting sick when the hallmark symptom of that sickness is the loss of feeling."[21] Or, a bit differently, what looks like denial might actually be, as in Meri Danquah's experience, an effort on the part of the afflicted to play by centuries-old historical-cultural values.

I beat up on myself for not being able to get with the program. After all, I'd tell myself, I was not the first woman to work and

19. Jamison, *An Unquiet Mind,* 58–59.
20. Clifford W. Beers, *A Mind That Found Itself: An Autobiography,* 5th ed. rev. (Garden City, N.Y.: Doubleday, Doran & Co., 1944), 50.
21. Thompson, *The Beast,* 112.

raise a child simultaneously. Black women have been doing that for ages, with and without partners. Some even held down two jobs while raising three and four children. No one ever made mention of these women griping about depression. It was a luxury that they couldn't afford. What made me think I was so special?[22]

If you have ever been puzzled about why emotional suffering springs up—in your life or in someone you know—when everything seems to be going well, the memoirists shed light on this experience. They tell of experience when the timing of spiritual agony is counter-intuitive. Sometimes this is because psychiatric disorders are never cured, always threatening recurrence. As in the previously noted example of Martha Manning, who had what she called "smaller depressions," sufferers may experience episodic recurrences that require adjustments in medication or rehospitalization. Also, as Sharon O'Brien reminds us, counter to our expectations, anguish can, rather startlingly, first emerge full-blown after the satisfaction of our hearts' desires—"after moving into longed-for retirement, after getting tenure, after the party is over and the guests have left. The gain is also a loss—not just of the completed project, but also of the identity and purpose invested in it."[23] For O'Brien, it happened when depression struck her right after a success—her biography of Willa Cather was published, "bringing to fruition fifteen years of work." Of his breakdown and hospitalization the famous preacher Harry Emerson Fosdick says that "it was not trouble that slew me but happiness—the excitement of the most exhilarating opportunity I had ever had": the start of his seminary studies.[24] In retrospect, Henri Nouwen surmises that though the timing of his breakdown seemed irrational, his pained soul had a logic of another kind.

> The strange thing was that this [most difficult period of my life] happened shortly after I had found my true home. After many years of life in universities, where I never felt fully at home, I had become a member of L'Arche, a community of men and women with mental disabilities. I had been received with open arms,

22. Danquah, *Willow Weep for Me*, 195.
23. O'Brien, *The Family Silver*, 208.
24. Harry Emerson Fosdick, *The Living of These Days: An Autobiography* (New York: Harper and Brothers, 1956), 72.

given all the attention and affection I could ever hope for, and offered a safe and loving place to grow spiritually as well as emotionally. Everything seemed ideal. But precisely at that time I fell apart—as if I needed a safe place to hit bottom![25]

IMAGES AND METAPHORS

Images and metaphors for suffering are numerous and very personal—only a small sample of our memoirists' descriptions will be noted here. Indeed, if you or a loved one have known psychic anguish, there may well be a symbol or other representation that is very meaningful to you but that doesn't appear in our discussion. There are, however, a few common characterizations of psychic turmoil, and the most common is of striking theological significance: severe psychospiritual suffering is hell. For example:

> Norma Swetnam: Some theologians interpret hell as alienation from God. I have experienced such a hell while in the throes of depression—a terrible sense of aloneness and isolation from everything, from everybody and from God. This results in a loss of hope for the future, and without hope what is there?[26]

> Betty Holder: As I walked into his hospital room, Alan intoned in a sepulchral voice, "Abandon hope, all ye who enter here!" Recognizing the inscription over the gate to Hell in Dante's *Inferno*, I knew that my son, always a bookish person, was telling me that he was in Hell. At that moment, I did not doubt that he was, indeed, in Hell.[27]

> Susan Gregg-Schroeder: I had descended into hell. The Apostles' Creed suddenly took on new meaning and significance for me—Jesus descended into hell. And I was in my own personal hell. I could not will my way out of this deep darkness, and so I had to learn how to abide in the shadow.[28]

---

25. Henri J. M. Nouwen, *The Inner Voice of Love: A Journey through Anguish to Freedom* (New York: Doubleday, Image Books, 1996), xiii–xiv.

26. Norma G. Swetnam, "My Journey through Hell," in *Presbyterians Today Online* (August 1998), http://www.pcusa.org/today/archive/features/feat9808d.htm (accessed August 1, 2006): 1.

27. Holder, "Living on the Edge," 156.

28. Susan Gregg-Schroeder, *In the Shadow of God's Wings: Grace in the Midst of Depression* (Nashville: Upper Room Books, 1997), 30.

Dan Hanson: Living with someone who is mentally ill is living with constant fear that conflict will erupt and things will fall apart. And for me that is like living in hell.[29]

It may be tempting to defuse this characterization by treating it as metaphor only. However, to do so is theologically unwise, since these narratives relentlessly enumerate evidence that the concept of hell may indeed name an actual dimension of human suffering and not either a mere metaphor or an imagined future threat. In the experience of severe psychospiritual suffering, "hell" is less a place of the soul's possible punishment after death and more the everyday and endless pain of a psychospiritually sick soul with no hope that suffering will ever end *except*, ironically, in death.

In narratives of severe psychospiritual suffering, "hell"—whether in the future or the present—has a distinctive torment: the illnesses themselves often cause afflicted ones to feel that they are elementally corrupt, in contrast to being unfairly or accidentally wounded. Tracy Thompson's depression, which emerged while she was in grammar school, caused her to feel deficient and led to a precise long-lasting religious certainty, despite the fact that she was "born-again": "I was not going to heaven. I could not remember a time when I did not know that."[30] Science has proven that many sufferings once explainable only as demonic possession or deserved divine punishment are in fact disorders of the brain or treatable emotional disabilities. Nonetheless, the nonrational sense of wrongdoing and self-blame is a common symptom or side-effect of psychiatric illness. For many people living with the often invisible, still mysterious, soul-betraying symptomotology of severe psychospiritual suffering, every day is "judgment day."

Biblical literature provides other images of the anguish. Joshua Shenk turns to Psalm 38: "I am often 'bowed down greatly.'"[31] Divisions within the black community regarding psychiatry and the mental health system make poignant sense of why Meri Danquah uses Song of Solomon 1:6–7 (KJV) as the epigraph for her memoir: "Look not upon me, because I am black, because the sun hath looked upon me: my mother's children were angry with me; they made me the keeper of the vineyards; but mine own

---

29. Hanson, *Room for J*, 37.
30. Thompson, *The Beast*, 20.
31. Shenk, "A Melancholy of Mine Own," in *Unholy Ghost*, 250. Psalm 38:6 (KJV).

vineyard have I not kept." The biblical accounting of Jesus' birth and life suggests a possibility of some greater meaning in the experience of the Hansons.

> J believes that he was Jesus in another life, and is therefore, God. We know that he is not, but, still we can't help but notice in some ways he does resemble the biblical Jesus. Like Jesus, J does not fit in this world. There is no room for him in any "inn" we know of. The only way for J to be accepted by our world is to become just like the rest of us, and that is something he cannot do.[32]

Readers of his memoir will sense the love and respect Dan has for J, and the plea to the rest of us, when he inverts the negative biblical image in the title to his memoir. In *Room for J*, Dan also uses a biblical reference to convey the depth of his own anguish. When J's delusions are endangering his life, Dan and Sue Hanson call the police and have their son hospitalized and medicated against his will. Feeling as if he has betrayed J, more than once Dan identifies himself with the biblical character of Judas.[33]

Sometimes the titles of memoirs convey meaningful images of the anguish their authors have experienced. Depression is the beast[34] and the noonday demon.[35] A woman institutionalized for schizophrenia is nobody's child.[36] A hospitalization against one's will because of mania is the loony-bin trip.[37] A minister suffering depression says his is a soul under siege.[38] Cycling mania and melancholy lead to an unquiet mind.[39] Bulimia is the monster within.[40] Families describe themselves as the outsider[41] and

---

32. Hanson, *Room for J*, 89.
33. Hanson, *Room for J*, 32, 43–44.
34. Thompson, *The Beast*.
35. Andrew Solomon, *The Noonday Demon: An Atlas of Depression* (New York: Scribner, 2001).
36. Marie Balter and Richard Katz, *Nobody's Child* (Reading, Mass.: Addison-Wesley, 1987).
37. Kate Millett, *The Loony-Bin Trip* (New York: Simon & Schuster, 1990).
38. C. Welton Gaddy, *A Soul Under Siege: Surviving Clergy Depression* (Louisville: Westminster John Knox Press, 1991).
39. Jamison, *An Unquiet Mind*.
40. Cynthia Joye Rowland, *The Monster Within: Overcoming Bulimia* (Grand Rapids, Mich.: Baker Book House, 1984).
41. Nathaniel Lachenmeyer, *The Outsider: A Journey into My Father's Struggle with Madness* (New York: Broadway Books, 2000).

hidden victims.[42] Other titles capture the ambiguity of madness: the daughter of a woman with schizophrenia is her mother's keeper[43]; bipolar disorder is a brilliant madness.[44]

Other images are less boldly conveyed but carefully articulated within pages of explanatory description. Henri Nouwen's suffering was "one long scream coming from a place I didn't know existed."[45] Sharon O'Brien describes the emergence of her depression: "I'd lie in bed as long as I could, submerged in a dark, clotted lake. Sounds were muffled, voices remote; I was living underwater."[46] Howard Stone: "I am lost in an immense underground cavern with tangled, unending passageways. . . . Earlier I tried mightily to get out, to find the light of day again, but it is no longer possible and I no longer care. I am very, very tired. . . . I have no real hope for the direction I am going . . . God is absent."[47] Lauren Slater: "How do you describe emptiness? Is it the air inside a bubble, the darkness in a pocket, snow?"[48]

We must be cautious not to allow prevalent images to distract us from the uniqueness of each person's suffering. For example, especially for the suffering of melancholy, darkness is a common image. The familiarity of two illustrations makes the point: Winston Churchill called his depression "the black dog"; William Styron titled the meditation he wrote on his melancholy *Darkness Visible*. But for Meri Danquah, this common image says nothing about her depression, nor even carries any negative connotations except perhaps that it hints at the way emotional fears and racism feed on one another.

> You've heard descriptions of depression before: A black hole; an enveloping darkness; a dismal existence through which no light shines; the black dog; darkness, and more darkness. But what does darkness mean to me, a woman who has spent her life surrounded by it? The darkness of my skin; the darkness of my

---

42. Julie Tallard Johnson, *Hidden Victims: An Eight-Stage Healing Process for Families and Friends of the Mentally Ill* (New York: Doubleday, 1988).

43. Tara Elgin Holley, with Joe Holley, *My Mother's Keeper: A Daughter's Memoir of Growing Up in the Shadow of Schizophrenia* (New York: Avon Books, 1997).

44. Patty Duke and Gloria Hochman, *A Brilliant Madness: Living with Manic-Depressive Illness* (New York: Bantam, 1992).

45. Nouwen, *The Inner Voice of Love*, xiv–xv.

46. O'Brien, *The Family Silver*, 45.

47. Stone, *Depression and Hope*, 1.

48. Slater, *Prozac Diary*, 16.

friends and family. I have never been afraid of the dark. It poses no harm to me. What is the color of my depression?[49]

One of Danquah's descriptions reminds us that for some people emotional suffering has not one face but many.

> Depression offers layers, textures, noises. At times depression is as flimsy as a feather, barely penetrating the surface of my life, hovering like a slight halo of pessimism. Other times it comes on gradually like a common cold or a storm, each day presenting new signals and symptoms until finally I am drowning in it. Most times, in its most superficial and seductive sense, it is rich and enticing. A field of velvet waiting to embrace me. It is loud and dizzying, inviting the tenors and screeching sopranos of thoughts, unrelenting sadness, and the sense of impending doom.[50]

Finally, while most images of the suffering are unequivocally characterized by pain's costs, some painful images have within them intimations of healing to come. His therapist offered Parker Palmer an image that proved so crucial that Palmer says now it "helped me eventually reclaim my life."

> "You seem to look upon depression as the hand of an enemy trying to crush you," [my therapist] said. "Do you think you could see it instead as the hand of a friend, pressing you down to ground on which it is safe to stand?"[51]

"Impossibly romantic, even insulting," Palmer says of this image's first impression on him in the context of depression's onslaught. But in the same moment he scoffed at it, Palmer writes that the image was able to start its gradual remedial work because "something in me knew, . . . knew that down . . . was the direction of wholeness."

Reflecting on his life through the image, Palmer began to perceive that his suffering had started before his depression struck. He had been

49. Danquah, *Willow Weep for Me*, 22.
50. Danquah, *Willow Weep for Me*, 22.
51. Parker J. Palmer, *Let Your Life Speak: Listening for the Voice of Vocation* (San Francisco: Jossey-Bass, 2000), 66.

living an ungrounded life, he says, "living at an altitude that was inherently unsafe."

> The problem with living at high altitude is simple: when we slip, as we always do, we have a long, long way to fall, and the landing may well kill us. The grace of being pressed down to the ground is also simple: when we slip and fall, it is usually not fatal, and we can get back up.[52]

He retraced the climb: operating out of his head, not inhabiting his whole body; inflating his ego to ward off fears of his insufficiency; embracing an ethic of "oughts" rather than of humanness and authenticity; and—perhaps this one, especially, allowed the others to go unreformed in this person of faith—accepting abstractions about G-d more than seeking experience of G-d. He also saw that depression seemed an enemy primarily because he had for so many years ignored sociable efforts by his interior life to get his attention. He began to imagine within him this friend, who had something life-saving to say but, because Palmer refused to listen, the friend, and the messages, had to become increasingly emphatic. At first, the friend just waved and shouted from a distance, then came closer to tap him on the shoulder. Still ignored, the friend became desperate, given what was at stake, and threw stones at Palmer's back and struck him with a stick. Nothing. Finally, depressing Palmer was the last-ditch effort of the friend to save Palmer's inner life, to get him to "turn and ask the simple question, 'What do you want?' When I was finally able to make that turn—and start to absorb and act on the self-knowledge that then became available to me—I began to get well."[53] In part 5 we will see that the wellness this image set in motion included greater wholeness in his notion of G-d.

PHYSICAL ASPECTS OF ACUTE ANGUISH

In acute phases, psychic turmoil often reveals the error of our dualistic thinking about mind and body. For some sufferers, the acute episode is precipitated by a physical crisis, not an emotional or spiritual one. Especially in the case of depression and mania, acute episodes can be pre-

---

52. Palmer, *Let Your Life Speak*, 66.
53. Palmer, *Let Your Life Speak*, 68.

cipitated by physical processes of chemistry and neurology. Unexpectedly, some people in the grip of melancholy feel their emotional pain in their bodies.

> One day it might be a "grief knot" in my throat. On another it might be chest pains that could easily be mistaken for a heart attack. Other days it might be an awful heaviness in my eyes, pressure in my head, feelings of sadness in my cheeks, shaky hands and legs, or even some combination of all these. On my most difficult days I was constantly aware of my body, monitoring from minute to minute whether things had become better or worse.[54]

After Lauren Slater's writings gained some public attention, she was interviewed on television and radio.

> "What is depression like?" interviewers ask, and you answer obediently, laying out all the horrifying things you did to yourself, to your skin, when what you really wish they'd ask is, "Where did it hurt?" and you would say, "In my throat, at the backs of my eyes, deep down in my gut, in every tooth."[55]

Though it happens far less often than stereotypes suggest, acute breakdown sometimes brings physical violence. Especially as a mental health professional, and in light of the stereotypes and stigma attached to such behavior, especially for females, Kay Redfield Jamison is notably courageous to include this part of her story in her memoir. I include the following remarkable passage in its entirety because it captures—in the voice of a primary sufferer—the many forms of violence experienced, its devastating aftermath—including the devastation to one's ability to trust oneself—and the capacity of some relationships to recover from violence.

> Both my manias and depressions had violent sides to them. Violence, especially if you are a woman, is not something spoken about with ease. Being wildly out of control—physically assaultive, screaming insanely at the top of one's lungs, running frenetically with no purpose or limit, or impulsively trying to

---

54. David A. Karp, *Speaking of Sadness: Depression, Disconnection, and the Meanings of Illness* (New York: Oxford University Press, 1996), 7.
55. Lauren Slater, "Noontime," in *Unholy Ghost*, 80.

leap from cars—is frightening to others and unspeakably terrifying to oneself. In blind manic rages I have done all these
things, at one time or another, and some of them repeatedly; I remain acutely and painfully aware of how difficult it is to control
or understand such behaviors, much less explain them to others.
I have, in my psychotic, seizurelike attacks—my black, agitated
manias—destroyed things I cherish, pushed to the utter edge
people I love, and survived to think I could never recover from
the shame. I have been physically restrained by terrible, brute
force; kicked and pushed to the floor; thrown on my stomach
with my hands pinned behind my back; and heavily medicated
against my will.

I do not know how I have recovered from having done the
things that necessitated such actions, any more than I know how
and why my relationships with friends and lovers have survived
the grinding wear and tear of such dark, fierce, and damaging
energy. The aftermath of such violence, like the aftermath of a
suicide attempt, is deeply bruising to all concerned. And, as with
a suicide attempt, living with the knowledge that one has been
violent forces a difficult reconciliation of totally divergent notions of oneself. After my suicide attempt, I had to reconcile my
image of myself as a young girl who had been filled with enthu-
siasm, high hopes, great expectations, enormous energy, and
dreams and love of life, with that of a dreary, crabbed, pained
woman who desperately wished only for death and took a lethal
dose of lithium in order to accomplish it. After each of my violent psychotic episodes, I had to try and reconcile my notion of
myself as a reasonably quiet-spoken and highly disciplined person, one at least generally sensitive to the moods and feelings of
others, with an enraged, utterly insane, and abusive woman who
lost access to all control or reason.[56]

DIFFICULTY OF ACCESSING TREATMENT

In acute emotional anguish, help is difficult to access. As we have noted,
sometimes cognitive distortion interferes with the sufferers' capacity to

---

56. Jamison, *An Unquiet Mind*, 120–21.

recognize the need for help. Even more often, sufferers silence themselves because of cultural and personal expectations of self-reliance—"I must not disgrace my family," and "I should be able to handle this on my own." The strength of this last obstacle is illustrated by the nonsequitur in Kay Redfield Jamison's thinking about getting help.

> I decided early in graduate school that I needed to do something about my moods. It quickly came down to a choice between seeing a psychiatrist, or buying a horse. Since almost everyone I knew was seeing a psychiatrist and since I had an absolute belief that I should be able to handle my own problems, I naturally bought a horse.[57]

Other sufferers withdraw, even hide, because of the stigma against emotional difference and how it is complicated by other prejudices. As we addressed in part 2, some people of color find asking for help to be fruitless or dangerous, because racism has made "help" ambiguous, at best. Others face related systemic issues, for example, no one speaks their language or understands their culture. Some fear prejudice against or incompatibility with their religious beliefs, but sometimes religious teaching and ethnic tradition intertwine to make mental health treatment irrelevant, as in Sharon O'Brien's family.

> [T]he religious and cultural ethic of Irish Catholicism stresses silent suffering. "Offer it up," people used to say about some tragedy or setback, which might, if endured well, grant you "a higher place in Heaven," as if the hereafter were organized by the reverse of earthly values. If you're Irish, suffering is supposed to make you a better person: you're supposed to endure it, not seek help to deal with it.[58]

But even for those willing to use the mental health system when acute suffering first emerges, getting the help they need is not assured. Not uncommonly, primary sufferers and their loved ones haven't faced such a situation before and don't know where to turn for help—An emergency room? A mental health clinic? A psychiatric hospital? A doctor?—and, if so, what doctor deals with emotional emergencies? In situations where

---

57. Jamison, *An Unquiet Mind*, 55.
58. O'Brien, *The Family Silver*, 159.

the primary sufferer or others are in danger of physical harm, some families call 911 or the police; we will reflect later on the special anguish experienced by families who, for the sake of safety, have their loved ones hospitalized, medicated, or in other ways treated involuntarily.

THE SHOCK OF LOSS

The losses of acute phases are devastating and, usually, seem to come out of the blue. Certainly, most devastating and shocking is loss of life, and the lives of suicide survivors have a stark before-and-after quality—"Suicide [of a loved one] bisects your life with a thick dark line."[59] Similarly, as Jamison described previously, acute psychic turmoil can cause a loss of innocence that can never be regained: one experiences or witnesses in a loved one overwhelming and oftentimes terrifying changes in emotion and behavior—violence, but also desolation or mania—that seem to have obliterated the person's previous personality, habits, and values. Primary sufferers and their loved ones are left with shattered assumptions and demolished naiveté. Almost as disturbing is loss of the primary sufferer's capacity to reason and assess danger, which tends to result as well in loss of relationship: the efforts of loved ones to convince the primary sufferer that she or he is behaving nonrationally can break down the closest ties.

However, for family members, this loss of capacity to exert beneficial influence in the life of the suffering loved one reaches beyond trying to exert rational influence—in acute phases, even one's love seems to have lost its effectuality. In an effort to comfort her, Martha Manning's teenage daughter Keara was reassured that she had no responsibility for her mother's clinical depression. For Keara, however, this also meant she was helpless to ease her mother's pain. "One of the worst things was seeing my mom in so much pain and being constantly reminded that it wasn't my fault and there was nothing I could do to make her feel better."[60] Acute episodes rob not only the primary sufferer of a capacity to exert self-control. Family members young and old lose their sense of control, too, and any illusions they had about others' ca-

---

59. Albert Y. Hsu, *Grieving a Suicide: A Loved One's Search for Comfort, Answers, and Hope* (Downers Grove, Ill.: InterVarsity Press, 2002), 20.
60. Martha Manning, "The Legacy," *Family Therapy Networker* (January–February 1997): 40.

pacity to provide decisive intervention. No one is in charge, no one can be blamed, no one has a solution.

SPIRITUAL AND RELIGIOUS DISTRESS

Finally, spiritual and religious distress is a common aspect of acute psychic turmoil. We will attend in parts 4 and 5 to how religious and spiritual experiences provide for some people sources of care and healing. But even then, much of the spiritual wisdom won from soul-suffering starts in—not simply after—the most acute phases of the anguish. This makes the suffering itself ambiguous.

The best known among the negative effects are religious or spiritual perceptions that occur as part of altered states of consciousness. Some primary sufferers agree with their families and clinicians—usually after the experiences abate—that these religious or spiritual experiences are unhealthy, precisely because it is clear that the experiences cause suffering to themselves or others. They agree that their beliefs during such periods are indeed "psychotic" or "delusional." While we tend to think delusions have to do with otherworldly misperceptions, for some the delusion is of being estranged from or persecuted by that which is sacred. Physician David Hilfiker says that "I've come to recognize that my sense of great distance from God is a delusion of my mental illness."[61] Martha Manning describes an experience while she was hospitalized that illustrates the more familiar religious delusion—identification with the divine—but also that illustrates the spiritual loss more typical in soul-suffering. Trying to relax in a hot bath, she can hear a man in the seclusion room next door exhorting heathens to repentance. She says, "I am engrossed in his ravings. I envy him his energy, and the righteousness of his rage. I wish I could feel his connection to the God who abandoned me so long ago."[62]

In some cases, however, the effect of the religious content of altered states of consciousness—what some see clearly as delusion or psychosis—is more ambiguous, and the line between delusion and religious truth more difficult to enforce. The opening sentence of Dan Hanson's memoir speaks to the centrality of religion in the upheaval his family experi-

---

61. David Hilfiker, "When Mental Illness Blocks the Spirit," *The Other Side* (May and June 2002), 13.
62. Manning, *Undercurrents*, 117.

ences: "It's been almost ten years since our son Joel declared that he was Jesus in another life and is, therefore, God."[63] J Hanson does not see his belief as delusional, and the only suffering his belief causes him is when forced hospitalization and medication cause him to fail his "calling." But his beliefs certainly bring suffering to the souls of his parents: his belief in his invincibility causes him to put himself in life-threatening situations in which Dan and Sue Hanson intervene against his will. Both the danger and the intervention cause distress to Dan and Sue, and sometimes to J as well. Even when he is not in danger and safely goes through his everyday life operating from his belief that he is God, Dan and Sue suffer the loss of their son as they knew him. But even as his memoir conveys so powerfully the anguish the family feels in response to J's religious ideas, Dan is also moved by the values at the heart of his son's delusions. "I have grown to wonder more and more if our world would not be a better place if there were fewer 'normal' people and more gentle souls with J's visions of how this world could be more loving."

> The truth is, J's delusion has made us look at spirituality in new ways. He challenges tradition and forces us to re-define our relationship with God. As you might imagine, it is hard to take God to church with you. But we have discovered that J's belief, even though it is delusional, has strengthened our own connection to that which transcends our understanding. We have been forced to see God in new, even bizarre ways.[64]

Persons familiar with psychiatric diagnostic categories see in J a serious case of schizophrenia. At the same time, persons familiar with the Bible will also recognize that J has carried to a serious length a biblical affirmation—that all persons are made in the image of God and should strive to embody that image increasingly. Similarly, when Sascha Garson's son is in the grip of mania, his apparently irrational behavior causes fear in others, or breaks the law. But sometimes he has in mind a religious teaching. Once, he received a citation for soliciting without a license because he was asking passersby for money. A short time earlier, however, he was *giving* the small change he had to passersby, since

---

63. Hanson, *Room for J*, 1.
64. Hanson, *Room for J*, 99, 112.

our religion recommends that the giver try to be anonymous to avoid shaming the poor. Withholding nothing for himself, he opens his full hands and heart to strangers and then asks others to help him with his own needs.[65]

The holy basis of this philanthropist's logic is imperceptible to the officer who tickets him. As his mother observes, the police have training to enforce laws, not "to be aware of the exhortations of the prophets." Here we see that religious values, when fully lived out to their logical, literal ends, can run afoul of expectations in secular society. The consequent social and legal penalties thus become part of the soul-suffering judged to be illness.

But it is not only the drama of delusion or psychosis that causes religious and spiritual issues to be part of soul-suffering. Some memoirists experience their illnesses as getting in the way of meaningful spiritual life. David Hilfiker has been dedicated to developing his spirituality: "an hour of quiet time daily, tithing, weekly worship, silent retreat, and participation in corporate mission." He has been a preacher and worship leader in his congregation and, having left his medical practice in Minnesota to care for homeless people in Washington, D.C., become an inspiration to other religious people. "But still, no real relationship with God. No real joy in my work. No sense of relationship with God."[66] As Hilfiker said, he now realizes that his illness causes the delusion that he is distant from God, but

> [n]onetheless, at times my depression overwhelms my spiritual life. I am sometimes unable to sit through a church service. Listening to sermons about Christian life or watching others in the community relate to each other is too difficult. I feel acutely aware of my distance, my lack of relationship. Sometimes just being there is intolerable, and I have to leave.[67]

Depression undermines spiritual life through isolation, but also by undermining a sufferer's sense of adequacy as compared to others. Hilfiker: "At times, I have kept myself outside of the faith community.

---

65. Sascha Garson, "The Sound and Fury of Mania," *Newsweek* (April 13, 1987), 10.
66. Hilfiker, "When Mental Illness Blocks the Spirit," 12.
67. Hilfiker, "When Mental Illness Blocks the Spirit," 13.

Since I felt no sense of authentic relationship with God, I didn't want to be a hypocrite."[68] For others in the midst of soul-suffering, familiar religious language can take on ominous new meanings.

> When the leader [of the study on the life of Jesus] offered the question: "What does commitment mean to me?" all I could think of in answer was the commitment of a mental patient to a mental hospital or the committal service that places a body in the ground.[69]

Beliefs that had seemed secure—even deeply considered—are found not just inadequate but painful. Fuller Theological School Professor Dean Gilliland relates his experience during a period when his son, diagnosed with paranoid schizophrenia, went missing.

> I will never forget how for three days I was lecturing in my seminary classes on the God who can be found in any situation and who rewards any and all who seek him. At the same time, David was lost somewhere in Los Angeles. . . . This process forced me to ask a different set of questions and look for answers that I found I did not have. Sometimes I felt so stretched that it was almost impossible to stand in front of my classes.[70]

For some believers, the loss of religious meaning is more wrenching: amid the dire circumstances of mental health crises, they find that explicit religious care is not effective, relevant, or a priority. Stewart Govig, himself a clergyperson, found himself in the turmoil of his son's psychotic break.

> Our pastors called at the hospital psychiatric ward in the midst of chaos and confusion without consulting us for either information or advice (to say nothing of a home visit). By then medical and social work professionals had taken over. For crisis times these helpers formed my "church"—psychiatrists were the priests,

---

68. Hilfiker, "When Mental Illness Blocks the Spirit," 12.

69. Florence Lerrigo, "What the Christian Faith Can Mean to a Deeply Troubled Mind," unpublished essay, 2.

70. Lois M. Gilliland and Dean S. Gilliland, "A Crisis of Faith in Parenting," *Theology, News and Notes: Fuller Theological Seminary Newsletter* (December 1998), 15.

health professionals were the staff support, and other parents the fellow congregational members. Faith was in science.[71]

Another danger is that theology and illness become mutually reinforcing. Without comment, Professor Sharon O'Brien chose this segment of the Baltimore Catechism as an epigraph for one of her chapters.

Q: Besides depriving the sinner of everlasting grace, what else does mortal sin do to the soul?

A: Mortal sin deprives the soul of the right to everlasting happiness in heaven, and makes it deserving of everlasting punishment in hell.[72]

For some sufferers, such an articulation of the reality and consequences of sin reinforces their sense of worthlessness and hopelessness, and vice versa. The Baltimore Catechism assumes a believer able to take advantage of the grace offered through confession and absolution and thus able to exit this cycle of despair. But for those not taken into account by such an assumption—many soul-sufferers—religious emphasis on human sinfulness and the demoralization caused by psychic turmoil become a toxic combination. Tracy Thompson was depressed and a born-again Christian by age eleven: "I was so convinced of my sinfulness, and so certain that I would never be anything but a sinner, that a public confession of my failings seemed agonizing and pointless."[73] Years later, as an adult, her depression and her theological conviction remained firmly linked, undermining her hope even as she sought treatment of her illness. "I still didn't believe I was sick. I was defective. . . ."[74]

Given the arbitrary and severe nature of the suffering, it is not surprising to find a few sufferers trying to make sense of why the anguish struck them and not someone else: "Why me?" "Why us?" What *is* surprising is that most sufferers do *not* devote space in their memoirs to such questions. As we will see later, many sufferers wrest a blessing out of these horrific experiences, and that may account for why, at least by the

---

71. Stewart D. Govig, "Chronic Mental Illness and the Family: Contexts for Pastoral Care," *Journal of Pastoral Care* 47 (Winter 1993): 406.
72. O'Brien, *The Family Silver*, 86.
73. Thompson, *The Beast*, 51.
74. Thompson, *The Beast,* 156.

time they compose a memoir, they are not mired in the unfairness of their situations. However, painful questions and dispiriting hunches about the nature and location of God do become part of their suffering. As we have seen, especially in the acute phase, some Christian sufferers understand their turmoil within one of the most widespread theological frameworks provided by the church to explain suffering: God is a punisher, they have been taught, and so their suffering becomes even sharper because they assume that it has a divine origin. Even more frequently, God is experienced as absent during their suffering, and for some believers this is a radical, agonizing departure from their previous religious experience. "All my life I've had a strong, unshakable faith in God," Lois Bloom says.[75] That her faith was unshakable does not mean that there had been no previous upheavals—tragic sickness and death had plagued her family before. But when her son, Sammy, killed himself, her faith was shaken, deeply. "Where was God?" "Why hadn't God intervened?" "Has God forgiven and accepted our son?" "There were so many questions and so little energy to work on them. . . . Questioning God at that time, I seemed to get few answers—at least not the preconceived answers I wanted." Other sufferers imply that such questions are more appropriately asked not of G-d but of their religious communities: "Where was my pastor?" "Why didn't my congregation get involved?" "Will the church accept my loved one?"[76]

---

75. Lois A. Bloom, *Mourning, After a Suicide* (Cleveland: Pilgrim Press, 1986), 18.
76. Bloom, *Mourning, After a Suicide*, 4, 18.

LONGER-TERM DYNAMICS OF THE ANGUISH

Within the broad understanding of soul-suffering we are using, some kinds of anguish do resolve. Karen Armstrong's case is such an example: a medical illness—which produced symptoms that for years doctors misdiagnosed as psychiatric illness—was finally treated effectively; normal developmental stages delayed by life in a convent and her novitiate were eventually worked through; years of vocational uncertainty led, unexpectedly, to a meaningful career as an independent scholar and authorship of numerous widely read books, such as *A History of God.*[77] But in most of the soul-anguish we are considering, and especially where psychiatric disorder is a factor, there are no cures, and thus these chronic conditions require long-term coping, which lead to additional dynamics in the suffering. Primary sufferers and their loved ones typically experience cycles in which, to differing degrees, acute turmoil appears and recedes. In between those most excruciating times are additional hardships that make it hard to keep going, day after day, with no end in sight. "I didn't think of [depression] as a sickness," Virginia Heffernan says. "I thought of it as work."

> Unless you are rich, . . . you have to keep going when you're depressed. . . . For every twenty-four hours I got about three, then

---

77. Karen Armstrong, *A History of God: The 4000-Year Quest of Judaism, Christianity, and Islam* (New York: Alfred A. Knopf, 1993). The story of her misdiagnosis is told in Karen Armstrong, *The Spiral Staircase* (New York: Alfred A. Knopf, 2004).

two, then *one* hour worth of life reserves—personality, conversation, motion. I had to be frugal . . ."[78]

Heffernan is right that some wealthy sufferers do get quicker respite from depression, as well as other forms of anguish. It is similarly true that poverty and lack of access to services, such as that suffered by the homeless or new immigrants, make it worse. But resources, education, and social status make surprisingly little difference relative to the main point Heffernan is making: emotional suffering drains the human spirit of personality, conversation, motion. There are legions of people in emotional pain—primary sufferers but also their family members—who struggle just to get through each day. "Imagine the worst moment in your life. Extend it to an hour. A day. A month. A Year. Years on end, moments stacked up and lost forever. This is the stultifying process of madness."[79] This is all the more true for those many families where more than one member is affected by emotional turmoil. What are the particulars of this drudgery? As we will see, memoirists who must deal with psychiatric disorders in themselves or in loved ones say that, in the long-term, the most exhausting and aggravating factors are the insufficiencies of the mental health system. Other factors of a more personal nature, however, are almost as prominent.

THE UNKNOWN

First, though the emergence of acute anguish seems to cry out for decisive action, there are many uncertainties and few solutions to the problems posed by soul-suffering. We know that genetics and environment each play a role in the development of soul-suffering. But almost nothing can be said definitively about why a person does or does not develop an illness or find some healing. There are no cures for dis-ease of the soul. Even in the case of psychiatric illness, medications and other treatment are debated, not widely agreed upon and, besides, they affect symptoms, but not the disease itself. Philosopher Ranier Maria Rilke urged humans to "live the questions," but for Dan Hanson, living the questions is anguish when it means that you are a parent without any answers for

---

78. Heffernan, "A Delicious Placebo," in *Unholy Ghost,* 9, 13.
79. Rae Unzicker, "On My Own: A Personal Journey Through Madness and Re-Emergence," *Psychosocial Rehabilitation Journal* vol. 13, no. 1 (July 1989): 71.

the questions and problems devastating your family.[80] As can be heard in the plaintive question of Lois Bloom, suicide survivors know acutely the anguish of being without answers: "What was so terrible in our son's life that he felt the need to end his life?"[81]

And even as it develops answers, science raises new uncertainties that cause some soul-sufferers concern about long-term implications. For example, the discovery of a genetic component in the development of some psychiatric disorders raises the specter of genetic selection. Kay Redfield Jamison tells of the doctor who said to her "in an icy and imperious voice, . . . as though it were God's truth, which he no doubt felt that it was— 'You shouldn't have children. You have manic-depressive illness.'" Jamison was devastated by his implication: "Even in my blackest depressions, I never regretted having being born."

> Now and again, despite my strong commitment to track to down the genes for manic-depressive illness, I have concerns about what finding the genes might actually mean. . . . Will prospective parents choose to abort fetuses that carry the genes for manic-depressive illness, even though it is a treatable disease? . . . Do we risk making the world a blander, more homogenized place if we get rid of the genes for manic-depressive illness—an admittedly impossibly complicated scientific problem? What are the risks to the risk takers, those restless individuals who join with others in society to propel the arts, business, politics, and science? Are manic-depressives, like spotted owls and clouded leopards, in danger of becoming an "endangered species"?[82]

Unpredictability keeps one's nerves on edge and is another long-term aspect of soul-suffering. Sufferers cannot predict acute phases, nor whether their condition will, in the long run, deteriorate, level off, or improve. By definition, a chronic illness is always present, even in remission, and recurrence is a persistent threat to any easing of the suffering. Lauren Slater puts it simply—"I know, have always known, that I could

---

80. Hanson, *Room for J,* 35. See R. M. Rilke, *Letters to a Young Poet,* 1903.
81. Bloom, *Mourning, After a Suicide,* 3.
82. Jamison, *An Unquiet Mind,* 191, 193–94.

go back."[83] "Feeling normal for any extended period of time raises hopes that turn out, almost invariably, to be writ on water," says Kay Redfield Jamison,[84] and with some conditions, this turns out to be true even when medications are found that "control" symptoms. As the father of a son diagnosed with schizophrenia, Stewart Govig describes the devastation this cycle wreaks on families.

> Rather than being a static condition, the situation of the chronically ill individual and his or her relatives is in fact an up and down disability *process* of being continually heartened but then defeated and rendered incapacitated by circumstances surrounding the struggle.[85]

Not all soul-suffering is a "disability process" as Govig describes it. However, we do not grasp the seriousness of soul-suffering where it involves a psychiatric disorder if we gloss over this point: in the case where an illness goes untreated because treatment is unavailable, unsuccessful, or not utilized—all of which happen too often with schizophrenia and other major disorders—the course of illness is usually devastating. Remission, if it comes at all, turns out to be "a deceptive respite from the savagely recurrent course that the untreated illness ultimately takes."[86] "Each episode takes its toll on the brain, erodes it that much more; bouncing back gets harder, and harder still."[87]

One measure of the enormous burden of the unknown is the enormous relief that comes from getting useful information. Learning from books brought to Tracy Thompson by her boyfriend that there are connections between depression and chemical processes in the brain turned out to be one of the most helpful effects of her hospitalization.[88] Being educated about the biology of schizophrenia was similarly powerful for Dan and Sue Hanson, perhaps especially in its capacity to help them have some well-founded empathy for themselves. After J became ill, they

---

83. Lauren Slater, *Welcome to My Country: A Therapist's Memoir of Madness* (New York: Random House, 1996), 182.
84. Jamison, *An Unquiet Mind*, 69.
85. Govig, "Chronic Mental Illness and the Family," 407.
86. Jamison, *An Unquiet Mind*, 56.
87. Slater, "Noontime," in *Unholy Ghost*, 92.
88. Thompson, *The Beast*, 187ff., 220.

sometimes feared they were to blame. Dan includes in his book some excerpts from Sue's journal:

> When we first learned Joel had a mental illness we both went back over and over and over what we possibly could/should have done differently. . . . One day early in J's illness, we were speaking with Joel's psychiatrist and the doctor looked at Dan and me and very kindly told us J's illness was/is biological. Period. What a blessed gift that phrase was. I suspect there's still an impact that a good or bad home life can have, but how wonderful to hear those words from a doctor.[89]

SHAME AND RESPONSIBILITY

Over time, questions about shame, blame, guilt, and responsibility develop for many living with soul-suffering. While we will see that taking responsibility for one's *recovery* is a healing act, questions about who or what is liable for one's *suffering* can rarely be answered, only fester or be relinquished. Parents of primary sufferers are especially vulnerable to the no-win self-interrogation Dan Hanson recounts: "Did we overindulge or under-indulge?" "Were we over-protective or too lenient?"[90] Similarly, Lois Bloom interrogates herself about her son's suicide: "Could I have prevented his death?"[91] The sense of guilt is not rational: despite the fact that her son was genetically predisposed to the depression he developed, Pam Martin says,

> I felt on trial as a parent. "Surely the parents of a depressed seven-year-old must have twisted this child's personality; they must have mishandled him," accused a mocking voice from within.[92]

Dan Hanson uses a biblical reference to convey the depth of his own guilty anguish and conflicted feelings about responsibility. When J's delusions are endangering his life, Dan and Sue Hanson call the police and have their son hospitalized and medicated against his will. More than once Dan

---

89. Hanson, *Room for J*, 53.
90. Hanson, *Room for J*, 41.
91. Bloom, *Mourning, After a Suicide*, 5.
92. Pam Martin, *Touch the Angel's Hand: A Family's Struggle with Depression* (Oak Park, Ill.: Meyerstone Books, 1988), 30.

identifies himself with the biblical character of Judas, whose actions are construed as a betrayal assuring that Jesus would die. Dan feels like a Judas, even while acknowledging that he takes this action for opposite reasons, so that his son will *not* die.[93]

As we will address in a moment, the loss and grief that are part of soul-suffering account in large part for the relentless and nonrational quality of feelings of guilt, responsibility, and blame. But their power and persistence is also fueled by what Stewart Govig calls the "leprosy within"[94]—the *internalized* shame and stigma. In most social and cultural contexts, those who develop psychiatric illness or are afflicted with other forms of soul-suffering are treated as a disgrace and often actively shamed. It is said that guilt is the feeling we have when we have *done* something wrong, and shame is the feeling we have when we think we *are* something wrong. To be shamed by others is to be treated as one flawed. Thus, another long-term aspect of psychic turmoil is that sufferers are so often disgraced: societies typically revoke grace from people whose agony doesn't go away. Even in the case of those who function well or heal, forever after, grace toward them is in short supply. Not infrequently, they are the victims of widespread impatience, judgmentalism, suspicion, and the failure of advocacy. As Martha Manning observed, madness becomes, like a crime, part of her "permanent record." Sometimes, though, the permanency of a record of psychiatric care affects not only attitudes but opportunities, as for several memoirists who report being denied theological education and service in the church because, though recovered, they had once been hospitalized for their emotional suffering.

The revocation of grace does not have to be done directly by society or individuals, however, because internalized stigma will do the job indirectly. Tragically, the psychiatrically ill often dis-grace themselves by internalizing the judgment, fear, and disrespect most societies direct toward the psychiatrically ill, or by mentally differentiating themselves from the "really" sick people. Before her illness surfaced, Kay Redfield Jamison and one of her colleagues used to discuss their moods and why they didn't need medication, an attitude that later caused costly delays in her acceptance of the treatment that saved her life.

---

93. Hanson, *Room for J*, 32, 43–44.
94. Stewart D. Govig, *Strong at the Broken Places: Persons with Disabilities and the Church* (Louisville: Westminster John Knox Press, 1989), 40ff.

Antidepressants might be indicated for psychiatric patients, for people of weaker stock, but not for us. It was a costly attitude; our upbringing and our pride held us hostage.[95]

Those with psychiatric illnesses withhold from themselves the grace of friendship, aid, and regard for themselves as sacred beings—which increases the costly delay in healing. Conversely, Sharon O'Brien observed while attending a support group for people with depression that its capacity to empower its members was, in part, because it served as a space to admit and wrestle with the internalized shame and stigma.

> People are drawn together by their illnesses . . . and by their struggle to let go of the story that depression *is their own fault.* Yes, intellectually everyone . . . knows that depression and manic depression are inherited, . . . that we should compare our illnesses to diabetes and equate our antidepressants with insulin. Yet at the same time, emotionally most of us are still afflicted by the contradictory belief that we're weak-willed. We're just not strong enough to overcome our illness: if we were only better people, we'd be normal.[96]

SOCIAL ISOLATION

As time goes by, anguish isolates primary sufferers and the people who love them. This is caused in part by two dynamics just addressed: social shunning, and also the wariness many primary sufferers have toward treatment. As Jamison noted, wariness toward treatment is costly, in two ways. On the one hand, repeated acute episodes tend to get worse each time they happen, whereas, if some effective intervention can be found, treatment tends to stop or reverse that downward slide into disintegration, which can become life-threatening. But also, a treatable illness left untreated brings unnecessary and unrecoverable losses. Kay Redfield Jamison:

> It took me far too long to realize that lost years and relationships cannot be recovered, that damage done to oneself and others cannot always be put right again, and that freedom from the control

---

95. Jamison, *An Unquiet Mind*, 54.
96. O'Brien, *The Family Silver*, 260.

imposed by medication loses its meaning when the only alternatives are death and insanity.[97]

More benignly, there is the social gap that always yawns between the one
unfortunate to have been afflicted with suffering of any kind, and all others. When faced with another's suffering, rather than lessening the gap
with a kind word or act, we wring our hands: "I don't know what to do."
When we are suffering, rather than lessening the gap with a direct request, we do not risk: as a civil rights organizer, James Farmer gave
much of himself, but when depressed, "I was never able to ask for help.
No, no. Me? Too much pride."[98] Jyl Felman captures the vicious circle: "I
am afraid to ask someone to stay with me. Sleep over in the guest room.
And no one offers."[99]

So, in an effort to avoid being stigmatized or burdensome, soul-
sufferers usually hide and, as an indirect and unfortunate side effect,
end up hiding themselves and helpful information from each other.
Given that suicide is the eleventh most frequent cause of death in the
United States,[100] Lois Bloom did not have to feel, months after her son's
suicide, alone and different, that no one could understand.[101] Social isolation is only one of many other isolating factors. It is remarkable how
many memoirists speak of a silence within their families about soul-
suffering, a silence that sometimes goes back generations and is a knot
of cultural, familial, and personality patterns that cannot be untangled.
Albert Hsu discovered a generation-old silence in his family, and
within his father.

> After my father's suicide, . . . I learned from my mother that my
> family has some history of mental illness. My father's mother be-
> came schizophrenic when he was five or six years old. This was
> in rural Taiwan right after World War II, a place and an era in

---

97. Jamison, *An Unquiet Mind*, 6.
98. James Farmer, quoted in Kathy Cronkite, *On the Edge of Darkness: Conversations about Conquering Depression* (New York: Dell Publishing; Delta Trade Paperbacks, 1994), 147.
99. Felman, "Nurturing the Soul," 51.
100. This statistic pertains to the year 2000. National Institute of Mental Health, "In Harm's Way: Suicide in America," http://www.nimh.nih.gov/publicat/harmsway.cfm (accessed July 13, 2006).
101. Bloom, *Mourning, After a Suicide*, 4.

which no one really knew how to deal with mental disorders. My grandmother was institutionalized in an asylum for the mentally ill . . . and died there when my father was a teenager. "Your dad never, ever talked about it," my mom told me.[102]

During her girlhood, Sharon O'Brien's family moved to a new community. She was aware that her parents did not make friends in the new community as they had in the old one. Years later, after her own experience with depression, and studying her family history, it made sense: her father's depression and consequent loss of job had forced the move, and the stigma of depression and unemployment isolated her parents in the new community. But there was also a silence within the family, within her parents' marriage.

> "Did Daddy ever tell you what he talked about with the psychiatrist?" I once asked my mother.
> "No," she said.
> "You never asked him?"
> "No," she said, looking away . . .[103]

In both cases, there is also isolation within Hsu's and O'Brien's fathers, imposed by the depression that caused their soul-suffering. Isolation is a symptom of many forms of psychic turmoil, but persons with depression are especially able to describe the isolation.

> Parker Palmer: Depression is the ultimate state of disconnection—it deprives one of the relatedness that is the lifeline of every living being.[104]

> Martha Manning: In depression, the lights are off, but somebody's definitely home. She just can't make it to the door to let you in.[105]

> Sharon O'Brien: I began to experience increased dissociation, a kind of eerie numbness that separates your body from your soul. After a while my soul was hovering on the ceiling, looking down

---

102. Hsu, *Grieving a Suicide*, 49.
103. O'Brien, *The Family Silver*, 159.
104. Palmer, *Let Your Life Speak*, 61.
105. Manning, "The Legacy," 40.

as I struggled to perform the rituals of ordinariness, like daily conversation. But I didn't want to talk because I had nothing interesting to say. Who wanted to hear about how hard it was becoming to get out of bed on days when I didn't have school?

Maybe the ultimate irony is this: depression—soul-crusher, destroyer of days, thief of life and love and time, violator of the will, unloving companion—is, at the bottom of its chill and useless heart, a ferociously *boring* torturer.[106]

Sharon O'Brien provides one of the most unexpected and telling accounts of the isolation imposed by internal and external silences—a story about the year the Modern Language Association conference had a panel called "Professors on Prozac." The pun was intended—"professors might be taking the antidepressant as well as talking about it." Since scholars were increasingly using the first person in their academic writing, would anyone be willing to "reveal themselves"? Only one panelist spoke of her illness; the rest engaged in social analysis of various kinds, critiquing the drug industry. No one spoke of the despair of suffering until a therapist present stood and spoke of depression's anguish and that antidepressants can help alleviate the suffering that drives some people to suicide.

> When I look back on this session, . . . I am sure that many people in that room besides me . . . must have been taking Prozac as well as thinking or writing about it, many must have understood depression from the ground up. But in the context of an academic conference, where speech was supposed to be intellectualized and theoretical, they—like me—could find no way to speak.
>
> I know at least one other person there understood suffering—the organizer of the session, a brilliant scholar who had just published an important book. A few months later she would kill herself. . . .
>
> . . . I can't help wondering whether it's not just the suffering of depression that leads to suicide—it's also the isolation. And yet the ultimate sadness, the ultimate irony, is that the potential for community is there all along. But it's hidden, and we cannot find it unless we challenge the stigma and speak.[107]

---

106. O'Brien, *The Family Silver*, 216.
107. O'Brien, *The Family Silver*, 258, 259.

Because of the risk within communities of color of compounding racism and sexism by admitting soul-sickness—especially psychiatric illness—Meri Danquah's isolation was made even more complex. She had difficulty locating any memoirs written about depression by black people, so she read ones by white people.

> If I were to say that reading all the books by those depressed white people did not have a profound impact on my ability to come to terms with my own battle against depression, it would be disingenuous. Each one was like a mirror. Even if the external reflection looked nothing at all like me, what I saw of the internal reality was an accurate representation. The disease was the same, the symptoms were the same. The resulting confusion and hurt were the same.
>
> None of that was enough though. I craved wholeness.[108]

All these voices help us hear the multiple layers of isolation implied by the lines O'Brien quotes from a soul-sufferer we heard from earlier—Emily Dickinson: "I had a story / I could tell to No one."[109] Stewart Govig, who has roundly criticized the church for its inadequate response to persons dealing with psychiatric disorders, admits that even when pastors tried to listen, he and his family had trouble telling.[110]

DAMAGED RELATIONSHIPS

The prevalence of social isolation implies the damage done to more personal relationships, arguably the most devastating long-term dynamic. We considered previously Kay Redfield Jamison's honest accounting of the violence she has done—to and in the presence of—her loved ones, and not knowing how her relationships survived. "Madness . . . most certainly can, and often does, kill love," she writes, "through its mistrustfulness, unrelenting pessimism, discontents, erratic behavior, and, especially, through its savage moods."[111] In its most virulent forms, it leaves in its wake splintered families, shattered romances, and sapped friendships. In addition, there are so many compromised ties with the very people

---

108. Danquah, "Writing the Wrongs of Identity," in *Unholy Ghost*, 176–77.
109. O'Brien, *The Family Silver*, 158.
110. Govig, "Chronic Mental Illness and the Family," 406.
111. Jamison, *An Unquiet Mind*, 174.

who are most important. For Meri Danquah, among all the relational damages her illness has caused, she feels the most grief that there have been times when she was so ill that she inflicted her illness on her young daughter:

> More than any of the appointments that I've cancelled, friends that I've lost, or projects that I have bungled on account of depression, what I most regret are the times that I was unable to properly tend to my daughter's needs. When I could, I found someone else to take care of her. But many times, . . . she stayed by my side, trapped in my depression with me.[112]

More often than not, primary sufferers are conscious of the enormous toll their anguish and need for help takes on their loved one(s). Lizzie Simon says that as a child she had a fear of being kidnapped and now she sees it as a premonition: "[I] knew somehow that it would all happen, that one day I'd be stolen, and that getting me back would drain everybody around me and give me a guilt I'd never completely shrug."[113] Because she is single, Sharon O'Brien is especially conscious of her need for friends, and fearful of wearing them out. When her illness is causing her to feel emotionally impoverished, her support group meetings are especially helpful because, she says,

> I don't have to be upbeat, the way I am sometimes with friends whose patience I fear is running thin. Maybe I've asked for too much, maybe I haven't given enough back; you start thinking in terms of emotional economy when you have a chronic illness. Have you invested enough to be able to make a withdrawal? Have you overdrawn your friendship account?[114]

Family and friends find themselves torn, their love for the primary sufferer tested. They are all at once fierce activists for their suffering loved ones and also among those alienated by some of the behaviors induced by psychiatric disorders. Faithfulness to their loved ones forces revision of their deepest values, as Dan Hanson conveys.

---

112. Danquah, *Willow Weep for Me*, 144.
113. Simon, *Detour*, 77.
114. O'Brien, *The Family Silver*, 256–57.

I have grown to wonder more and more if our world would not be a better place if there were fewer "normal" people and more gentle souls with J's visions of how their world could be more loving. . . . I grow angry, at times, with those who fail to appreciate our son. Then, I remind myself that even I, his father, could not appreciate J until I let go of some of my preconceived ideas about what is "normal."[115]

Or family members fear that actions they feel forced to take out of love will cost them the relationship. When William Hulme, in a delusional state and physical decline, refused the only treatment the doctors had to offer, Lucy Hulme was forced to get a court order to have her husband treated against his will. She feared that "signing the document might mean the end of [their] marriage."[116]

Even given these honest admissions, it is also true that, for the most part, the memoirs we are studying are stories of relational resilience, the dynamics of which we consider in parts 4 and 5. At the end of her memoir, Lizzie Simon is headed back to her "biggest messiest burnt bridge"—her family.[117] Because of her isolation, and annoyed with her parents, Lizzie Simon went off in search of her "herd," traveling around the country to interview other young people with bipolar disorder. What she found, though, was that, even with the burning, the bridge held. "My family is, of course, the original herd . . . the herd I'd always had, and when I was done wandering, they became the herd that welcomed me back. For that I am truly blessed."[118] Many of our memoirists echo her sentiments.

We must be mindful, then, that not well-represented in the memoirs is soul-suffering's capacity to obliterate relationship. Our memoirists suffer lost and damaged relationships, yes, but in almost every case it must be said that they can write their stories in part because loved ones have stuck by them. In contrast there are legions of soul-sufferers who have no family or friends buoying them up with love and advocacy. Sometimes they have out-lived or been abandoned by their family. There are also

---

115. Hanson, *Room for J*, 99–100.
116. Hulme and Hulme, *Wrestling with Depression*, 35.
117. Simon, *Detour*, 199.
118. Simon, *Detour*, 205.

legions of family and friends who wanted relationship but have been dealt with so cruelly by their troubled loved ones that they have withdrawn for their own safety. Or, their loved one has disappeared, or died. Most of these people do not write memoirs, and yet their isolation is arguably most profound of all.

LOSS AND GRIEF

Finally, then, we come to a dynamic that is, in a sense, a capstone to all the long-term dynamics of soul-suffering: loss and its attendant grief. Perhaps it is because the losses are of such breadth and depth that, of all the emotions described in reaction to soul-suffering, grief is arguably dominant, if not obvious. Other emotions, of course, are strongly at play: fear, anger, shame, regret—to name a few. However, as we will see in part 5, healing, if it comes, relies to a large degree on dealing with the losses, moving from static grief to active mourning. By inference, then, we see the prominence in soul-suffering not just of the losses themselves but of the expression of anguish we call grief.

The loss of one's old self-understanding begins in the acute phase but continues in the long term. But over the long term, other losses pile up, as Meri Danquah describes.

> Each wave of the depression cost me something dear. I lost my job because the temp agencies where I was registered could no longer tolerate my lengthy absences. Unable to pay rent, I lost my apartment and ended up having to rent a small room in a boarding house. I lost my friends. Most of them found it too troublesome to deal with my sudden moodiness and passivity so they stopped calling and coming around.[119]

Soul-sufferers often lose other aspects of their health besides their psychospiritual health. Their psychic turmoil may have its own negative physical effects—inability to sleep or to eat and exercise healthfully, for example. If their psychic turmoil leads to unemployment and to loss of health insurance, or because their anguish leaves them unable to make and keep the necessary appointments, pre-existing health problems may be exacerbated. If medications are taken to ease the psychic turmoil, suf-

---

119. Danquah, *Willow Weep for Me*, 30.

ferers usually have side effects so significant that the body they once knew is no longer recognizable. Even where no dangerous side effects are experienced, loss of pleasure in one's body is common, especially loss of sex drive. And finally, ironically, if the soul-suffering resolves, one also loses the illness, which may have brought some good things into one's life. For example, people who have never experienced mania find it hard to comprehend how difficult it is to surrender the vitality and pleasure of such energizing periods. As Kay Redfield Jamison puts it, "the intensity, glory, and absolute assuredness of my mind's flight made it very difficult for me to believe, once I was better, that the illness was one I should willingly give up."[120]

---

120. Jamison, *An Unquiet Mind*, 91.

THE SPECIAL ANGUISH OF SUICIDALITY

Soul-suffering can be fatal. It's more to the point to say that people die from psychiatric illnesses than to say that they die from suicide. Most people think Anne Sexton died by suicide, but Linda Gray Sexton, her daughter, says, "My mother died of depression."[121] In such cases, suicidality is a direct symptom of an illness. In other cases, suicidality is not so much a symptom of the illness as a response to the endlessness and pointlessness of the suffering. Parker Palmer minces no words: "I understand why some depressed people kill themselves: they need the rest."[122] Martha Manning describes the forced labor:

> Every inch of me aches. I can't believe that a person can hurt this bad and still breathe. . . .
>
> I want to die. I can't believe I feel like this. But it's the strongest feeling I know right now, stronger than hope, or faith, or even love. . . . It's not that I want to die. It's that I'm not sure I can live like this anymore.
>
> I was always taught that suicide is a hostile act, suggesting anger at the self or others. . . . But I think that explanation excludes the most important factor—suicide is an end to the pain, . . . as devastating as any other "act of God." I don't want to die because I hate myself. I want to die because . . . I love myself enough to have compassion for this suffering and to want to see it end.[123]

---

121. Linda Gray Sexton, *Searching for Mercy Street* (Boston: Little, Brown, 1994), 295.
122. Palmer, *Let Your Life Speak*, 58.
123. Manning, *Undercurrents*, 99.

But Manning's compassion is not socially sanctioned. There are only two circumstances in which physicians or police can hospitalize a person against their will: being a danger to others or a threat to one's own life. As Kate Millett puts it, your life is not your own.

> You must not commit suicide—that is absolutely forbidden. Your life does not belong to you but to the doctors, the relatives, the state: the social circle. Show any symptoms of suicide, and they'll pick you up like a thief.[124]

However caring it is to try to prevent suicide, successful prevention means that a person is forced to endure further what ultimately may be a terminal illness. It is a curious contrast that in most modern societies one is considered cruel to force animals to suffer futile pain but principled to expect the same of human beings. But others agree with Manning: some people in psychic agony come to the point where mercy is the only acceptable course of action. As Kay Redfield Jamison planned her suicide, she remembers thinking that "it was . . . the only sensible thing to do for myself. One would put an animal to death for far less suffering."[125] In contrast, suicidality is stigmatized and shamed.

As Manning notes, suicide is often thought of as a hostile act, if not against the self, then against others. What is less often realized is that suicide is sometimes contemplated or carried out as an act of care for others. When Jamison was a girl, a pilot losing control of his plane in the skies above her school thought he would injure the children if he tried to reach the airstrip and instead deliberately crashed the plane. He died in the crash and was seen as a hero for his sacrifice. "In a perverse linking within my mind I thought that, like the pilot whom I had seen kill himself to save the life of others, I was doing the only fair thing for the people I cared about."[126] Of course, there is no heroism associated with suicide as an act of love—not by society, and usually not by the sufferer either. Ed Cooper explains:

> You seek the end because you see not only what it has done to you, but also what it is doing to the ones you love. The fear of death fades because, to a large degree, you already feel dead. You

---

124. Millett, *The Loony-Bin Trip*, 259.
125. Jamison, *An Unquiet Mind*, 115.
126. Jamison, *An Unquiet Mind*, 115.

are not able to [interact], nor are people willing to interact with you as they once did. In fact, it feels like you have fallen so low even the devil has deserted you.[127]

Suicidality is sometimes a "cry for help." Under such circumstances, it is judged to be manipulative, which is, of course, the point of it. What is less often decried, however, is the neglect and abuse that give rise to the cry. Meri Danquah writes of being abused by her stepfather, Jonathon, and trying to get help.

The summer before ninth grade, I tried to kill myself by swallowing some pills. Not a lot, not even enough to cause minor damage. My attempt at suicide was a rather austere means to a much-desired end. Because of the abuse, I was already in the process of dying. I was fading into the pastels of walls, the blues and greens of the outside world. I wanted someone else to notice this, to help me reverse what was happening. I thought if my family and friends knew that I was miserable enough to want to die, they would rush to my aid with love and attention. I thought that things would change. And they did. They got worse.

My mother responded to my suicide attempt with "tough love": I was chastised and placed on punishment. She never knew what the real source of my troubled behavior was because I never told her. I didn't tell anyone. . . . The way I saw it, all of the adults in my life were either physically or emotionally unavailable. All except Jonathan.[128]

The same can happen among adults and professionals. Before her epilepsy was diagnosed, scholar and writer Karen Armstrong suffered for years from unexplained lapses of consciousness, which her psychiatrist ignored in favor of psychoanalytic interpretation. She writes of the aftermath of swallowing a nonlethal handful of pills.

I felt ashamed and could understand the scarcely veiled contempt of the nurses. When you are caring for people who are mortally

---

127. Ed Cooper, "To Touch the Untouchable," *Mental Illness Awareness Worship Resources* (St. Louis: Pathways to Promise).
128. Danquah, *Willow Weep for Me*, 125.

ill and struggling desperately to live, it must be almost insup-
portable to have to deal with people who want to throw it all
away. But I did not believe that I had really wanted to die. . . .
This strange act had been another cry for help. What I was un-
consciously trying to do that night was to make clear the depths
of my desperation. . . .

The trouble is that when people decide that what looks like a
suicide attempt is "only" a cry for help, they sometimes conclude
that this appeal need not be answered. Indeed, they even decide
that it is better not to respond, because the patient must not be encouraged to give way to such neurotic exhibitionism. He or she
must learn to express pain simply and directly, without resorting
to such outlandish symbolism. But I had tried to explain my fears
and bewilderment as clearly as I was able, and no aid was forth-
coming.[129]

Theological, ecclesial, and social prohibitions against suicide are remarkable for their power to eclipse compassion for persons for whom life
and death are not neatly divided. William Styron observes that whether
a person actually kills him- or herself, attempts it, or only threatens it,
"the sufferer . . . is often, . . . unjustly made to appear a wrongdoer."[130]
The person's family members, too, often feel shame and disclaim the
truth: "the stigma of self-inflicted death is for some people a hateful blot
that demands erasure at all costs."[131] Thus suicide is interpreted as a
Judas-like betrayal of family and religious values. Where persons succeed in committing suicide, it is legal to penalize their families: insurance
companies will pay family survivors for death from homicide, accident,
or any other medical condition except suicidality.

---

129. Armstrong, *The Spiral Staircase*, 125.
130. Styron, *Darkness Visible*, 30.
131. Styron, *Darkness Visible*, 31.

FAMILIES' DISTINCTIVE ANGUISH

F amily and friends of the primary sufferers are often unsung heroes. Though onlookers tend to focus on the anguish of the primary sufferer, we have been discussing just as much the enormous psychospiritual price paid by loved ones when psychiatric disorder or other psychic turmoil strikes. Interestingly, much of the suffering is similar in type, if not in degree. There are, however, some dynamics that are particular to loved ones, especially the closest family members.

SUICIDE SURVIVORS

Most obviously, when someone commits suicide, all the people who love and survive the victim are left with a distinguishing kind of suffering. Albert Hsu, whose father committed suicide after a stroke, describes suicide's devastation: "There may be one primary victim, but as with a bomb thrown into a crowd of people, the collateral damage done to others nearby is massive."[132] There is the initial shock wave. Some loved ones discover the body, as did Albert Hsu's mother: she found her husband's body in their bedroom. Others hear the news from family or friends, as did Albert, whose mother called him, wailed into the phone, "Daddy killed himself," and then walked off sobbing. Still others are informed by police officers, as was Lois Bloom. Though the outcome is obviously less bad, even in cases where suicide was attempted but not completed, this shock wave is the first "collateral damage."

---

132. Hsu, *Grieving a Suicide*, 9.

A very few survivors are not surprised. In such cases, the victim is known to be struggling, perhaps having tried suicide before, and there may even be a feeling of dread, feeling the loss is almost inevitable. Lloyd Carr's daughter-in-law had been at risk for years.

> For me Kate's death was a shock, but not a surprise. She had undergone several years of professional counseling, but she still found it difficult to integrate her experience and low self-esteem with the expectations of family, church, and society. Nor did her chosen circle of friends provide much help. She had attempted suicide before, but failed. We tried to help, to encourage and care, but bit by bit she withdrew from all of us. We sensed, but could not really know, how deeply she was hurting. By mid-summer I had known instinctively it would only be a matter of when and how. From early September, every time I went out I expected to arrive home to hear the news. Every time I saw a road accident my heart skipped until, relieved, I saw it was not a small blue car that was involved.[133]

But most survivors are truly shocked. In some cases they are shocked, not because the loved one had not been struggling in a way obvious to the onlooker, but because there had been some improvement. This was the case for Lois Bloom, who did not realize that, as in the case of many people with suicidal depression, her son's initial improvement put him at greater risk.[134] Others are shocked because they had absolutely no warning—the suicide is the first knowledge they have of their loved one's deep anguish. Others are shocked because suicide is so horrifying and unacceptable—some loved ones find themselves thinking it would be better if the loved one had been murdered.[135]

Albert Hsu points out that bereavement specialists differentiate between "typical grief" and "complicated grief"—where the loss is exacerbated by an additional trauma.[136] For suicide survivors, grief is always "compli-

---

133. G. Lloyd Carr, with poetry by Gwendolyn C. Carr, *The Fierce Goodbye: Hope in the Wake of Suicide* (Downers Grove, Ill.: InterVarsity Press, 1990), 27.

134. Bloom, *Mourning, After a Suicide*, 3. A slight improvement in the depression of suicidal persons sometimes gives them energy to carry out suicidal actions they were previously too depressed to set in motion.

135. Hsu, *Grieving a Suicide*, 18.

136. Hsu, *Grieving a Suicide*, 26.

cated." The grief of most suicide survivors is immediately complicated by the stigma against suicide, especially within their religious traditions. Planning the funeral—a painful matter in any circumstance—also becomes fraught with complicating questions: Should the cause of death be addressed in the funeral? If so, how will religious leaders deal with the religious prohibitions against—and judgments in the event of—suicide? Is the victim in some way now outside divine mercy? The initial days are a blur—filled with funeral preparations and receiving friends and family, all complicated because of the shock. Even at the funeral, some survivors find themselves already caught in the troubling feelings that characterize the complicated mourning in the case of suicide. For example, the anger toward the dead loved one that descends on many suicide survivors is, for Lloyd Carr, just under the surface of his feelings and words even at the funeral.

> I stood beside the coffin a few moments, my brain a turmoil of confusion. Grief, loss, and pity flooded over me, but the most overwhelming feeling was one of waste. For those who are desperately ill, death can be a welcome relief. Sudden death by accident or heart failure always shocks and devastates. But suicide, deliberate self-destruction, especially of a talented and gifted young person, appalls. The unfulfilled dreams, the unfinished work, the uncompleted promise, mock like demons.[137]

Long before the shock wears off, nagging questions descend. "Why did my loved one do this?" Gwendolyn Carr, Kate's mother-in-law, worked on this question in the poetry writing she did as part of her grief work. Here is one answer she gave to her question, in a poem titled, simply, "Why?":

> You revelled deeply
> in your pain,
> until, with only death
> to gain,
> gave one last cry
> to sever hurt—
> then one last fierce goodbye.[138]

---

137. Lloyd Carr, *The Fierce Goodbye*, 27.
138. Gwendolyn Carr, *The Fierce Goodbye*, 24.

The fierceness of the goodbye, the shock, the waste, the feelings of abandonment and rejection—it all combines for many survivors into a distressing sense of betrayal by the dead loved one. "We have been victimized by our own loved ones," as Hsu puts it.[139] But they fear as well, that they have failed their loved one—the "if onlys," Lois Bloom calls them. "If only I had known! If only I had gotten home earlier! If only I hadn't said _____ ! If only _____ !"[140]

These do not exhaust the complications. For those people whose loved one had been through years of turmoil that threatened to destroy the family, they may wrestle with feeling not only grief, but that there has been a needed reprieve. Lloyd Carr:

> There is, for some, another disturbing element: the sense of relief that the successful suicide brings to the survivors. That relief is real, even with the mourning and the loss, but that in itself often compounds the guilt. We sense, although we do not always ask ourselves, the question: "Is it *right* to be relieved at another's death?" Of course this question is broader than just suicide.[141]

Finally, for those whose religion does prohibit suicide, there are particular questions if not complications. Some religious people find their love and compassion for the victim a meaningful rebuttal to any religious prohibitions and punishments, a rebuttal that frees them from anguish over their loved ones' eternal fate. Others find their loyalties more conflicted and work to find a stance that honors both their loved one and their religious beliefs. Lloyd Carr devotes several chapters in his memoir to a detailed study of all biblical texts that mention suicide and finds that nowhere is suicide explicitly condemned, much less seen as an "unforgivable sin." "It is an act which we do not want to condone or encourage," he concludes, but "the gospel is the good news that proclaims mercy and grace."[142] Albert Hsu also devotes a portion of his memoir to wrestling with biblical texts, as well as other theological sources, trying to reconcile his love for his father with his conviction that suicide is wrong. Ultimately, he comes to the position that suicide is a tragedy, "a situation where a good

---

139. Hsu, *Grieving a Suicide*, 112.
140. Bloom, *Mourning, After a Suicide*, 11.
141. Lloyd Carr, *The Fierce Goodbye*, 105.
142. Lloyd Carr, *The Fierce Goodbye*, 97–98.

person's human frailties and failures lead to self-destruction."[143] Given the number and seriousness of the particular challenges faced by the loved ones of suicide victims, it is not surprising that some of them feel vulnerable to their own suicide. Having lived close to someone who lost her or his life in a battle with emotional suffering, it is all too clear how powerful the undertow of soul-suffering can become. "We wonder if we will be consumed by the same despair that claimed our loved one."[144]

OTHER FAMILIES' DISTINCTIVE SUFFERING

While there are many similarities in the anguish of primary sufferers and their loved ones, there are a few important distinctions. Especially in those cases where the anguish leads to the primary sufferer's inability to carry out his or her responsibilities, families are weighed down by worry, efforts to help, and extra responsibilities. To the surprise of most, their devotion to the primary sufferer is shaky ground for the trials to come. "Love did not prepare me for 1985," Rose Styron says, referring to the year in which her husband William Styron began his descent into melancholy. "I . . . seesawed hopelessly between bafflement and anger, between immediate compassion for Bill and despair for his future."[145] In the most serious cases, families deal every day with upheaval and unpredictability: "[mental illness] takes over lives and turns them upside down. Nothing is ever the same again."[146] Loved ones are information central: they are expected to keep everyone informed—professionals, family, acquaintances. Given what we will hear in part 4 about the limitations of the mental health system, it is not surprising that families find themselves watchdogging the treatment their loved one receives and always on the hunt for new options. Families are not always in agreement about the treatment a loved one should receive and are often of divided opinion toward the loved one's condition—some empathic and forgiving, others hard-nosed and skeptical. Though there are "oases," and some find healing, living with suffering loved ones is for many families a "wilderness."[147]

143. Hsu, *Grieving a Suicide*, 107.
144. Hsu, *Grieving a Suicide*, 10.
145. Rose Styron, "Strands," in *Unholy Ghost: Writers on Depression*, ed. Nell Casey (New York: HarperCollins/Perennial, 2002), 129, 130.
146. Hanson, *Room for J*, 1.
147. Stewart D. Govig, "Wilderness Journal: Parental Engagement with Young Adult Mental Illness," *Word & World* vol. 9, no. 2 (Spring 1989): 147–153.

Gwendolyn Carr's poem "And still they come" captures how, even for suicide survivors years past their loss, a day can suddenly be upended.

> On some small day
> when life sits still,
> thoughts arrive unbidden,
> meddle with the memory,
> ruffle what I hoped lay hidden:
> rousing sorrow to a storm,
> and that small day,
> to devastation.[148]

Especially where illness causes the sufferer to engage in potentially dangerous actions, families go through especially excruciating suffering. Some can see that the illness threatens the life of their loved one. Because J feels himself to be invincible, Dan and Sue Hanson's "most vivid nightmare is having to identify J in a morgue, a victim of his own inability to know his own limits."[149] Sometimes the illness threatens the physical and emotional well-being of the loved ones: Jay Govig was occasionally physically violent and verbally assaultive at home.[150] Though J has never been violent, the Hansons fear another horrific reality faced by some families. They tell of reading an editorial written by a woman after the police shot to death a mentally ill man. "Why didn't his parents make sure that he took his medication?" she wrote. Her words reveal her ignorance about the limited power anyone has to make an unwilling adult take medication and about medication's efficacy. But her words also communicated to the Hansons, who have dedicated themselves to the care of their son, "that if something bad happens, it is as much [the parent's] fault as it is the person's who is ill, . . . [a] full load of responsibility . . . that can seem impossible to bear at times."[151]

There are wrenching dealings with police and the legal system. Families are chagrinned to sometimes rely on forced hospitalizations and guardianship of their adult relatives, just to assure their safety. As we

---

148. Gwendolyn Carr, *The Fierce Goodbye*, 118.
149. Hanson, *Room for J*, 91.
150. Stewart D. Govig, *Souls Are Made of Endurance* (Minneapolis, Minn.: Fortress Press, 1994), 5–6.
151. Hanson, *Room for J*, 42.

have seen, when J endangers himself, the Hansons call the police to force the hospitalization that will lead to forced medication. Sascha Garson experiences painful ironies as she tries to care for her son, who has bipolar disorder. For example, she hopes that her Phi-Beta-Kappa, college-graduate son will be judged unable to care for himself, so that she will be granted conservatorship. As her words communicate, her son's illness forces other incongruities on her that seem to distort a mother's love.

> I have other perversities. When my son is jailed I relax. When he is hospitalized, I feel relieved. . . . In a hospital, [he] will receive treatment for [his] illness; in jail, protection, perhaps, from being beaten or raped.[152]

Other times, the police and legal system add to their problems. As noted previously, Garson's son was arrested for soliciting on a city street, even though he was in the middle of an episode of mania. Until he is shepherded home safely by his siblings, Ruth Sullivan is in anguish that Joseph's decision to take off on his own after church might lead to an encounter with police unable to deal appropriately with actions induced by her son's autism.

> Without an advocate, Joseph, with very deficient social skills, would quickly have escalated the situation, possibly causing the officer to either chase him, shoot at him, or put him in handcuffs and haul him to jail. This has actually happened to a few autistic people I know.[153]

When soul-suffering strikes in the form of serious psychiatric illness, the demands of care place special burdens on parents, spouses, and adult siblings and children of the primary sufferer—a poignant and weighty combination of desire to help, limited ability to intervene, and legal responsibility.

Illness often leaves a person unable to find a partner with whom to share life, and parents continue to have primary responsibility for the care of their adult children, even as the parents age and need more help them-

---

152. Sascha Garson, "The Sound and Fury of Mania."
153. Ruth C. Sullivan, "Rain Man and Joseph," in *High-Functioning Individuals with Autism*, ed. Eric Schopler and Gary B. Mesibov (New York: Plenum Press, 1992), 249.

selves. The combination, over many years, of the sick person's bizarre behavior, the inadequacies of the mental health system, the limits of their
ability to influence their adult children, and worry who will care for their
child after their death leaves many parents hobbled by the load. Though
resources are improving since Sascha Garson wrote in 1987, too many
parents of children with serious psychiatric illnesses still experience
themselves, as she says, "a tongue-tied, self-castigating, silently grieving
subculture."[154] The harshness of this self-description suggests another
pain particular to parents: some are tongue-tied and self-castigating over
the possibility that they bear blame for their child's illness. Intellectually,
these questions may be rebuffed, but the feelings persist. We noted earlier Dan Hanson's self-interrogation, despite the fact that here he succinctly identifies insufficient logic in old theories:

> For years the psychiatric profession believed that over-protective
> parenting was one of the causes of mental illness. Perhaps they
> had things turned around. Maybe over-parenting was not the
> cause, but rather the result.[155]

When there is a partner or spouse, the illness and demands for care
test and often threaten the bond. Novelist Russell Banks saw in retrospect that he had fallen in love with characteristics in his wife, poet Chase
Twichell, that were symptoms of her illness. Then, again in retrospect,
he realized that when he found himself unable to cure his wife's symptoms, he took symptoms of her illness on himself.

> My reaction to all this was to blame my wife—to be angry at her,
> first, for not having allowed me to cure her of her depression, and
> then for infecting me with it. Crude, I know, but not uncommon.[156]

Periods of remission give only limited relief. Donald Hall's description of
the effect on their marriage of Jane Kenyon's illness is illustrative:
"Depression was a third party in our marriage. There were many happy
third parties. . . . Yet depression's ghost was omnipresent for both of us,
in dread if not in actuality."[157]

---

154. Garson, "The Sound and Fury of Mania."
155. Hanson, *Room for J*, 77.
156. Russell Banks, "Bodies in the Basement: An Ars Poetica with Attitude," in *Unholy Ghost*, 36.
157. Donald Hall, "Ghost in the House," in *Unholy Ghost*, 170.

As the parents or spouse of the primary sufferer age, if there are siblings or adult children, they come to bear more and more responsibility—voluntarily and/or because the legal system requires it of them. In most families, this passing on of responsibility leads to some conflicted feelings on all sides. A parent describes the typical dynamic:

> Under no circumstances do we want Howard to live with any of [his siblings]. They need to get on with their own lives. However, we do expect them to take care of his emotional needs . . . to continue to love and support him, to see that he has a place to live, warm clothes, dinners at their homes, and an occasional movie.[158]

Even before they are adults, many children of ill parents become caretakers. Gloria Steinem's childhood interactions with her ill mother are illustrative of the dynamics for many children.

> [W]hen I was growing up . . . [my mother was] someone to be worried about and cared for; an invalid who lay in bed with eyes closed and lips moving in occasional response to voices only she could hear; a woman to whom I brought an endless stream of toast and coffee, bologna sandwiches and dime pies, in a child's version of what meals should be. . . . Our roles were reversed.[159]

But quite apart from any role as caretakers for their anguished loved ones, children and siblings mourn the losses and their limited ability to help. Dan Hanson includes in his memoir reflections written by J's siblings. Troy, J's older brother:

> It's like my brother died. . . . In order to relate to J in his world, I must become "Buddha," the role he has created for me. . . . Unless I was willing to enter his world on his terms . . . there was no place for me or anyone else. . . . In a way it is like seeing a living ghost who forces you to either detach or go through the grieving process every time you see him. . . . Except I am a doctor now and I am supposed to try and save people, or at least

---

158. Anne C. Handler, "Living on the Edge: Experiences of Family Members," in *New Directions in the Psychological Treatment of Serious Mental Illness*, ed. Diane T. Marsh (Westport, Conn.: Praeger, 1994), 147.

159. Gloria Steinem, *Outrageous Acts and Everyday Rebellions*, 2nd ed. (New York: Henry Holt, 1995), 140–41.

ease their suffering. . . . I have an idea for a movie title: "Schizophrenia: Invasion of the Soul Snatcher." . . . I have so many questions and so few answers. . . . Having a loved one with schizophrenia is very painful. . . ."[160]

J's older sister, Heidi, writes to J:

> When we were kids I would sit with you for hours. It was calming for me. You always had that in you. . . . We connected, a big sister with her little brother. Those memories of fishing, playing tennis, video games, comfort me on some days, while other days they make me weep. I wish I had known how truly precious those times would be for me. I would have paid closer attention so that I could remember every detail later and relive it as if I was still there. . . . As an RN, I know that [the medications] cause serious side effects and will likely hurt you. . . . In the last eight years, I don't think of us as being connected anymore. I can't ask you for advice. You know very little of the things I deal with on a daily basis. . . . If you could only accept that you are ill perhaps then you could live in my reality, but you either refuse to accept or can't. And so we can't have a relationship, not here in this world anyway.[161]

Whatever their relation to the primary sufferer, however, loved ones share similar nagging questions and challenges arising from their efforts to care. How much care is enough, how much too much? The Hansons are regularly in a bind: they must balance the necessity to intervene for the sake of J's safety and—though J has never before endangered others—the safety of others; they also want to refrain from interfering unnecessarily in J's adult freedom and decision making, both of which are essential elements in J becoming more able to choose wisely for his life.[162] How do we deal with our horrified reactions to the behavior of the person we love? Stewart Govig's memoir is a story of tireless care for Jay, his son diagnosed with schizophrenia, but Stewart

---

160. Hanson, *Room for J*, selections from 57–62.
161. Hanson, *Room for J*, selections from 62–64.
162. Hanson, *Room for J*, 38.

is also candid about horrid challenges to the family's devotion to Jay: for example, "we have cringed at his compulsive, bizarre behavior, stood mute in its presence. . . . We have gagged at body odor and watched his teeth decay to the point of extraction."[163]

And then there are loved ones' particular losses. Sometimes the primary sufferer is lost to suicide, but many more times the sufferers are alive but still lost. Sometimes they are literally lost—their whereabouts are unknown because the illness drives them to homelessness or to sever relationships. But protracted emotional illness can cause the ill person to seem missing, even when physically present. Some loved ones experience the diagnosis of serious psychiatric disorders to be like the death of the loved one. When her son was diagnosed with schizophrenia, Betty Holder says that "in that moment we had lost the son we thought we knew as surely as if he had been struck by a train. I felt as if our son had died."[164] Though he has felt the same way, Dan Hanson restrains himself from making such statements, because he has seen the anguish of parents who have actually lost their children to death.

> I say to myself, at least Joel is still with us. But the truth is that the son we once knew is no longer with us. What's more, the life that we imagined for J will never be realized. . . .
>
> Perhaps it is the dreams that die when someone becomes mentally ill.[165]

Even where the primary sufferer is not completely lost to the anguish, relationships may be, or seem to be. "I seemed no more important to him than a chair," says Ruth Sullivan about how the autism of her son, Joseph, affected her relationship with him.[166] Given all the danger untreated illness can cause, fighting over treatment not infrequently causes terrible estrangements, as Dan Hanson's lament captures.

> I hate the medication. I hate what it does to J. I hate fighting with J to take it. I hate what fighting over medication has done to my relationship with J. . . . It is hard for me to feel rejected by my own son. I doubt that J will ever appreciate our efforts to

---

163. Govig, "Chronic Mental Illness and the Family," 405.
164. Holder, "Living on the Edge: Experiences of Family Members," in *New Directions*, 152.
165. Hanson, *Room for J*, 15.
166. Sullivan, "Rain Man and Joseph," in *High-Functioning Individuals with Autism*, 247.

help him. Part of me doesn't blame him, but that doesn't make it any easier.[167]

Jane Kenyon's depression caused her to put off the plans made with friends and family, but she couldn't cancel them herself. "It was generally I who telephoned, at Jane's request," says her husband, "because she could not herself make the calls."[168] There may be resentment and competition for attention, especially understandable from the other children when parents are preoccupied with a sick child. With her parent's attention centered on her sister Maud's depression and hospitalization, Nell remembers that "I whispered spitefully in my mother's face, 'Do I need to check myself into a mental hospital to make you pay attention to my problems?'"[169] When there is no adequate treatment, there are layers of lost dreams. Betty Holder describes this from the perspective of a mother of a son whose schizophrenia is only moderately alleviated by medication.

> [O]ne grieves for one's own unrealized dreams for one's child and has also to watch and endure as he grieves for his own lack of fulfillment. . . . Grandparents grieve not only for their grandchild but also for the anguish of the grandchild's parents, their own child. Family gatherings . . . are tinged with sadness for the young person suffering from mental illness and his parents and siblings.[170]

As if the excruciating, incurable, isolating suffering that primary sufferers and their loved ones endure were not enough, one final point must be made. When their loved one is enduring such horrific and untreatable illness, and this horror takes over their own lives as well, some family members find themselves wondering, in their most private and anguished thoughts, whether it wouldn't be better for their loved one to be dead. Or they find themselves wishing their loved one were dead. After they have waged noble war against the suffering we have been consider-

167. Hanson, *Room for J*, 36, 39.
168. Hall, "Ghost in the House," in *Unholy Ghost*, 170.
169. Nell Casey, "Wish You Were Here," in *Unholy Ghost*, 279.
170. Holder, "Living on the Edge," in *New Directions*, 154–55.

ing, those feelings deserve compassion from those of us on the sidelines. Ironically, such thoughts and feelings are born of love—desire for their loved one's suffering to be ended. They are born of an indescribable exhaustion of body and soul and a future likely comprised of a never-ending grief and sense of doom. Lloyd Carr was admirably honest to admit his mixed feelings about his daughter-in-law's suicide after her protracted illness: "is it *right* to be relieved by another's death?" But some family members must confront such thoughts and feelings prior to the death, and there may be no greater heartache than to wrestle with such feelings toward a loved one's life.

In this portion of the book, in order to give our full attention to the most personal dimensions of the suffering, we have allowed the sociocultural matters that cause and/or complicate soul-suffering to stay mostly in the background of our discussion. We have sought to better understand soul-suffering "from the inside out." That their lives are touched so substantially by suffering is a moral summons to all others that we should care and offer assistance. In the next portion of the book, then, we return our attention to suffering's social contexts as well as its interpersonal contexts, and turn to the question of what in the experiences of soul-sufferers comprises care—helpful and otherwise.

PART FOUR

CARE

Hillel's Golden Rule . . .

tells you to look into your own

heart, find out what distresses you,

and then refrain from inflicting

similar pain on other people.

—Karen Armstrong
The Spiral Staircase

SOUL-SUFFERING IS VERY RARELY A SOLITARY EXPERIENCE we survive on our own. Most often anguish of soul presses us so deeply and for so long that we are thrown into greater reliance than ever before on the care of others. This is certainly the case for our memoirists, and in part 4 we reflect on the dynamics of care they encounter with other persons. We typically assume the word "care" to have positive connotations. But many of us know from our own most troubled times that a person's desire to give us care, or their expertise in some helping profession, does not necessarily make that person capable of caring. That which is intended to be caring can often be quite uncaring, either because it proves to be irrelevant or because it injures further. Thus, we can speak of care that harms and care that helps. In this part of the book, we seek to understand what characterizes inauthentic and authentic care as described by persons who have experienced their own psychospiritual suffering or that of a loved one.

The first half of part 4 focuses on care that harms. We do this by reflecting on failures of care in the two main contexts where our memoirists seek help: the mental health system and religion. In one way, this is an unfortunate place to begin our reflection on mental health care and religious care, because there are so many resources and professionals in mental health and in religion that provide excellent, appreciated care. But in another way, it is entirely appropriate to first wrestle with the limits and failures in care, because that is what most of our memoirists first encounter. Reeling from the impact of inner anguish, most also experience, in their initial encounters with mental health and religious systems, inadequacy, disappointment, or even further injury.

As a reader, you may again feel weighted down in the first section but, as before, allowing ourselves to feel the anguish in these difficult stories is necessary if we are to comprehend soul-suffering and any wisdom therein. Also, comprehending these alienations and disappointments will make us more able to offer helpful care to others and to ourselves. In the second half of part 4, we will reflect on stories that describe helpful care. We will find there that the standards for helpful care are demanding, but they are also largely common-sense—"look into your own heart, find out what distresses you, and then refrain from inflicting similar pain on other people."

CARE THAT HARMS

As we enter into a discussion of care that harms, we start with the memoirists' admission that they sometimes do the very things they criticize in others. They are plain-spoken in their critique of the mental health and religious care they receive, but not usually self-righteous. In fact, in their memoirs comes through a kind of wonderment that, even though they have experienced harmful care in regard to their own soul-suffering, they cannot always find in themselves the helpfulness they expect from others. When her beloved aunt Ruth fell into months of keening and melancholia after the death of her husband, Sharon O'Brien could not meet Ruth in the place of her grief, even though—perhaps because—she, too, knew the despair Ruth was embodying.

> I did not say this to anyone at the time—how could I admit that I couldn't be more compassionate to a bereaved woman in her seventies?—but I found Ruth's presence almost unbearable . . .
>
> Looking back, I think now that I was also feeling the unacceptable emotion of anger: depressed people can make others furious. *Snap out of it!* I probably wanted to say to Ruth, as others must have wanted to say to me during long periods of chronic depression. *Stop wallowing! Everybody has problems! Get a life!* But I didn't say any of these things. . . . Instead I offered suggestions: *Find a grief support group: I'll call around for you. Meet a friend for coffee twice a week. Go to lunch at the senior center—I'll*

take you. Ruth would look at me, eyes glazed with tears and numbness, uncomprehending. I wasn't speaking her language.[1]

THE ANGUISH OF MENTAL HEALTH TREATMENT

Not all sufferers seek help from the mental health system. If they do, they have an enormous variety of experiences and opinions about the experience. A few survivors of mental health care find it categorically devastating, but the majority have both strongly positive and strongly negative experiences. The criticisms are hard to hear, especially if one is a caregiver, because responsible professionals often rail against the same problems articulated by the sufferers.

The Unknown

Mental health care sometimes misses the mark because so much is unknown about psychic anguish and its alleviation, even when it takes the form of the psychiatric disorders recognized by mental health professionals. The ubiquitous television advertisements of medications, the confident reporting of scientific discoveries about genetics and neurology, the widespread use of various therapies—all these are increasingly illuminating. However, they do not change the fact—and maybe even mask it—that so much remains unknown or uncertain. Much more than the average person is aware, knowledge about emotional suffering and about appropriate medical and psychological care is rudimentary at best.

For example, cultural competency in mental health care—knowledge about how to make mental health care appropriate and accessible to diverse cultures—is in its infancy. Psychiatric diagnosis is educated hypothesizing; however accurate the hypothesis, mental health professionals have no definitive diagnostic tests by which to determine that someone has a particular psychiatric disorder: no blood tests, no brain scans, no motor skill assessments definitively associated with a diagnosis. Rather, a person is usually diagnosed with a psychiatric condition because professionals observe in her or him certain behaviors or emotional patterns. We have developed reliable information about probable causes and helpful treatments for some illnesses—depression, for example—but about some other illnesses—dissociative identity disorder, for example—

---

1. Sharon O'Brien, *The Family Silver: A Memoir of Depression and Inheritance* (Chicago: University of Chicago Press, 2004), 105.

there is not full agreement among professionals about whether the illness even exists, much less how it ought to be treated. Significant progress has been made in the development of new and improved medications, but so much remains unknown and otherwise problematic that a later section is dedicated to this topic. Some people have an illness that is, technically, treatable but, in their case, for reasons no one understands, remains stubbornly "treatment resistant"—nothing eases the anguish enough to make life livable. All this accounts in part for why the suicide rate does not decline, despite our advances in understanding and treating psychiatric disorders—so much about psychic anguish and its mitigation remains unknown and untreatable.

The Mental Health System

Dan Hanson does not mince words: "If the illness doesn't break you, the system might."[2] A story that illustrates the most egregious errors in care by the mental health system is provided by William and Lucy Hulme. We have thus far reflected mostly on their experience related to Bill's depression. But as mentioned in part 1, many years before Bill's illness the Hulmes had a devastating encounter with the failures of the mental health system when their eight-month-pregnant daughter hung herself while a patient in a psychiatric hospital. During the last weeks of pregnancy, she had made a suicide attempt while suffering from delusional prepartum psychosis. Her husband took her to her obstetrician, who referred her to a psychiatrist, who recommended hospitalization. Less than twenty hours after she was hospitalized, she hung herself in her room. Even though the psychiatrist and the admitting staff knew of her previous suicide attempt, she had been left alone. "Our daughter need not have died. . . . It was a tragic example of what can happen when specific acts of carelessness reflecting weaknesses in the current state of health care come one upon another."[3] His family's experience shows how brokenness in the mental health system can leave sufferers without care.

First, Hulme declares the system broken when the physician functions as unquestioned authority. As Hulme puts it, "The closest we seem

2. Daniel S. Hanson, *Room for J: A Family Struggles with Schizophrenia* (Edina, Minn.: Beaver's Pond Press, 2005), 81.
3. William E. Hulme, "Our Daughter Need Not Have Died," *Christian Century* 91 (December 4, 1974): 1144.

to come to 'Thus saith the Lord' is 'The Doctor says.'"[4] The hospital staff allowed Hulme's daughter to be alone because the psychiatrist, who did not consider hers to be a serious case, had not put her on suicide watch, and the staff didn't question the absence of the order. Hulme notes that it is not just that physicians cultivate this role. "People encourage it." We supply "strong cultural supports" for the attitude that the doctor is God because we need—"perhaps all of us at times"—the reassurance of a doctor's presumed "inerrancy," the hope that the physician has answers that will heal us and those we love.[5] The death of the Hulmes' daughter illustrates a broader truth—in the situation of psychic anguish, mental health care is broken when the authoritative expertise of psychiatrists, which is increasingly limited to drug therapies, is allowed to dictate the direction and substance of care.

A second break in the care offered by the mental health system is, as William Hulme puts, "discounting the family as a positive influence." If the physician is at one end of a spectrum of respect in the mental health system, families often experience themselves as being at the opposite end. Even though families are not blamed for their loved ones' illnesses as often as they once were, strong cultural supports still lock in negative assumptions about families, rather than positive ones.[6] At the same time that their daughter was alone in her room and ending her life, the Hulmes' son and second daughter were sitting in the hospital lobby. The hospital barred her siblings from seeing her because of a hospital rule that only her husband could visit. Her siblings, unwilling to leave, remained in the lobby for five hours, until told by hospital staff of their sister's death.[7] While their exclusion rarely has such dramatically deadly results, most family members feel that the immense amount of information they develop about the primary sufferer's history and current condition is disrespectfully disregarded. Not all families want to be more involved, certainly. But neither are family members like Marjorie Kerns, who is the mother of an adult daughter and a stepson with schizophrenia, all that unusual. Her pleading conveys the yearning many loved ones express to be respected and included in treatment planning.

4. Hulme, "Our Daughter Need Not Have Died," 1144.
5. Hulme, "Our Daughter Need Not Have Died," 1144.
6. Hulme, "Our Daughter Need Not Have Died," 1145–46.
7. Hulme, "Our Daughter Need Not Have Died," 1145.

We have much valuable information to share. Many of us know which medications have been effective and which ones have not. We have an overview of our family member's illness at our fingertips, something that few clinicians have time to research from past records. Let us be a part of the solution.[8]

Hulme writes about a third break in the system, what he calls "gaps in interprofessional teamwork" and others describe as a fragmentation in services overall. The mental health system is, Dan Weisburd says, "a bewildering, Kafkaesque maze of difficult-to-access programs."[9] After inquiries into their daughter's death, the Hulmes were left to conclude that their daughter had died because "she had fallen through the cracks of a hastily contrived but basically fragmented interprofessionalism."[10] Decades later, there is still little continuity in mental health staff: "There is always someone new looking at him, trying to figure him out," Anne Handler says of the treatment given her son Howard.[11] Very frequently, memoirists decry the factionalism in the branches of mental health care where, to use Susanna Kaysen's comment as example, "the analysts are writing about a country they call Mind and the neuroscientists are reporting from a country they call Brain."[12] The gaps and factionalism mean that holism in care plans and coordination between caregivers is often absent; holistic care, if it happens, is created through the advocacy of loved ones or the primary sufferers themselves (though, obviously, many of them are in too much anguish to be able to advocate for themselves). Advocacy turns out to be a full-time job, and because, as Dan Hanson observes, those without advocates usually end up on the street or—in ways we have yet to fully explore—victims of the system,[13] many family members exhaust themselves trying to be such an advocate. Sue Hanson gives us a sense of what it involves.

8. Marjorie A. Kerns, "Living on the Edge: Experiences of Family Members," in *New Directions in the Psychological Treatment of Serious Mental Illness*, ed. Diane T. Marsh (Westport, Conn.: Praeger, 1994), 163.

9. Dan E. Weisburd, "Planning a Community-Based Mental Health System: Perspective of a Family Member," *American Psychologist* vol. 45 (November 1990): 1245.

10. Hulme, "Our Daughter Need Not Have Died," 1147.

11. Anne C. Handler, "Living on the Edge: Experiences of Family Members," in *New Directions*, 146.

12. Susanna Kaysen, *Girl, Interrupted* (New York: Vintage Books, 1993), 143.

13. Hanson, *Room for J*, 82ff.

> I telephone . . . I call until I can't call anymore—doctors, thera-
> pists, social workers from the hospital, social workers from the
> county, social workers from the group home, attorneys for the
> county, attorneys for the hospital, medical assistance, Social
> Security, and the list goes on and on. Sometimes, I think I call too
> much. But if I don't, who will?[14]

If navigating the system is this sort of challenge for loved ones, it is easy
to understand why few primary sufferers—many of whom are already
struggling with confused thinking—can do it for themselves, even
though taking responsibility for oneself is a goal of mental health care.

Pam Martin—primary sufferer, mother and wife of primary sufferers, and active Episcopalian—succinctly names another dynamic in the
factionalism—"science ignores religion, and religion snubs science."[15] In
the context of mental health care, this means that mental health professionals, except in those rare contexts where a chaplain is a part of the
treatment team, have no way to assess how spiritual struggle might serve
the ends of good mental health care. An incident during Rev. Susan
Gregg-Schroeder's second hospitalization illustrates the absurd extent of
the gap and its cost to care.

> I was walking the exercise track with the other patients. I sud-
> denly realized that the hospital where I had done my clinical
> pastoral education (CPE) was just next door. I felt a real need to
> connect with my CPE supervisor and to visit the chapel that was
> so familiar to me. I sensed an urgent need for a spiritual connec-
> tion in this time of great turmoil. So I set out for the chapel in the
> adjacent hospital . . .
>
> I returned to the track before our group time was up and
> began participating in the next activity—art therapy. . . . While
> feeling deeply introspective, I tried to sort out all that had pre-
> cipitated my unexpected hospital readmittance.[16]

But her introspection was forcibly interrupted. Someone had notified the
hospital that she had left the grounds. Her doctor and the staff assessed

---

14. Hanson, *Room for J*, 51–52.
15. Pam Martin, *Touch the Angel's Hand: A Family's Struggle with Depression* (Oak Park, Ill.: Meyerstone Books, 1988), 72.
16. Susan Gregg-Schroeder, *In the Shadow of God's Wings: Grace in the Midst of Depression* (Nashville: Upper Room Books, 1997), 25.

her action to indicate a lack of impulse control and decided that she needed to be taken to a locked unit. Four male attendants dragged her to the unit, where she was strip-searched and then left alone in a room to suffer through the flashbacks of being physically abused by her mother and also through being approached sexually by another patient. "To this day," Rev. Gregg-Schroeder writes, "I am not sure if anyone really understood that I had left the track because of my need for spiritual connection. I still have nightmares about that experience."[17] If the mental health staff was unable to include a clergywoman's spiritual needs in their formulation of her case, it is easy to imagine the size of the gap that exists between laypeople's mental health care and their spiritual care.

A fourth sign of the mental health system's brokenness identified by Hulme is that it as a whole is contaminated with politics, machinations that rarely serve the sufferers. The Hulmes encountered these politics when they could find no official who would take or assign any responsibility for the death of their daughter. More common manifestations of the political nature of the system's brokenness are the fragmentation and, even more, the economics of mental health care and the lack of public outrage. Remember Stewart Govig's "cardiac breakdown" analogy described in part 2: we would never—and do not have to—tolerate for cardiac patients the uncoordinated and underfunded care given to psychiatric patients. The movement that began in the early 1960s to improve mental health care by decreasing institutionalization and establishing community mental health clinics is experienced by most sufferers as flawed and dangerous. Given the marginalized nature of the population to be served, government and the private sector had no political motivation to provide the extensive funding needed to set up the number of clinics actually needed. Now, not forced to accept it because they are not hospitalized, many sufferers elect to forego the treatment they found inadequate. Untreated, many are unable to work sufficiently to earn the money needed to buy themselves shelter and food on the open market, and they end up in the "the revolving-door syndrome" in which Stewart Govig had to watch his son Jay be trapped: "from psychiatric ward to an apartment to the street or shelter to a congregate care facility, back to the street or jail, then to the hospital once more."[18] The

---

17. Gregg-Schroeder, *In the Shadow of God's Wings,* 26.
18. Stewart D. Govig, *Souls Are Made of Endurance* (Minneapolis: Fortress Press, 1994), 54.

public erroneously assumes that personal recalcitrance is the primary reason for their deterioration.

Safety is also compromised by the politics. Formerly, treatment was too often forced in violation of a person's civil rights. Now, concern for civil rights is overriding, and new problems are created. Once people were institutionalized for too little reason, now sufferers may not receive the hospitalization they need. Today, unless sufferers voluntarily seek treatment—and their comprised cognition may prevent them from seeing the necessity of it—treatment can be forced on them only if they pose a danger—and it normally must be a life-threatening danger—to themselves or others. This means that, under the current standards, families and physicians must watch as primary sufferers decline until they become dangerous. If they are hospitalized, in most states, professionals and loved ones have only seventy-two hours to make decisions about whether the sufferer is safe enough to be discharged or whether the court must be petitioned for permission to force a longer hospitalization. Because the courts permit such extensions only under limited circumstances, seventy-two-hour "holds" mean that the focus of hospitalizations is usually on quick release, even if that means persons are discharged without adequate after-care plans. Stewart Govig speaks with the outrage of a father whose son is harmed by the system supposedly designed to help him.

> Given the quality of life these civil liberties afford on release, it is easy to conclude that ideology has replaced both compassion and common sense. On the Western frontier, people died with their boots on. Today, people die "with their civil rights on."
>
> I advocate a change: instead of the criterion "danger to oneself or others" for involuntary hospitalization, make it "unable to care for oneself."[19]

Another father allows that there are also genuinely competing, confusing interests at stake. Dan Hanson:

> As a society, we fail to help those who need our help the most. Maybe it's because we are mixed up. We don't know whether to push the burden on the person who is ill or on society. . . . We

---

19. Govig, *Souls Are Made of Endurance*, 54–55.

can't decide when to protect the rights of the individual and when to step in and protect those who cannot care for themselves or keep them from harming themselves or others. We close institutions that restrict the freedoms of those who are ill, yet we fail to provide the community support they need in order to function in society. We force parents to testify against their own children in order to satisfy a system that seems as mixed up as we are. . . .

Until we as a society decide to care enough about the mentally ill to do something about our mixed up motives and mixed up systems, families will continue to bear the burden alone.[20]

Other aspects of the system are experienced by these burdened families and other sufferers as maddeningly uncaring. Not only physicians but also caregivers and bureaucrats fail to remember—as Kay Redfield Jamison reminded herself when worried that her illness or the stigma against it might prevent her from working as a psychologist—"The privilege to [treat patients] is exactly that, a privilege; it is not a right."[21] Too often, however, sufferers describe treatment regimens, bureaucracies, and professionals that are patronizing at best and inhumane at worst. For example, when William Hulme's delusions caused him to refuse (on no rational basis) the ECT treatments his doctors and wife, Lucy, saw as his only hope of recovery, it took a full month to get the first legal hearing required to proceed with the treatment—a month in which the seventy-year-old Hulme and his family suffered through his further, precipitous decline.[22] Depressed and strapped financially, single mother Meri Danquah tried to access the only care she could afford, the mental health system provided by the government for its low-income citizens: "All of the programs that I looked into had waiting lists of six months to two years and upwards. For someone suffering from depression, six months to two years might as well be a death sentence."[23]

---

20. Hanson, *Room for J*, 84, 85.

21. Kay Redfield Jamison, *An Unquiet Mind* (New York: Random House, Vintage Books, 1995), 207.

22. William Hulme and Lucy Hulme, *Wrestling with Depression: A Spiritual Guide to Reclaiming Life* (Minneapolis, Minn.: Augsburg Books, 1995), 25.

23. Meri Nana-Ama Danquah, *Willow Weep for Me: A Black Woman's Journey Through Depression—A Memoir* (New York: W.W. Norton, 1998), 189.

These are not "assembly-line" illnesses, and so "the one-size-fits-all philosophy does not apply" when it comes to treatment.[24] Yet when the system makes care available, often sufferers feel the treatment is mass-produced, not able to respond to their unique needs or take advantage of their unique resources. Generic care cannot, of course, be adequately culturally appropriate. Many, many sufferers undergo treatment in a second or third language, or are expected to participate in treatments that violate their cultural values. Tracy Thompson writes, for example, about Akmal, another patient during her hospitalization. His English was limited and no one at the hospital spoke his language. And then there was Movement Therapy.

> Somebody hauls out the tumbling mats and we all—or most of us—lie down on them while Evalina turns out the light. Akmal, a good Muslim, makes tracks for the door: none of this immoral business of men and women lolling about together for him.[25]

An area of improvement in mental health services involves medications. Many primary sufferers and their families affirm that they owe their lives to these improved drug treatments. However, the majority of them also communicate that the mental health system is now characterized by too much of a good thing. In contrast to the sufferers' experience that medications bring their own anguish, some professionals are enamored of their use—"promiscuously proscribing," William Styron calls it.[26] William Hulme identified professionals' overreliance on medications as another weakness of the "care" contributing to the suicide of his pregnant, hospitalized daughter.[27] As in her case, professional overreliance is sometimes a dangerous level of trust in the medication's efficacy. But for sufferers, this overreliance also communicates what Parker Palmer experienced as dismissiveness toward "the inner life," a willingness to settle for symptom reduction and anesthetization of pain rather than healing, and insufficient concern about the medications' negative effects.

---

24. Hanson, *Room for J*, 118.
25. Tracy Thompson, *The Beast: A Journey through Depression* (New York: Penguin, Plume, 1995), 174.
26. William Styron, *Darkness Visible: A Memoir of Madness* (New York: Vintage Books, 1990), 71.
27. Hulme, "Our Daughter Need Not Have Died," 1145.

The broken mental health system will never be repaired without more financial and political commitment to research. Dan Weisburd conveys the yearning of all sufferers who are not appeased by tinkering with it, partly because they know the mechanics aren't backed up by adequate information. As Weisburd says, "the book of knowledge about the brain and how it works has too many blank pages."[28] But other forms of treatment and the larger horizon of healing also need to be more vigorously addressed. For example, in part 5 we will see just how healing it is to be treated with respect, do meaningful work, earn an income. But the system sets stringent limits on this, as Dan Hanson was amazed to learn: "It seems as if the system goes against J by setting limits on what he can earn and still receive financial and housing assistance."[29] The mental health system has been reformed in many ways, and it has turned its considerable resources to develop the science of psychopharmacology. But the lack of commitment to this relatively simple and yet vital source of healing—opportunity for those with psychiatric illnesses to have appropriate work—seems a holdover from the old notion of rest cures. Charlotte Perkins Gilman's famous and somewhat autobiographical 1892 story of a woman who sinks further into insanity because she is confined to rest in a room with nothing more to occupy her than its yellow wallpaper drew attention to the problem of prescribed inactivity for those with psychiatric illnesses.[30] But as Dan Hanson describes, little positive change has occurred.

> Our long-term goal is to help J find a place in this world, a way to live *in* this world even though he will never be *of* this world. The hope for . . . all who struggle with mental illness is that they will find meaningful work and supportive relationships. Many of the programs for the mentally ill are designed to do just that. But the truth is that much of the work is demeaning and the relationships patronizing.[31]

---

28. Weisburd, "Planning a Community-Based Mental Health Center," 1247.
29. Hanson, *Room for J*, 99.
30. Charlotte Perkins Gilman, "The Yellow Wall-paper," *New England Magazine* vol. 5 (September 1891–February 1892): 647–56.
31. Hanson, *Room for J*, 92.

Diagnosis

"What's your diagnosis?" The directness of the question makes it seem simple. Yet, it is not uncommon for memoirists to recount circumstances in which diagnosis and the treatment it suggests are revealed to be elusive or illusive. That a physician suffered from his illness going undiagnosed is sobering evidence of the elusiveness of comprehension and care. David Hilfiker:

> Since no one stumbled onto the diagnosis for the first twenty years of my illness, I was left without a name for my experience, which is almost worse than the experience itself. I didn't understand what was happening to me.[32]

The illusiveness of diagnosis and the harm incorrect diagnosis can do are revealed in scholar and writer Karen Armstrong's agonizing tale of having her epilepsy go undiagnosed and untreated for years, leading to years of misery in body and, especially, soul. All the while, she was being misdiagnosed as having a psychiatric problem for which she was treated with psychoanalysis, drugs, and hospitalizations. Also, the notion of a singular, stable diagnosis is a chimera. Mr. David Waldorf, who has spent most of his adult life as a patient at Creedmoor State Hospital in Queens, New York, and is also a painter whose work has been featured in a documentary film, says, "I have suffered through every single aspect of mental illness. That's why it's very hard to diagnose me. I've been through *everything*—psychosomatic, suicide, manic-depressive, schizophrenic—every single aspect of mental illness, I've been there."[33] Multiple, shifting diagnoses reflect disagreements between doctors and, also, the fact that human suffering won't cooperate with diagnostic categories.

Another concern our memoirists voice is that diagnoses are individualistic and fail to adequately account for the interpersonal and social contexts in which psychic turmoil is created, defined, and endured. As we discussed in part 2, some observe that "crazy" social conditions lead to "crazy" people. A few go further and argue that behaviors and atti-

---

32. David Hilfiker, "When Mental Illness Blocks the Spirit," *The Other Side* (May and June 2002), 12.
33. Dawn Parouse, prod., Jessica Yu, dir., *The Living Museum* (Filmworks, 1999). Interview of David Waldorf.

tudes designated as "crazy" are those that are unbearable to whoever holds power and has dominance. This opinion was validated for Susanna Kaysen by her doctor. She devotes a chapter of her memoir to reflection on the meaning of her diagnosis, borderline personality disorder, which she calls "the charges against me":

> What does *borderline personality* mean, anyhow? . . . To quote my . . . psychiatrist: "It's what they call people whose lifestyles bother them."
>
> He can say it because he's a doctor. If I said it, nobody would believe me.[34]

Evidence that diagnostic categories correspond to social preferences and prejudices is that they fluctuate with changes in those social attitudes. A recent example is provided by the change made regarding homosexuality: after homophobia and social intolerance declined sufficiently, homosexuality was no longer considered by most professionals to be a psychiatric disorder. Unfortunately, bigoted attitudes are not easily removed from the diagnostic or treatment processes.

Finally, even when the memoirists find their diagnoses helpful, or at least don't dispute them, to a person they speak with resentment when they are treated as if their diagnosis is the sum total of their personhood. Listen to the psychologist Martha Manning overhearing her colleagues.

> In the midst of discussing cases with several colleagues, someone refers to a patient as "a thirty-five-year-old manic depressive." I cringe. . . .
>
> I think about the difference between *having* something and *being* something. They are only words, but I'm struck by how much they convey about the manner in which the shorthand of mental illness reduces the essence of people in ways that labels for other serious illnesses do not.
>
> People say, "I have cancer." They don't say, "I am cancer." . . . Call someone "a schizophrenic" or "a borderline" and the shorthand . . . lulls us into a false sense that those words tell us who the person is, rather than only telling us how the person suffers.[35]

---

34. Kaysen, *Girl, Interrupted*, 150, 151.
35. Martha Manning, *Undercurrents: A Therapist's Reckoning with Her Own Depression* (San Francisco: HarperSanFrancisco, 1994), 169–70.

Medications

Our memoirists are well aware that the science of psychopharmacology offers crucial and unique help, especially in those cases where illness has a biochemical basis. For some, medication may give the first real relief from symptoms, and they are grateful. Especially to loved ones and other observers, who can see positive effects of the drugs without being directly encumbered with the drugs' negative effects, medications can seem almost miraculous. Their positive effects evoke religious language in some of our memoirists who are religious. Pam Martin describes her experience several weeks after her husband Tony started taking antidepressants: "like Mary watching Lazarus emerge from the darkened tomb, I watched a silent resurrection unfold."[36] Even when the results are modest, the desperation of loved ones is meaningfully eased: Rev. Dr. Stewart Govig entitles a chapter "Give Us This Day Our Daily Meds," because "taken faithfully and according to the directions, the treatment at least gave [Jay] a respite from the frenzy that turned into punched holes in dormitory room walls."[37]

The primary sufferers' appreciation, however, is usually more measured. David Karp says about his antidepressant medication that "through the years my attitude toward drugs has remained steady—a mixture of hostility and dependence."[38] Those of us who do not have to take these medications can become quite easily exasperated by sufferers who refuse medications or stop taking them but, as we are about to see, taking medications consistently poses many challenges and can yield very little experience of being cared for.

There are impossibly conflicted cultural messages about drugs—not just illegal drugs but drugs of any kind, even prescribed medications. On the one hand, one cultural message is that the strongest and best people don't *need* drugs, *shouldn't* need drugs. Drugs are, as Kay Redfield Jamison reminds us, crutches for damaged people.

> I genuinely believed—courtesy of strong-willed parents, my own stubbornness, and a WASP military upbringing—that I ought

36. Martin, *Touch the Angel's Hand*, 27.
37. Govig, *Souls Are Made of Endurance*, 42.
38. David A. Karp, *Speaking of Sadness, Depression, Disconnection, and the Meanings of Illness* (New York: Oxford University Press, 1996), 79.

to be able to handle whatever difficulties came my way without having to rely upon crutches such as medication.[39]

On the other hand, another and conflicting cultural message is that people with psychiatric disorders should take their meds without fail, resistance, or question. Despite culture's judgmentalism against medication, their failure to comply is seen as personal recalcitrance and, especially if they don't control their emotional difference in some other way, an affront to society. No wonder people in psychic anguish are conflicted about medications.

Our memoirists agree with the cultural maxim that is it necessary to be analytical about taking medications, and they are. For example, Sharon O'Brien cautions that the biochemical model of depression is necessary because depression does so often have a genetic or other physical source—as does hers—but that "this model may also have achieved dominance because it fits so neatly with the marketing power of the drug companies, and because it keeps the focus on the individual rather than the larger society."[40] And, in addition to the socioeconomic issues, so much about the drugs is unknown. Given that their bodies and psyches serve as a kind of laboratory, it's not uncommon that the primary sufferers feel like they *are* the experiment, as Martha Manning's plaintive words convey: "We are fooling with medicines again. I feel like a science project. A little of this, a touch of that, and maybe we'll make me right again. I long to be right again."[41] Even those professionals with the greatest skill and highest standards of care end up making educated guesses: which drug(s), which psychotherapy, which psychotherapist, how much hospitalization, what kind of after-care?

The fearfulness of trying uncertain and unfamiliar treatments, the frustration of having to start over again with a new therapist or on yet another medication, the desperation of wondering if anything will work—all these introduce into mental health care a level of harmfulness that is no one's fault and everyone's heartache—sufferers and professionals alike. Dan Weisburd conveys the poignant pain of our partial and yet limited knowledge when he describes how trying a new medication

---

39. Jamison, *An Unquiet Mind*, 99.
40. O'Brien, *The Family Silver*, 263–64.
41. Manning, *Undercurrents*, 84.

affected his son, David, whose life had disintegrated due to years of ineffective treatment for schizophrenia.

> There was one day when he was perfectly well—normal, or 99% so. It happened in the hospital, in a research ward at the University of California, Irvine, under the care of a gifted and empathetic psychiatrist . . . who had obtained permission to try David on the research protocol of the breakthrough medication, Clozapine. I will never forget that day. . . . There were serious risks involved. . . . [But] David had opted to try the medication. . . . And then came the day when David stood before me, wide-eyed, a look of wonderment on his face. . . .
>
>> It's as if I awoke from a nightmare, Dad. And I'm so grateful. I don't want to waste a second crying. But I want to tell everybody, *this* is really me and I'm back; that I'm not my illness, that I'm David; that I'm not a schizophrenic. I'm a person.[42]

But David developed the life-threatening side effects about which he had been forewarned and had to go off the drug. Dan goes on: "Bravely, [David] said, 'If I've had this one day, then I know others are possible sometime, I hope soon. And I hope I'll remember what it feels like. Please, help me to remember.'"[43]

Dan Weisburd concludes the story with a personal word—"I live in the hope spawned by that good day." That he can muster years of hope on the basis of one day when his son was tantalizingly returned and then abruptly revoked is a measure of his agony, his strength, and his grace toward those who are trying to help amid all the uncertainty.

Some people outside the community of memoirists worry that psychiatric drugs are being prescribed to people who don't need them. Tracy Thompson, like most memoirists, thinks the much larger problem is that "millions more who could benefit from these drugs are too frightened or ashamed to seek them out."[44] If people do take psychiatric drugs for the purpose of miraculous transformation, they are very likely to be disap-

---

42. Weisburd, "Planning a Community-Based Mental Health System," 1246–47.
43. Weisburd, "Planning a Community-Based Mental Health System," 1247.
44. Thompson, *The Beast*, 281.

pointed because initial strong effects can level out, as was true for Lauren Slater. "While it is a fact that Prozac, at least in my case, had strong transformative powers in the beginning, it rather quickly, to use the phrase of the medical community, 'pooped-out.'"[45]

Medications are not the panacea the general public tends to think they are—medications sometimes add to the anguish of mental health treatment. Even if they get more than the one good day given to David Weisburd and his father, Dan, for many the tantalizing promises of medication are short-lived and broken many times over by many different medications. Martha Manning paints with words a still life of her medications, a study that suggests that the hopes for power over psychic pain—shared by all those who manufacture, prescribe, and/or take psychiatric drugs—are for some melted by the heat of the wound inside.

> The kitchen windowsill is littered with bottles of pills. Lovely party-pastels in circles and squares with strong vanquishing names like Prozac and Xanax. Or sweet promising ones like Halcion and Asendin. And all these potions make me big for a while, but the sweetness of their promises melts like kisses somewhere inside me.[46]

Then for all those who take medications to ease their anguish, there is the new anguish of side effects—known and not-yet-discovered. Millions of people are putting into their bodies medications about which it will be decades before we have data that will show long-term side effects. There are other problems drugs can't touch. With schizophrenia, for example, there are drug treatments that work for some people, but we know little about how to deal with the ways that side effects of the medications diminish quality of life. In the best of circumstances, when helpful drugs are found, they introduce unknowns into the sufferers' self-knowledge: in almost all cases, to different degrees, memoirists say that the medications or their side effects make them, to some degree, into people they do not recognize.

It isn't just that some of our memoirists have to take near-toxic amounts to get an effective dose, though some are faced with this diffi-

---

45. Lauren Slater, *Prozac Diary* (New York: Random House, 1998), 189.
46. Manning, *Undercurrents*, 106.

cult choice. Even at low doses, our memoirists seldom mince words about the misery drugs can cause. The suffering differs according to drug, dose, person, and time, but Kate Millett's description of what lithium cost her conveys common themes: the suffering is physical, public, private, psychic, present, and future.

> Why quit taking lithium? Six years of diarrhea. Six years of hand tremor in public places, . . . at the moment one is watched and observed. Six years of it in private while trying to draw, . . . Six years of being on a drug that made one sluggish, the mind sedated, . . . Rumors that it isn't good for you in the long run, the kidneys, the liver, maybe even the brain.[47]

Millett's difficulty with drawing—her creativity—is illustrative of a final crucial point about side effects: they don't just add negative things to the lives of sufferers. The medications that make them "well" may rob them of their greatest pleasures. For example, most medications interfere with memory and comprehension; scholar Kay Redfield Jamison, who once read three or four books weekly, was unable to read a serious book cover to cover, whether fiction or nonfiction, for more than ten years.[48] Most recent antidepressants interfere with sexual pleasure; as Lauren Slater points out, recent drugs that are hailed as wondrously successful in returning millions of people to normalcy rob most of those persons of the ability to function normally in one of the arenas of life deemed central to mental health and happiness—sexuality.[49] Very little is yet known about the effect of psychopharmacological drugs on fetuses; any sufferer who wants to have a biological child must make terrible choices, as Lauren Slater did: "They said it would be more dangerous for me to go off my medication than for the fetus to be on it, but even as they announced this, I saw a look of alarm in their eyes."[50]

We can see from all these factors that while medications sometimes help enormously, even save sufferers' lives, they do not cure. In fact, when they do their best work, medications reveal the need for more healing, which—as we will explore in part 5—is *work*. For most sufferers, med-

---

47. Kate Millett, *The Loony-Bin Trip* (New York: Simon & Schuster, 1990), 31.
48. Jamison, *An Unquiet Mind*, 95.
49. Slater, *Prozac Diary*, 154.
50. Lauren Slater, "Noontime," in *Unholy Ghost*, 79.

ications do not simply return them to themselves but rather, to different degrees, set them on an unfamiliar course. One is faced with discovering oneself again, finding what will anchor but not drown—akin to the awkward formation of adolescence, which few of us would choose to repeat.

Finally, medications interfere with care when they dominate treatment and supersede human interaction. Sufferers often get the impression that mental health professionals care more about the medications than about them. Overreliance on medications lends an air of impersonality to mental health treatment, as Lauren Slater describes:

> Psychopharmacology is the one branch of medicine where there is no need for intimacy; neither knives nor stories are an essential part of its practice. And in its understandable glee that it might finally move psychiatry into a position as respectable as surgery, it risks forgetting, or maybe never learning, what even many a surgeon knows: that you must smooth the skin, that you must stop by the bedside in your blue scrub suit, that language is the kiss of life.[51]

All this medication-related anguish details the many good reasons sufferers question and sometimes resist simple compliance with medications. Resistance to medication is human nature: as Kay Redfield Jamison points out, we can see this in the hordes of "normal" people who fail to take medication as prescribed and stop taking it the second they feel better.[52]

Psychiatrists and Psychotherapists

We have already identified much of the anguish that attends our memoirists' encounters with psychiatrists and psychotherapists: in the case of physicians, misuse of their unquestioned authority, failure to respect the information sufferers and their families have about their own situations, failure to engage in teamwork with professionals in other fields, overreliance on medications. Just a few more points are needed to adequately represent the ways that relationships with psychiatrists and psychotherapists yield "care" that is not helpful, or even harmful. First, sufferers

---

51. Slater, *Prozac Diary*, 11.
52. Jamison, *An Unquiet Mind*, 101.

want from their psychiatrists and psychotherapists far more education than they usually get. Just as most sufferers want to be as informed as possible about their treatment, most sufferers want to have knowledge about their suffering. Perhaps psychiatrists and psychotherapists overestimate the information that sufferers have about mental health issues, or perhaps they underestimate the degree to which information can aid recovery. But in either case, a lack of information too often causes insufficient prevention, additional suffering, or mediocre healing.

> I did not . . . get well. I got functional, which is another condition altogether (though not, on the whole, one to be sneezed at). My ignorance of the difference, which almost cost me my life, I attribute to my doctors, none of whom taught me the first thing about depression.[53]

Nancy Mairs left the hospital without knowing that depression can recur and that depression can be much less dramatic than the condition that got her hospitalized. So, not knowing she was still depressed, she failed to get further help until, thirteen years later, she fell into another dangerously acute months-long depression. As we saw with the Hansons, education about the biological aspects of emotional suffering is also desperately needed and can be dramatically healing. Without that information, too many sufferers continue to try to use professional psychotherapy or their own rational analyses to ease symptoms that, because they are rooted in neurology, are beyond the reach of insight.

Especially in their dealings with psychiatrists and psychotherapists, sufferers find that the impersonal nature of the mental health system flies in the face of care; the medical model in which psychiatrists and many psychotherapists are trained emphasizes professional distance. Lauren Slater captures the effects of this distance both on the human interaction between herself and her doctor and on the way he is likely thinking and writing about her—in "case" notes.

> He had all the right gestures. His knowledge was impeccable. He made eye contact with the subject, meaning me. But still, there was something about the way the Prozac Doctor looked at me, and the very technical way he spoke to me, that made me

---

53. Nancy Mairs, *Plaintext*, 147.

feel he was viewing me generally—swf, long psych history, five hospitalizations for depression and anxiety-related problems, poor medication response in past, now referred as outpatient for sudden emergence of OCD—as opposed to me, viewing me, in my specific skin.[54]

Slater left the Prozac Doctor's office with pills in hand but was left on her own to do the soul-work necessary to actually take the medication. Meri Danquah is like many more sufferers who, given impersonal instructions, simply ignore them and grow in their resistance to seek help, especially if the instructions come from someone of a different racial-ethnic or social class. Danquah—remember she is an immigrant of Ghanaian heritage—finally worked up the courage to call a therapist. At the end of their second session, Sylvia—a white woman—instructed a tearful Meri that before their next session, Meri was to see a psychiatrist for an antidepressant.

Asking someone who doesn't even take aspirin to take medication that will alter her brain chemistry is like asking an atheist to go on a pilgrimage to Mecca. . . . I was dizzy with regret. . . . It had all been a big mistake: going there, telling her all my business, bawling like that. This woman probably thought I was a compete basket-case. I was seized with feelings of shame. . . . That was the last session I had with Sylvia.[55]

Finally, psychiatrists and psychotherapists too often fail to meet sufferers in the heart of their anguish, or even their delight. Absorbed in theoretical agendas, past experience, or concrete expectations, they can miss priceless opportunities for connection and the cultivation of hope. Lauren Slater's depression lifted remarkably when her Prozac "kicked in." She waited four days and, still incredulous at how much better she felt, Slater called her doctor.

"I'm well," I told him.

"Not yet," he said. "You only started nine days ago. It may take a month, or even more, to build up a therapeutic blood level."

---

54. Slater, *Prozac Diary*, 6.
55. Danquah, *Willow Weep for Me*, 194.

"No," I said, "I'm well." I felt a rushing joy as I spoke. "I've, I've actually never felt better."

There was a pause on the line. "I'm not sure that's possible, so fast," he said.

So fast.[56]

The doctor missed the point. His patient had called him, not about the drug or even about being well, really, but about her joy, after such a long siege. However, when psychiatrists and psychotherapists miss the mark, it is more often because their own agenda prevents them from meeting sufferers at the place of their pain. In a crisis with her depression while on research leave and away from home, Sharon O'Brien seeks out a new therapist. In their first session, Will asks Sharon to describe her childhood experience of her parents—"intense, scary mother; calm, bookish father," she offers—and learns that she isn't interested right then in a long-term relationship with a man. Will then launches into a comparison between her situation and a fairy tale about a witch-mother who tries to destroy her children's sexuality.

> "Now you have to kill off the witch," [he says]. . . . "Neither parent helped you become a woman," he adds. "Your father didn't give you the rose."
>
> "The rose?"
>
> "It's the sign in the fairy tale that the father's helping the daughter become a woman."
>
> ". . . Your journey is to reclaim your sexuality and your femininity, the gifts your parents stole from you" . . .
>
> I had just wanted someone to help me through this depression, but now it seems that my depression won't lift until I kill the witch, get the rose, and reclaim my femininity. This could take a long time, and my sabbatical is over in August.[57]

Hospitalization

When it comes to the anguish of mental health treatment, the general public may be most familiar with the anguish of hospitalization. Historic scan-

---

56. Slater, *Prozac Diary*, 31.
57. O'Brien, *The Family Silver*, 296–97.

dals associated with psychiatric hospitalization have publicized the fact that some sufferers have been hospitalized too quickly, for too little reason, and that others have experienced harrowing incarcerations under horrible conditions. Those problems have not been completely solved, but other problems are more often encountered by our memoirists. We will hear in part 5 that hospitalization can be a part of healing, so the problems noted here are arguably most tragic because they represent lost opportunity.

Hospitalized sufferers are too often treated without respect. They tell of being treated like children, coerced into undignified activities, herded into compliant behavior, badgered into emotional expression. William Styron was, on the whole, comforted by his hospitalization, but this is remarkable, given the mortification he experienced.

> Art therapy . . . is organized infantilism. Our class was run by a delirious young woman with a fixed, indefatigable smile. . . . Unwinding long rolls of slippery mural paper, she would tell us to take our crayons and make drawings. . . . For example: My House. In humiliated rage I obeyed.[58]

Illustrating the cost to other forms of treatment when sufferers feel disrespected, Styron contemptuously returns the contempt he felt directed toward him.

> Group Therapy did nothing for me except make me want to seethe, possibly because it was supervised by an odiously smug young shrink, with a spade-shaped dark beard (*der junge Freud?*), who in attempting to get us to cough up the seeds of our misery was alternately condescending and bullying . . .[59]

Like Styron, other sufferers regularly report being subjected to what might be called emotional extortion: given respect, peace and quiet, or minor privileges only in exchange for emotional self-revelation. Martha Manning expands:

> Adults come onto a unit with a number of "rights," some of which must be curtailed for their own protection. However, I have often seen rights turned into privileges and conferred on

---

58. Styron, *Darkness Visible*, 74.
59. Styron, *Darkness Visible*, 73.

people for compliance, rather than health. In the space of one hour, the right to set out walking whenever I please has become a privilege, something that must be bestowed upon me. How do I earn it? By behaving myself, spilling my guts, providing a shining example?[60]

More respectful and healing than this focus on revocation would be direct and clear statements about how a patient can increase her power, rights, and autonomy.

Whereas the problem was once that soul-sufferers were hospitalized for too little reason and for too long, now some memoirists say that the problem is the opposite—they are hurried out of hospitals. Compared to investments being made in medications, the mental health system and insurance companies invest very limited resources in hospitals or programs for learning how to be well. Lauren Slater writes of the need to put the "rushing recovery" medications sometimes provide into a broader context of care. "At the risk of nostalgia," she writes, we need to consider the value of the sanatoriums and convalescent homes provided (to those who could afford them) in the late eighteenth and early nineteenth centuries. These served, she writes, as the halfway houses of their era.

> The old-fashioned convalescent home, chairs stretched by the salty sea, isolated from the world and yet close on the cusp of it, acknowledged the need for a supportive transition, moving the patient incrementally from an illness-based identity to a health-based identity, out of the hospital, not yet home, hovering, stuttering, slowly learning to speak the sanguine alphabet again.[61]

Finally, a few words must be said about a specific treatment that has historically been part of the horror of psychiatric hospitalization: ECT—electroconvulsive therapy. We might expect this infamous treatment to be scathingly critiqued by our memoirists but, for the most part, this is not the case. In part 5 we will reflect on the improvements made in this treatment, which probably account for why some of our memoirists speak of the help it provided them and very little of problems associated with it. Here we will note that our memoirists who received the treatment many

60. Manning, *Undercurrents*, 115.
61. Slater, *Prozac Diary*, 36, 37.

years ago suffered then with a treatment that was terrorizing in the method, number, and strength of its applications. Nancy Mairs, who received twenty-one treatments, tells a story to illustrate one of the most common critiques of ECT, its diminishment of short-term memory.

> I had once, many years later, a string of black clay Mexican beads on a nylon thread that snapped suddenly, in the middle of a class I was teaching, scattering little fish and birds and balls every which way. My students scrambled, retrieving many of them, and my foster son restrung them, in a new pattern necessitated by the missing pieces, into a shorter necklace. One can, to some extent, recover one's losses, but the bits that roll under the shelves, into the corners, out the door are gone for good.[62]

Mental health treatment sometimes causes anguish by inflicting challenges that would try any person's soul. It is ironic, of course, that mental health treatment—designed to care for those in psychic anguish, staffed by many well-intentioned professionals—should be itself a source of soul-suffering. Much has improved, but what Clifford Beers observed in the 1908 first edition is still on the mark: "Is it not, then, an atrocious anomaly that the treatment often meted out to insane persons is the very treatment which would deprive some sane persons of their reason?"[63]

THE ANGUISH OF RELIGIOUS CARE

Stewart Govig, the Lutheran professor and minister whose son, Jay, is diagnosed with schizophrenia, implies that he and his family have a relationship to a local congregation and pastor. Yet, he barely mentions these ties to religious life and community in his memoir. Govig admits that this absence is due in part to him and his wife, in the crisis of Jay's illness, having "surrendered to professional expertise and ignored resources within . . . religious faith." Referring to his many disappointments in mental health treatment, he says, "Despite everything, I am still inclined to approach medical personnel like priests of healing whose

---

62. Mairs, *Plaintext*, 125–26.
63. Clifford W. Beers, *A Mind That Found Itself: An Autobiography,* 5th ed. rev. (Garden City, N.Y.: Doubleday, Doran & Co., 1944), 250–51.

words for Jay's illness become magical answers to the pain and dilemmas a parent such as I must face." Similarly, though a number of our memoirs are written by people active in religious community, religious life and care is a relatively minor theme, probably because, in the dire and urgent circumstances of mental health crises, religious care may not be a priority or even relevant. Most of our memoirists who are religious would say with Govig that, "before long, practical realities overtook my faith intangibles."[64] Though religious care is mentioned only infrequently, as compared to mental health treatment, memoirs of soul-suffering nonetheless reveal quite a bit about how religion and its representatives contribute to the anguish of soul-suffering. In part 5 we will reflect on ways that religion is part of healing. But here we focus on how memoirs of soul-suffering reveal that, in religious communities, we too often do unto others what we would not want done to ourselves.

Community

> Recently I broke a small bone in my foot and had to walk around with a cast and cane. Interestingly, I received more sympathetic concern over this tiny broken bone than I ever had with my broken spirit and wounded soul.[65]

Rev. Susan Gregg-Schroeder is not speaking here only of religious community, but neither is she excluding her wider church community. Even after she wrote an open letter to her congregation about her depression, she got relatively little response. Usually, the neglect happens because religious communities are no more proactive than any other social institution about educating their members to understand and react appropriately to psychic turmoil. Laypeople and clergy alike don't know what to say, nor what to do. Consequently, the experience of many soul-sufferers is like that of Stewart Govig: "Our church, aloof and silent, seemed irrelevant."[66] Silence is better than prying, prurient questions, of course. Lucy Hulme is candid about the lack of care given to her when she tried to go to church at the start of her husband's sudden, catastrophic depression.

---

64. Govig, *Souls Are Made of Endurance*, 46, 89, 51.
65. Gregg-Schroeder, *In the Shadow of God's Wings*, 39.
66. Stewart D. Govig, "Chronic Mental Illness and the Family: Contexts for Pastoral Care," *Journal of Pastoral Care* 47 (Winter 1993): 406.

I did not attend church after the first couple Sundays of Bill's hospitalization. He was very well known in the church and I would have found having to answer all the questions wearing and not helpful. "How is he getting along?" "No, he is no better." "What do his doctors say?" And on and on. Many of the questions were not helpful; people would press for details they did not need. To me this seemed offensive. I also observed . . . that many of these people were asking for themselves, as they were or had been depressed. Some were just morbidly curious. Some offered reassurances that they were in no position to offer; they rather needed to reaffirm their positive religious hope.[67]

Silence is also better than judgmentalism and theology dangerous to one's soul. "Several church people told my husband that I did not have enough faith or must have a poor relationship with God or that my mental illness was a form of 'demon possession,'" says Norma Swetnam. "Because of attitudes that still prevail, I am cautious about sharing my experiences. I fear people will consider me a lesser child of God—although I know that to God none of us is 'lesser.'"[68]

Care offered by religious professionals is not necessarily more helpful. Some of the clergy who appear in memoirs of soul-suffering remind us that too many pastors have insufficient education or skill regarding acute psychic turmoil. Church officials are slow to investigate pastoral misconduct, but when her superiors became aware of Rev. Gregg-Schroeder's depression, they held meetings to review her fitness for ministry. When Jay was hospitalized, the Govigs found pastoral response to be "reactive help, never a proactive initiative."[69] Psychologist Frederick Frese reports encountering priests on two occasions when he was having psychotic episodes. One priest gave him printed material about entering the priesthood. Another priest, after Frese knelt by the altar as mass was being said, threatened to call the police if Frese did not leave the church.[70]

The lack of responsiveness to the Gregg-Schroeder, Govig, and Hulme families was probably exacerbated because expectations abound

---

67. Hulme and Hulme, *Wrestling with Depression*, 15.
68. Norma G. Swetnam, "My Journey through Hell," in *Presbyterians Today Online* (August 1998), http://www.pcusa.org/today/archive/features/feat9808d.htm (accessed August 1, 2006), 2.
69. Govig, "Chronic Mental Illness and the Family," 407.
70. Frederick J. Frese, III, "A Calling," *Second Opinion* 19 (January 1994): 17, 20.

that religious professionals and their families are—or should be—of ex-traordinary strength-of-soul. They are supposed to give care, not need care. This judgment was even more maddening than the judgmentalism Norma Swetnam and her husband endured: "Most frustrating to both of us was the assumption that a minister's wife does not need pastoral care."[71] Especially in communities that portray religious faith as an inoculation against doubt and pain, religious leaders and their families are expected to be exemplars of faith and well-being.

Despite the prevalence of people in emotional anguish both within and beyond religious communities, the needs of those in psychic anguish are usually omitted from education, prayer, worship, and community advocacy. Some soul-sufferers are working to counter this. For example, Susan and Gunnar Christiansen—active Presbyterian laypeople and parents of a son diagnosed with schizophrenia—have founded FaithNet (see appendix), pouring their time and financial resources into establishing a national organization that educates clergy and religious communities regarding the needs of those with psychiatric disorders. Dr. Gunnar Christiansen undertook this work after realizing that "what was necessary for me was to ask for strength to forgive the Faith Community for the past wall of silence."[72] Religious persons thrust into the politics surrounding psychic upheaval—stigma, discrimination in health insurance, inadequate care—soon notice that the silence is not just local. Grassroots advocacy and support networks have developed within many denominations (see appendix), but the official structures of most religious bodies have been largely aloof and silent on both national and international levels. Rev. Dr. Govig writes about struggling not to drown in negative feelings, like these toward his denomination: "I am disgusted that my church trumpets justice in distant lands and ignores Lazarus (Luke 16: 19–31) on its doorstep."[73]

Theology

Most memoirists who comment on religious care note that its contributions to the anguish of soul-sufferers are a direct result of theology that

---

71. Swetnam, "My Journey through Hell," 2.
72. Gunnar Christiansen, "Spirituality and Religious Outreach," *The Journal of the California Alliance for the Mentally Ill* vol. 8, no. 4 (December 18, 1997): 6.
73. Govig, *Souls Are Made of Endurance*, 48.

is, at best, inadequate to address the realities of soul-suffering and, at worst, heartbreakingly cruel and unnecessary. First and foremost, psychic anguish pushes to consciousness excruciating implications of common teachings and truisms about G-d, many of which fail to disclose a caring G-d. As she felt herself slipping into depression, Virginia Heffernan went back to church for the first time since childhood. "I went to the earliest service, often fighting tears through the prayers and hymns. . . . 'God' always refused to become glorious, instead stubbornly remaining plain, a headache, a sorrowful knot of language."[74] Seeing a homeless woman who looks locked in a private psychic hell, Manning is reminded of the phrase "there but for the grace of God go I."

> When I think hard about the statement, . . . I find no comfort. Because if I've learned anything from Scripture, I've learned that what the Lord giveth, the Lord can sure as hell take away. . . . When I begin to feel myself slip, and know that I am more broken than whole, I have trouble assuming the grace of God. Instead, I panic, convinced that *this* time I will be at the end of the line. This time, the very last bit of God's grace will go to the person in front of me, and I will be turned (away) empty.[75]

Parents of children afflicted with psychic turmoil wonder if their lives are proof of a wrathful G-d, unappeased by their devotion. Stewart Govig remembers anew Deuteronomy 5:9 (NRSV).

> "I the Lord your God am a jealous God, punishing children for the inequity of parents, to the third and fourth generation" . . . Iniquities? We were, after all, praying, Bible-reading people. Had we taken for granted . . . our abilities to accomplish a biblical standard for family discipline . . . ?[76]

For those whose loved ones commit suicide, the untruth in the theological truism—God doesn't give us anything we can't handle—is no longer held at bay: if God does give us the suffering we experience then, as

---

74. Virginia Heffernan, "A Delicious Placebo," in *Unholy Ghost*, 13.
75. Martha Manning, *Chasing Grace: Reflections of a Catholic Girl, Grown Up* (San Francisco: HarperSanFrancisco, 1996), 120.
76. Govig, *Souls Are Made of Endurance*, 7.

Albert Hsu points out, many people, like his father, *are* "given" by God far more suffering than they can bear.[77]

Some memoirists' belief is shattered, because the ideas about G-d they have been taught can't stand the heat of soul-suffering. Or, perhaps worse, they are left trying to reconcile themselves to a G-d they have been taught is loving, omnipotent, omniscient, and omnipresent, but has let them down. Kay Redfield Jamison speaks for many who find that at the point of their deepest need, "God, conspicuously, was nowhere to be found."[78] Two months after Martha Manning's discharge from the hospital, many things are improved, but she writes that

> I confess to [my therapist Kay] that my spiritual life is in the toilet. I don't believe in anything anymore except luck—good and bad. I still feel like I am being punished for being a bad person, a weak person, a neurotic person. It is hard to reconcile my old concept of a merciful God with my recent experience of a hateful, spiteful God, or a totally indifferent God who plays fifty-two-pickup with people's lives. . . . Will I ever be forgiven?
>
> Kay listens to my rantings and smiles. "Martha," she says, "I don't think we're talking about God forgiving *you*. I think we're talking about you forgiving *God*."[79]

A second way in which theology adds to anguish is through traditional teachings about suffering. As we will see in part 5, sufferers often try to make meaning despite their suffering, or do something meaningful with the wisdom borne of suffering. But this is quite different from saying that the suffering itself is good. Some common teachings imply that suffering is good because it brings one closer to G-d. Dan Hanson speaks for those who do not find care in this theological notion.

> People tell us that in another time and place J could have been a shaman or a prophet. I am sure they are trying to make us feel better. But there are times when I resent their comments. What do these people know of mental illness, I ask myself. Have they

---

77. Albert Y. Hsu, *Grieving a Suicide: A Loved One's Search for Comfort, Answers, and Hope* (Downers Grove, Ill.: InterVarsity Press, 2002), 144.

78. Jamison, *An Unquiet Mind*, 122.

79. Manning, *Undercurrents*, 155.

lain awake all night wondering if their child will hurt himself or someone else? Do they know what it's like to live with someone who [proclaims] God and informs you in no uncertain terms that *he* has created *you*? Have they watched their child sit out in the snow for hours wearing only a light jacket, his arms stretched out to the heavens crying for the aliens to come and rescue him from a hard, cold world that doesn't recognize or appreciate him? Have they ever been forced to call the police on their own child because all of their efforts to persuade him to come in out of the cold have failed? Have they helped lock up someone they love in a psychiatric ward? Have they had their hopes dashed by a system that is not equipped to deal with . . . their ill child? How dare these people trivialize what we go through by simply stating "he could have been a shaman" as if conjuring up some spiritual role makes it all better?[80]

Other common teachings imply that suffering is good because it leads to spiritual growth. As Sharon O'Brien puts it, "suffering is supposed to make you a better person: you're supposed to endure it, not seek help to deal with it."[81] However, at least where a person has a psychiatric illness, the "endurance" that is supposed to make the person better can make the person worse if it keeps people from getting help that could alleviate the suffering. Especially with psychospiritual suffering, it becomes clear that it is suppression that is expected as much as endurance. If one actually feels or shows the suffering one is enduring, one's spiritual maturity is brought into question. David Hilfiker speaks for the many who are left feeling judged by implications in worship and other religious settings that g-dly people are serene and untroubled.

I need my community not to require that my spirituality bring me any particular joy—for if joy is some measure of spirituality, I'm a long way from home. If a relationship with God brings one peace and a sense of harmony with the world, then I have little relationship with God.[82]

---

80. Hanson, *Room for J,* 13–14.
81. O'Brien, *The Family Silver*, 159.
82. Hilfiker, "When Mental Illness Blocks the Spirit," 14.

Here we have entered into a third area in which theology is more hurtful than helpful: the conflation of curing and healing. Pam Martin observes that when there are prayers for those in psychospiritual anguish, too many churches do not distinguish between healing and curing, and judge and shun those whose illnesses do not go away.[83] The factionalism between religion and psychiatry shows up on the theological side when it is stated or implied that psychology can be replaced with religion and that prayer can cure what psychiatry cannot. As David Hilfiker says,

> We may have gotten beyond the belief that faith in God always brings material blessings, or even physical health. . . . But sometimes, I suspect, we still get hooked by the illusion that deep spirituality should bring emotional or mental health.[84]

The failure of the Christian community to distinguish between cure, which is the absence of illness, and healing, which is living with integrity in the presence of illness or other suffering, can lead soul-sufferers to despair. Lloyd Carr suspects that the absence of such distinctions in his daughter-in-law's religious community contributed to Kate's suicide.

> Her commitment was genuine, and, in the first few years of her conversion her life showed many signs of growth and progress in the faith, yet the old habits died hard. Nor was the task made any easier for her by the indoctrination of some of her friends, who taught her to think that if she only had "enough faith" all her problems would disappear. She tried to follow their lead, but when the problems would not disappear and the old temptations proved so strong, she found herself thinking that in fact she did not have "enough faith," nor could she ever get "enough."[85]

Finally, nearly every memoirist comments on a fourth area where theology and religion add to the heartache of soul-suffering, and that is in regard to suicide. As Carr's study after Kate's suicide revealed, in passages that address suicide the Bible neither supports nor condemns. Yet, doctrinal

---

83. Martin, *Touch the Angel's Hand*, 52.
84. Hilfiker, "When Mental Illness Blocks the Spirit," 12.
85. G. Lloyd Carr, with poetry by Gwendolyn C. Carr, *The Fierce Goodbye: Hope in the Wake of Suicide* (Downers Grove, Ill.: InterVarsity Press, 1990), 79.

prohibitions against suicide abound, arguing from the fundamental theological assertion that life is a gift from God that a faithful person never spurns, and from the Decalogue's commandment: you shall not murder.[86] These religious prohibitions sidestep the experience of suicidal persons, for whom life is not gift but agony. For persons in soul anguish, the gift of life is often defiled with pain, and love cries out for mercy. In the words we considered earlier, Martha Manning offers an alternative philosophy, one that respects both the suffering and the mercy of persons whose life is threatened by soul-suffering: "I don't want to die because I hate myself . . . [but] because . . . I love myself enough to have compassion for this suffering and to want to see it end."[87] This is the ultimate paradox, when life is deathly, and death is love. Those caught in this paradox often receive not grace or even much compassion, but usually judgment. Of course, for people in acute anguish, it is deeply ironic that the Christian tradition teaches that death is not to be feared and is the not the end of life.

These failures of religious community and theology to provide helpful care tend to have two effects. However hurt and disappointed, some soul-sufferers feel empowered to reform the church, revise theology, reinterpret traditional biblical interpretations, and create the new rituals and practices they need. Other sufferers, though, do not feel empowered or motivated to reinvent their religion, and they are driven out of the church by its failure to provide care or teachings that relate to their suffering with sufficient comprehension and compassion. In both groups, though, where religion falls short, many seek to formulate a spirituality that will endure. During a conversation about God with her sister, a recovering alcoholic, Martha Manning agrees with her sister's observation that "religion is for people who are afraid of going to hell. Spirituality is for people who have already been there."[88] Not all our memoirists would agree with this characterization of religion, but many would. However they feel about religion, many of our memoirists seek meaning, values, and soul-sustenance beyond formal religion. In part 5, we will consider the importance of both religion and spirituality in the lives of those soul-sufferers who find some healing.

---

86. Exodus 20:13; Deuteronomy 5:15 (NRSV).
87. Manning, *Undercurrents*, 99.
88. Manning, *Undercurrents*, 178.

CARE THAT HELPS

Memoirs of soul-suffering are full of stories that help us comprehend what sort of care helps. While expertise is sometimes insufficient among professionals and concern is sometimes insufficient within families and communities, memoirists' stories of harmful and helpful care reveal that a lack of these is not the most basic problem in caregiving. Rather, what matters most is the quality of the interpersonal interactions between caregivers and care seekers. Therefore, in this section we will assume expertise and concern, and push beyond those crucial dimensions to what seems to be more elusive—and more precious. Since beyond expertise and concern our memoirists want pretty much the same thing from all of us—loved ones, communities, and professionals—this section makes no distinctions according to role and is instead organized according to qualities that make the interpersonal dimensions of care most meaningful and powerfully healing.

Mostly we will find in these stories the truth articulated by the Golden Rule. The basics of care are found in doing unto others as we would have done to us and also the inverse—not doing, restraining ourselves from inflicting on others that which, honestly, we ourselves hate having done to us. We will find that these basics are harder to practice than we might initially think. As we noted earlier, soul-sufferers themselves often find it hard to practice the kind of caregiving they know from experience to be most needed. Yet, we will also be encouraged to find that our care need not be perfect. It needs to be, as the pediatrician and psychoanalyst D. W. Winnicott has famously called it, good-enough. The best care isn't perfect care: perfection may flatter the one caring, but it eventually weakens and even humiliates the one cared for. Rather, over the long haul, the best care is good enough to meet the needs of sufferers, but without overpowering their agency.

More than anything else, our memoirists cherish and are grateful for what, in pastoral care and counseling, we call the ministry of presence. This presence is a ministry because it yields the sacred gifts of accompaniment and empowerment, given from human soul to human soul. This presence is not easy to describe, though when Nishimoto Muneharu rewords the Beatitudes to specify a care-filled relationship between disabled persons and those desiring to assist them, specific actions begin to reveal the contours of the presence that ministers.

- Blessed are you who take the time to listen to difficult speech, for you help me to know that if I persevere I can be understood.
- Blessed are you who never bid me to "hurry up" and take my tasks from me and do them for me, for often I need time rather than help.
- Blessed are you who stand beside me as I enter new and untried ventures, for my failures will be outweighed by the times I surprise myself and you.
- Blessed are you who ask for my help, for my greatest need is to be needed.
- Blessed are you who understand that it is difficult for me to put my thoughts into words.
- Blessed are you who with a smile encourage me to try once more.
- Blessed are you who never remind me that today I asked the same question two times . . . or more.
- Blessed are you who respect me and love me as I am—just as I am, and not like you wish I were.[89]

The care conveyed here exemplifies both accompaniment and empowerment. It also testifies that persons who are willing to provide comforting accompaniment when pain cannot be alleviated are as much a blessing as

---

89. Stewart D. Govig, *Strong at the Broken Places: Persons with Disabilities and the Church* (Louisville: Westminster John Knox Press, 1989), 95–96, citing Nishimoto Muneharu, "A Whole Church Includes the Disabled," *Japan Christian Quarterly* 48 (Winter 1982): 37.

persons who take concrete actions that alleviate pain. Presence can be conveyed by both "being with" and "doing for." But discussions of the ministry of presence focus more on being than on doing. This is not because actions are unimportant. Rather, "being with" is emphasized because, for most of us, it is more difficult. It requires that the caregiver not insist on the heroic role of bringing solutions to pain but be willing to share with sufferers their vulnerability to pain's power, persistence, and poignancy. It is easiest to do this if one has experienced the kind of suffering that does not yield easily to solutions and the reluctance of others to sit with one in one's ash heap. William Hulme expresses what seems to be true: many people were helpful to him and his family, and the most helpful were those who had been involved in "a socially unacceptable trauma."[90] As we will see, however, what matters most is the caregivers' capacity to suffer with the sufferer, to embody compassion in any of its countless forms, and in so doing, to embody a divine love and, sometimes, hope.

BREATHING, AND OTHER ACTS OF BEING

"Having it Out with Melancholy"— the poem Jane Kenyon wrote about her battle with depression, a poem that has touched so many—includes a description of one caring interaction, and it is this:

> The dog searches until he finds me
> upstairs, lies down with a clatter
> of elbows, puts his head on my foot.
>
> Sometimes the sound of his breathing
> saves my life—in and out, in
> and out; a pause, a long sigh. . . .[91]

Caring relationships between humans and animals teach us much of what we need to learn. Reminiscent of the biblical texts about the woman who searches for a lost coin until it is found, and the shepherd who goes in search of even one lost sheep, the caregiver here—Kenyon's dog—puts effort into seeking her out. Every person matters, though not every person

---

90. Hulme and Hulme, *Wrestling with Depression*, 104.
91. Jane Kenyon, "Having it Out with Melancholy," in *Constance: Poems* (St. Paul, Minn.: Graywolf Press, 1993), 24.

desires it, and is worthy of being sought. Undoubtedly, Kenyon remembers this caregiver so lovingly, at least in part, because he is so low maintenance—willing and able to get little in return, unlike helpers who come armed with questions, answers and advice driven by their own needs. The caregiver here is not graceful—like most of us in these situations, he's all "clatter of elbows." But—because his record of loyal love precedes him, because the one in anguish is sure of the caregiver's love—this clumsy, noisy arrival appears endearing and not distracting. Kenyon's upstairs solitude and silence seem not to be interrupted by this caregiver's arrival. Indeed, this centered, loving presence seems to further hallow her seclusion and quietness. First, there is physical touch, which can be so iffy, but here is not, perhaps because it is so slight, so humble—like being annointed. But this touch is also safe enough because it is not the sufferer whose vulnerability is increased but the caregiver—his head on her foot. The encounter also seems hallowed by the caregiver's arrival because it draws Kenyon's attention to breathing, as in meditation. Except here, to the steady in and out, in and out, is added an important difference in emphasis. In meditation we are told to focus on our own breath, but here it is attentiveness to *his* breath that saves her. And it is not only the in-breath and out-breath that matters, but the pause—and then a long sigh. He keeps on breathing, despite the pauses, and the long sighs. Perhaps she thinks, "With him beside me I, too, can keep breathing despite the pauses, and my long sighs."

When Lizzie Simon was on her road trip, she asked her interviewees what advice they have for parents and friends about what they should do to help. Listening to them, and to her own deepest need, she comes to the realization that advice about what to do is not needed, at least not as much as encouragement about how to be.

> I'm starting to think it isn't about what they should do. What is there to do, anyway? It's how they could be. If parents could be any way we designed—if friends could be, if therapists could be—how would we design them . . . ?
>
> I'd put them there, here, right next to me, right in the middle of my loneliness and terror. I'd have them standing there or sitting beside me when the house is caving in and the ground is melting.[92]

---

92. Lizzie Simon, *Detour: My Bipolar Road Trip in 4-D* (New York: Washington Square Press, 2002), 156.

Providing undemanding, nonviolating physical presence and touch to sufferers is harder for humans than for animals, but when we can do it as humbly and bravely as pets, it is similarly healing. When her friend, Nick, is having a hard time, is crying, Lizzie remembers, "I want to wrap him up inside of me. I sit on the arm of his chair and put my hand on his back, to let him know I'm not afraid of any of this."[93] Parker Palmer says, "I do not like to speak ungratefully of my visitors. They all meant well, and they were among the few who did not avoid me altogether." But, too many of them came with words of "false connections": "It's a beautiful day. Why don't you go out and soak up some sunshine. . . . Surely that'll make you feel better." "But you're such a good person. . . . Try to re-member all the good you've done, and surely you'll feel better." "I know exactly how you feel. . . ." Parker was reminded of the biblical story of Job, and of all the times he, like Job's friends, tried to help but made things worse.

> Having not only been "comforted" by friends but having tried to comfort others in the same way, I think I understand what the syndrome is about: avoidance and denial. One of the hardest things we must do sometimes is to be present to another person's pain without trying to "fix" it, to simply stand respectfully at the edge of that person's mystery and misery. Standing there, we feel useless and powerless, which is exactly how a depressed person feels—and our unconscious need as Job's comforters is to reassure ourselves that we are not like the sad soul before us.[94]

Palmer tells one story to show us a different way, and it is a story about the presence offered by his friend Bill.

> [H]aving asked my permission to do so, [Bill] stopped by my home every afternoon, sat me down in a chair, knelt in front of me, removed my shoes and socks, and for half an hour simply massaged my feet. . . .
> Bill rarely spoke a word.[95]

93. Simon, *Detour*, 69.
94. Parker J. Palmer, *Let Your Life Speak: Listening for the Voice of Vocation* (San Francisco: Jossey-Bass, 2000), 61, 62, 63.
95. Palmer, *Let Your Life Speak*, 63.

NO SMALL THING

Many, many families and friends provide helpful care to soul-sufferers, and do so heroically. Sadly, some find their heroic care rebuffed by their loved ones. But many times, it is a family member, or families and friends and professionals pulling together, who save a life. And while their acts of heroism sometimes involve big things, their heroism is most often seen in the consistency of their everyday faithfulness in the "small" things, even when their own hearts are breaking. Here, from Kay Redfield Jamison, is one of countless examples.

> My mother . . . was wonderful. She cooked meal after meal for me during my long bouts of depression, helped me with my laundry, and helped me pay my medical bills. She endured my irritability and boringly bleak moods, drove me to the doctor, took me to pharmacies, and took me shopping. Like a gentle mother cat who picks up a straying kitten by the nape of its neck, she kept her marvelously maternal eyes wide-open, and, if I floundered too far away, she brought me back into a geographical and emotional range of security, food, and protection. Her formidable strength slowly eked its way into my depleted marrowbone. It, coupled with medicine for my brain and superb psychotherapy for my mind, pulled me through day after impossibly hard day. Without her I never could have survived. . . . Often the only thing that would keep me going was the belief, instilled by my mother years before, that will and grit and responsibility are what ultimately make us supremely human in our existence. For each terrible storm that came my way, my mother—her love and her strong sense of values—provided me with powerful, and sustaining, countervailing winds. . . .
>
> . . . It was as if my father had given me, by way of temperament, an impossibly wild, dark, and unbroken horse. It was a horse without a name, and a horse with no experience of a bit between its teeth. My mother taught me to gentle it; gave me the discipline and love to break it; and—as Alexander had known so intuitively with Bucephalus—she understood, and taught me, that the beast was best handled by turning it toward the sun.[96]

96. Jamison, *An Unquiet Mind*, 118–19.

Showing up and hanging out with suffering ones in pain is, really, the better part of valor. On the other hand, there are times a sufferer needs a good meal (or a foot massage). So, laying around and breathing isn't enough—caring presence is sometimes practical presence. It cannot be overemphasized that "doing something" is too often alienating, especially when the actions are touted as caregiving but are actually busyness to avoid dealing with the chronic pain of emotional anguish. But when sufferers perceive that actions are undertaken to move closer to them in their pain, then those actions serve presence and are often welcomed with gratitude.

As we will see in part 5, healing comprises many small and healthy steps, made into a whole life. So, when it comes to caring that serves healing, there are no small things. As in the case with Kay Redfield Jamison's mother, her actions were occasionally directed toward protecting her daughter and teaching her discipline—and note as well that Kay uses the word gentle, twice, to describe her mother in those roles. More often, she directed her practical actions toward supporting her daughter's strength by loaning to Kay some of her own. Kay implies that the food and chores and errands were important because—through it all—her mother conveyed love for her, body and soul, and values. To do this, she worked alongside Kay—not getting ahead of her, it seems, nor lagging behind—modeling the will, grit, and responsibility healing requires.

But "breaking" the wild horse of temperament is no end in itself—as we have seen, Kay finds too much value in her moods to have allowed that. Rather, her mother's way of helping reminds her of how twelve-year-old Alexander, son of Phillip II, king of Macedonia, had been able to befriend a wild horse no one else had been able to reach. This wild horse, Bucephalus, had been brought to the royal court, and no one, not even the king, had been able to tame it. But Alexander noticed that Bucephalus seemed frightened by his shadow. So, the boy brought the horse into sunlight, and after he stroked the horse gently—there's that word again—and whispered in his ear, Bucephalus allowed Alexander to ride him. They traveled together for many years, and it is said that Alexander believed that he became Alexander the Great only because of the help of the spirited Bucephalus.

EVERYONE NEEDS KEYS

Psychologist Lauren Slater ends one of her memoirs with a story that suggests many aspects of helpful caring, but none more than the importance of dignity, humanity, and mutual respect. She is meeting for the first time the patient assigned to her at the hospital where Slater was herself once a patient and had experienced the way hospital rules and regulations eat away at one's sense of value, dignity, and maturity. Another small thing that matters—literally and metaphorically—is having keys to the locked doors.

> "Linda," I say, as she comes close to me, I extend my hand. "Hello," I say, and I can hear a gentleness in my voice, a warm wind in me, for I am greeting not only her, but myself.
>
> We stand in front of the locked interview room and I fumble for the correct key. I start to insert it in the lock, but then, halfway done, I stop. "You," I say to my new patient, Linda. "You take the key. You turn the lock."
>
> She arches one eyebrow, stares up at me. Her face seems to say, *Who are you, anyway?* I want to cry. The hours here have been too long and hard. "You," I say again, and then I feel my eyes actually begin to tear. She steps forward, peers closely, her expression confused. Surely she's never seen one of her doctors cry. "It's OK," I say. "I know what I'm doing." And for a reason I cannot quite articulate at the moment, I make no effort to hide the wetness. I look straight at her. . . . "Take the keys, Linda," I say, "and open the door."
>
> She reaches out a bony hand, takes the keys from me, and swings open the door. The interview room is shining with sun, one wall all windows. I've been in this room too, . . . meeting with psychiatrists who tried to treat me. I shiver with the memory. Ultimately it was not their treatments or their theories that helped me get better, but the kindness lodged in a difficult world. . . .
>
> My patient and I sit down, look at each other. I see myself in her. I trust she sees herself in me.
>
> This is where we begin.[97]

---

97. Lauren Slater, *Welcome to My Country: A Therapist's Memoir of Madness* (New York: Random House, 1996), 197–98, 199.

Arguably more than any other single quality, our memoirists say, being treated with respect makes the difference between helpful and harmful care. Respect can be shown in many ways, but some of the basics are surely in the way Lauren Slater synthesizes within herself the standards of care from both "sides"—the sufferer's and the professional's. From start to finish, there is respect in the form of affinity—recognition of sameness as much as of difference. There is respect in the form of empowerment—Slater treats Linda like an adult, and encouraging Linda to unlock the door is symbolic of the work ahead for them both. Together they need to find the locked doors, but Linda will also have to believe she can act for herself. Respect is conveyed in the form of mutual vulnerability—Linda does not need to know the cause of Slater's tears to find them an undeniable sign of the humanness of this person to whom she is being asked to entrust her deepest self. The caregiver's tears can be inappropriate if they try to manipulate attention from the sufferer to the caregiver, but here it seems they are undemanding tears that convey not weakness or need but Slater's humanity and capacity to be moved. These are keys we all need to carry, and they open many, many doors: affinity, respect, and mutual vulnerability.

LIFE REALLY *IS* A MYSTERY

Psychic anguish is, as William Styron puts it, "mysterious in its coming, mysterious in its going."[98] "To me," Stewart Govig says, "mental illness carries an ultimate: it hints at the yawning, formless void present at the beginning before God's wind swept over and brought light to general disorder."[99] These survivors attest repeatedly to the limits of our knowledge: we do not know much at all about what causes this suffering, why it afflicts this person and not that one, why now and not then. Caring is helpful, then, when it joins sufferers in the mysteries. Parker Palmer describes one such joining.

> I once met a woman who had wrestled with depression for much of her adult life. Toward the end of a long and searching conversation, during which we talked about our shared Christian beliefs, she asked, in a voice full of misery, "Why do some people kill themselves yet others get well?"

98. Styron, *Darkness Visible*, 73.
99. Govig, *Souls Are Made of Endurance,* 83.

I knew that her question came from her own struggle to stay alive, so I wanted to answer with care. But I could come up with only one response.

"I have no idea. I really have no idea."

After she left, I was haunted by regret. Couldn't I have found something more hopeful to say, even if it were not true?

A few days later, she sent me a letter saying that of all the things we talked about, the words that stayed with her were "I have no idea." My response had given her an alternative to the cruel "Christian explanations" common in the church to which she belonged—that people who take their lives lack faith or good works or some other redeeming virtue that might move God to rescue them. My not knowing had freed her to stop judging herself for being depressed and to stop believing that God was judging her. As a result, her depression had lifted a bit.[100]

There are many ways to, as Parker Palmer put it earlier, "stand respectfully at the edge of [a] person's mystery and misery." Experienced soul-sufferers know—and the neophytes intuit—that their suffering really *is* a mystery, and what most soul-sufferers want is accompaniment in the not-knowing. When in their agony sufferers ask us "why?" the "why" is as much or more a cry as a question. So, it takes guts, but it is often the better thing to keep silence, or to utter three simple words—"I don't know." The silence and the not-knowing make us feel, as Palmer warned, useless and powerless. But we must take courage, even when the sufferer responds differently than the woman in Palmer's story, and remember that our not-knowing is more caring than simplistic answers. To admit to the mystery that pervades inner anguish is another way to stay present, to offer being as much as doing, to show respect, to support the sufferer in his or her not-knowing. Annie is another of Martha Manning's clients. On the day Annie finds out that her breast cancer has spread, she asks Manning what she believes about God answering prayers, about what happens when we die.

I, who pride myself on being able to use language to bullshit my way out of any number of awkward situations, can't find a word

100. Palmer, *Let Your Life Speak*, 59.

to say. . . . I owe this woman so much more than bullshit. I figure that all I can give her is honesty, so I admit that I really don't
know. I want to know. At times I've thought I've known. But
right now, I just don't know. She seems satisfied with this woe-
ful response. She tells me that she, herself, isn't totally sure, but
that she is trying hard to believe in a God who still hears her,
even if that God will not heal her in the way she is asking.[101]

Manning's capacity to bear the mystery of life and suffering were tested
by her own illness in the months that followed. But eventually, much as
she went with Annie into the unknown of late-stage cancer, she went for
her own sake into the unknown of treatment for late-stage depression—
ECT.

INCREASING PAIN THRESHOLDS

Sitting down together with mutual respect and shared vulnerability to
mystery and misery is where we begin. After that, though, helpful care
will require an even higher pain threshold. It is so much easier to talk
about pain tolerance than to have it when wounds are raw, pain excruciating, and care suspect. Another story told by Martha Manning makes
more visceral the challenge of care in the face of excruciating pain. Six
months after Manning's hospitalization for depression, she is trying to
resume her counseling practice. A woman is referred to Martha by an
oncologist, who says the woman is depressed.

She fumes at me for giving such lousy directions and makes it
clear that seeing me is not her idea and that she has no intention
of returning. Sometimes, in situations like these, I have the good
sense to keep my mouth shut long enough for people to tell me
their real stories. In the silence, her anger gives way quickly to
tears. She tells me about her mastectomy and the recurrence of
her breast cancer. The cancer is eating her up from the inside
out, resulting in ulcerations all over her chest. She wrestles with
words that could possibly convey her suffering. As she tries to
talk to me, deep wrenching sobs drown out the words. Her cries
come from that place in us where hell resides. . . .

---

101. Manning, *Undercurrents*, 23.

"Sometimes," I admit to her, "hell has no words."

Her sobbing quiets, her breathing deepens. She looks straight at me and begins to unbutton her blouse. I want to stop her and say, "Oh, no. I'm not that kind of doctor." But I realize she knows that already. She unbuttons her blouse and holds it open. She is wearing nothing underneath. What she shows me has no words. Her skin is ravaged with scars and huge sores. . . . Never have I seen anything so horrible, so painful.

She holds her blouse open and looks me in the eye with a mixture of pain and defiance. . . . She defies me. To what? Flinch? Turn away? Feel pity? Say something totally inept? I don't know. All I know is that I need to stare her right back in the eye and stop fighting so hard to keep my own eyes from filling up.

She tells me that she can't even show her husband and daughter the ravages of her cancer. In acknowledging the torment of her isolation, I understand what I have to do with her for the rest of this hour. I have to sit with her, with her blouse open, and her awful wounds, both visceral and psychic. I have to sit with her in her pain.

The quiet between us is punctuated by brief exchanges about her life. But it is clear that she doesn't really want my words. She wants my presence.

When the hour is up, she buttons her blouse. She straightens herself up, thanks me, and shakes my hand. She tells me that she doesn't think she'll be back and adds, "I wish you were a priest." I tell her that sometimes I wish that too. She says good-bye and leaves the way she came, bitching about my directions.[102]

Many of the dimensions of caring we have considered are illustrated again in this story. Manning's capacity to keep silence, initially, apparently conveys care, because the woman risks sharing a deeper level of her anguish. Manning's few words are no small thing—they, too, apparently convey care, because the woman goes farther still. Opening her blouse reveals more of her physical and spiritual agony, in a way that refuses the limits of the professional role for which Manning was trained. In that

102. Manning, *Undercurrents*, 171–72.

mysterious territory, there is much about which Manning is honest to admit "I don't know." The one thing she knows, importantly, is the value of her humanity shown, again, in tear-filled, unaverted eyes.

But do not think that it takes professional training or even your own good psychospiritual health to provide meaningful pain tolerance. In part 5, we will explore the ways that hospitalization can provide profound help on the way to healing, in part because of the community sufferers can provide to one another during hospitalization. This next story foreshadows that discussion by illustrating the kind of caring pain tolerance that it is possible to provide even when we ourselves are compromised. This story is also precious because it illustrates that sometimes we don't need the training of a therapist or the inborn gift of caregiving to do the right, caring thing. Sometimes what is needed is that we receive a painful story with simple listening and dignify it with our quietness. Among the other patients with whom the journalist Tracy Thompson found herself hospitalized was Hugo: in his fifties, alcoholic, thick bandages on his wrists, dressed in two hospital gowns wrapped around his considerable girth. One morning, two weeks into Thompson's hospitalization, Hugo refers in group to "the monkey on my back all these years," feeling responsible for his younger brother's death. Later that day, Hugo sat down beside Thompson and told her what had happened, how he had desperately wanted the affection of his stepfather, but the stepfather was cold to Hugo and doted on his natural son, Hugo's younger stepbrother. One day—this was when Hugo was five or six—he and his brother were playing in the front yard.

> A truck was coming down the street. Hugo remembered his little brother chasing him; he remembered making a conscious decision to dart across the street just in front of the truck.
>
> "I knew I would make it, and I knew he wouldn't." . . .
>
> I don't remember what I said. I think it was something like, "I'm sorry," or, "It's okay." What could anyone say to that?
>
> "I've never told the whole story to anybody before," he said. Then he got up and wandered away.
>
> *So why did you tell it to me?* I thought. But slowly, over the next day or so, I began to realize that he had given me a gift. Trapped behind my own glass wall, loathing my own isolation

and contemptuous of others in the same trap, I only wanted escape. I wasn't really interested in anyone else's pain, except to criticize it, . . . or observe it like some weird phenomenon. But hearing Hugo's story, I had for a moment entered somebody else's isolation. And in that moment, as simplistic as it sounded, he had offered me a fragment of that thing I craved: connection . . . out of dozens of people trapped with me inside that glass cage, one had stopped, turned to me, and said, "I am caught too. A connection with me may seem worthless to you, but it's the real thing. It's yours if you want it."[103]

More than our previous stories, these show the pain tolerance we must have in order to keep standing respectfully at the edge of soul-sufferers' misery. They speak of tolerating what happens when a sufferer is pressed to and beyond her or his pain threshold. Manning's story illustrates a common situation: when we try to care for someone in pain, that person may rebuff or scorn us; the pain tolerance caregivers must have is not only for the pain of others but for the pain we experience when our caregiving is rejected or the sufferer inflicts pain on us in some other way. Both stories suggest the pain we must tolerate when the sufferer needs a kind of care we cannot give. Both vividly illustrate how pain tolerance is at the heart of compassionate human interaction. They vividly illustrate that compassion requires suffering-with, *literally*, and that if we do stay alongside those who suffer, we sometimes will approach the hell of which those in psychic turmoil speak. More comfortingly, however, the stories also vividly illustrate that suffering-with creates profound human connection and, sometimes, for the caregiver, too, holy sanctuary—the most reliable of all asylums.

WHAT CAN WE SAY?

An implicit message in many of these stories is that having something to say is often overrated in situations of soul-suffering. Nonetheless, those of us wanting to offer care sometimes stay at a distance from soul-sufferers because we don't know what to say or worry about saying the wrong thing, so the question of what to say is an issue important to address in a discussion of care that helps. When the caregiver's words do play a posi-

---

103. Thompson, *The Beast*, 200, 201–2.

tive role in the stories we have been considering, it is important to note that they are few in number, and simple: "You take the key," and "I have no idea," and "Sometimes hell has no words." A few, simple words go a long way when the soul is in anguish. Also, the few words spoken by caregivers in these stories support the helpfulness of the care because the words are evoked primarily by the situation of the care seekers, not very much driven by the need of the caregivers. The few simple words are helpful also because there is no hint that they come out a sense of superiority on the part of the caregivers. Rather, the few simple words suggest that the caregivers are feeling a sense of common humanity with the care seekers, and are willing to join the care seekers in humility.

Admittedly, our memoirists do tell some stories that suggest that it is sometimes important to say *something*. As if to imply that saying the "right" thing is most likely to happen when we meet on the ground of our common humanity, some of the caring conversations that memoirists recount occur between themselves and relative strangers. Even fleeting encounters can convey care in a few simple words. Newly discharged from the hospital and getting back to work, Tracy Thompson was a little worried about how people would respond to her absence; she prepared herself to tell the truth. But mostly, there was silence. "There were only a few polite inquiries at the *Post* about where I'd been. The relative dearth of curiosity was a sign that everybody who was interested already knew; after all, newspaper people gossip for a living." But back at the courthouse, covering a story, she was surprised and moved by an interaction with one of the judges.

> "Where have you been?" he asked me one day, stopping in the corridor of the courthouse. "We haven't seen you around here for a couple of weeks." He had turned around to face me; his body language suggested that this was no casual "Howya doin'?" kind of query.
>
> "I've been in the hospital," I said, inwardly cringing, taken unaware and anticipating another excruciating social encounter. "I had a bad episode of depression."
>
> "I'm sorry to hear that." His next question surprised me. "Are you taking anything for it?"
>
> "Imiprimine and lithium," I said.

"You know, my sister is a manic-depressive, and she takes lithium," he said. "She says it's changed her life." We chatted about lithium for a moment; then he had to get back to his chambers. As he turned away, he said warmly, "Hope you start feeling better."

This was amazing. Here was someone—a public official, no less—who had freely talked about mental illness in his own family. He was matter-of-fact, he treated the subject seriously, and he hadn't pried. I felt, briefly, relieved.[104]

Again we see that caring can be conveyed by a few simple words, genuinely responsive to the situation of the other, spoken from a willingness to reveal our common human vulnerabilities. As in the encounter between Thompson and the judge, what we can say is given meaning and conveys care less because it is profound and more because we have made time, and centered ourselves on the other, and risked revealing ourselves in the process. The writer Anne Lamott tells a story that reveals similar caring dynamics, this time experienced with a religious professional. She is relating the story of her struggle with alcoholism, describing her habit of walking into town on the bike path to dispose of one bottle and buy another. This path took her every day past an Episcopal church, where her mother had taken her for midnight mass on Christmas Eve. She still sometimes attended services there. She had heard that there was a new pastor there.

> Then one afternoon in my dark bedroom, the cracks webbed all the way through me. I believed that I would die soon, from a fall or an overdose. I knew there was an afterlife but felt that the odds of my living long enough to get into heaven were almost nil. They couldn't possibly take you in the shape I was in. I could no longer imagine how God could love me.
>
> But in my dark bedroom . . . that afternoon, out of nowhere it crossed my mind to call the new guy at St. Stephen's.
>
> So I did. He was there, and I started to explain that I was losing my mind, but he interrupted to say with real anguish that he was sorry but he had to leave. He literally begged me to call back in the morning, but I couldn't form any words in reply. . . . There

---

104. Thompson, *The Beast*, 206-207.

was this profound silence. . . . Then he said, "Listen. Never mind. I'll wait. Come on in."

It took me forty-five minutes to walk there, but this skinny middle-aged guy was still in his office when I arrived. My first impression was that he was smart and profoundly tender-hearted. My next was that he was really listening, that he could hear what I was saying, and so I let it all tumble out—the X-rated motels, my father's death, a hint that maybe every so often I drank too much.

I don't remember much of his response, except that when I said I didn't think God could love me, he said, "God *has* to love you. That's God's job."[105]

We can only wish that Lamott would have said more about what gave her the impression that he was really listening. But what can we say? We only need to say, "Come in . . . I'll wait . . . God *has* to love you."

RENEWABLE RESOURCES

Helpful care is resilient and sustainable. Given the chronic nature of much soul-suffering, caregivers must pace themselves. Care does not need to be rationed; our capacity to care is a renewable resource. However, the renewal of our caring spirits does not happen on its own, and requires tough choices. David Hilfiker comments on how his marriage has survived, given his depression.

> One reason Marja and I have been able to maintain our marriage relationship over thirty years is that Marja has never taken on my emotional or spiritual health as her responsibility. At a certain point—after she has listened and tried to understand—she rolls over and goes to sleep. She gets on with her life. I need my community to come into my darkness with me, but I don't want them to get consumed by it.[106]

Despite David's praise, Marja may strike you as not very caring at all! But he is right. Of course, presence is about listening and trying to un-

---

105. Anne Lamott, *Traveling Mercies: Some Thoughts on Faith* (New York: Pantheon Books, 1999), 41–42.
106. Hilfiker, "When Mental Illness Blocks the Spirit," 14.

derstand. But one of the hardest lessons of caring through presence is that limits must be recognized and set. Presence is caring to the degree that it is resilient, and to be resilient, it must be sustainable, and to be sustainable, presence requires that the caregiver's psychospiritual and relational resources not be drained but be replenished. To stay present over the long haul, caregivers must reckon with their humanity and their own need for care. We will not be able to be present to others if our own needs are gnawing at us.

Like David and Marja, Dan and Sue Hanson try to be realistic about the limits of their responsibilities and resources. In fact, J's belief that he is God creates a ruefully humorous context that encourages Dan's limit-setting with himself: "I am not God. One God in the family is enough." As if he is indirectly modeling that we will probably need to keep reminding ourselves of the value of setting limits, Dan recites David Karp's "four Cs" twice in the course of his memoir. Karp offers these reminders to caregivers (though they are true as well for primary sufferers). Significantly, Dan Hanson adds a fifth:

> I didn't *cause* it.
> I can't *cure* it.
> I can't *control* it.
> All that I can do is learn to *cope* with it.
> I can *care* for myself and J.[107]

The fifth "C" is significant for our purposes because it leads Sue and Dan to share the boundary-setting they do as part of their efforts to renew their resources and stay resilient. Among other things, unless J has a real emergency, they set aside four hours every day during which they have agreed not to discuss J's situation, and they take regular weekend getaways to replenish themselves and their relationship. When Lizzie Simon is asked what advice she has for families, she emphasizes three things: "Be aggressive" in educating yourself about the particular kind of condition your loved one is dealing with, and encourage your loved ones to "be aggressive" about caring for themselves; encourage your loved ones "to be all the other wonderful things [they are] outside

---

107. Hanson, Room for J, 114, 115. Citing David A. Karp, *Burden of Sympathy: How Families Cope with Mental Illness* (New York: Oxford University Press, 2001).

of" their suffering, and, "Get counseling or therapy for everyone in the whole family, not just the 'sick' kid. No one ever wants to take this advice, but it's incredibly important."[108] This third strategy is "incredibly important" because it attends to the resilience of caregivers. But also, if caregivers admit their limits and seek professional help, the stigma attached to both the "sick" one and to seeking help is reduced.

⚛

In discussions of helpful caregiving, the importance of listening is often emphasized. But it is hard to describe, theoretically, what listening is or how to do it. Stories help, and though we haven't been discussing listening explicitly, these stories show listening in action. Listening is being together, sometimes just breathing, in silence and shared solitude. Listening is attentiveness to the small things that matter. Listening has several purposes, but the ultimate one, arguably, is to convey respect and help empower sufferers to take the keys that open locked doors. Listening is not for the purpose of answering, but for the purpose of providing companionship in common human questions. Listening requires a high pain tolerance, not least when our listening is unappreciated, or seems so. Listening, when done well, is hearing *and comprehending,* which prepares one to say a few words when necessary, a few, simple, humble words that say something needed. Listening is a gift we give to ourselves as well as others, the source of the wisdom that prompts us to renew our resources and, in turn, our capacity to give care to others that does not harm but helps.

In this portion of our study, we have been confronted with the sad irony that the care that harms is sometimes caused by malpractice but at other times is caused by best efforts. Memoirs of soul-suffering literally beg those of us who would be caring to listen not only to the criticism but just as much to their stories of care that helps. While such stories do not minimize the harmful care we have considered, these stories do give us al-

---

108. Simon, "A Conversation with Lizzie Simon," in *Detour*, 214.

ternatives and reasons to be hopeful that some forms of our caring can and will alleviate soul-suffering. In the next part of our study, we turn to another source of hope: the wisdom in soul-suffering is not just about what makes relationships authentically caring but also about the enormous resources persons find in themselves for the journey of healing.

PART FIVE

The world breaks everyone

and afterward many are strong

at the broken places.

—Ernest Hemingway
A Farewell to Arms

MEMOIRS OF SOUL-SUFFERING offer many moving and inspiring stories of healing. There is no cure for anguish of soul, and some sufferers find no relief. But other sufferers do find solace and renewal. In this portion of our study, we will reflect on stories told by primary sufferers and loved ones about the healing they experience. Where a person's suffering has the potential to be healed, what attitudes and actions awaken and sustain that potential? What are the values, dynamics, and choices that consistently coincide with healing? We will not find here the simplistic and saccharine attitudes that pervade so much discourse about healing. No amount of will, merit, love, or faith guarantees recovery from psychic turmoil. Some are lost even with the best of care, strenuous effort, and a lifetime of belief. Neither is science the answer. Medications and other treatments help, but not everyone and not consistently. Whatever we come to understand about healing, we will not finally unravel the mystery of which Parker Palmer speaks.

> I do not understand why [some] are able to find new life in the midst of a living death, though I am one of them. I can tell you what I did to survive and, eventually, to thrive—but I cannot tell you why I was able to do those things before it was too late.[1]

Coexisting with the mystery are stories like Palmer's, in which some memoirists describe the moments and processes that enabled them "to survive and, eventually, to thrive." We will learn that healing in the context of soul-suffering depends upon a constructive dynamism between caring contexts and relationships, the idiosyncratic aspects of a given person's suffering, the particular choices suffering people make in their existential aloneness, and some measure of luck. Since anguish is part of the human condition, and psychiatric illnesses are incurable, we will learn that healing is not "natural," it is chance, and always a challenge. Survivors have to "learn the landscape of health," as Lauren Slater puts it.[2] A remarkable number do.

---

1. Parker J. Palmer, *Let Your Life Speak: Listening for the Voice of Vocation* (San Francisco: Jossey-Bass, 2000), 58.
2. Lauren Slater, *Prozac Diary* (New York: Random House, 1998), 36.

Despite personal and social sicknesses, survivors find what the law student R.B. went looking for—"another reason to stay here." They find ways of living not in denial of the suffering but not dominated by it, either. They find a way of living that keeps excavating the divinest sense not only in madness but in all of life. Again, that these experiences enable healing for some is no indictment of those who continue to suffer—soul-sickness is mysterious and powerful enough to defeat the full arsenal of these approaches. But I am saying that if more people were supported to have the kind of experiences we are about to consider, healing would increase.

Because healing in the context of soul-suffering cannot rely upon cure, the initial moves toward healing typically rest primarily on the attitudes and actions of the sufferers, not professionals. Thus, we begin with changes that most survivors undertake on the way toward healing—turning points, acceptance of the need for healing, and the initiation of the personal healing work that makes long-term recovery possible and sustainable. We'll then turn to the contributions that mental health treatment, religion, and spirituality can make to the mystery of healing.

TURNING POINTS

Driving down my street, I pass a woman and her daughter stuffing scarecrows in their front yard. It is a cool bright yellow-orange kind of day and they are totally immersed in their creations. Their laughter is pure music and they are golden in their joy. I am seized with the most piercing sadness—that I have lost that capacity, for playing, for creating, for relishing beauty. I pull up in front of my own house and turn off the ignition. I lay my head against the steering wheel and my body shakes with wrenching sobs that have been contained for too long. I know now what I have to do. It is time. It is past time.[3]

The day after this incident, Martha Manning admitted herself to a psychiatric hospital.

Healing almost always comes in fits and starts. But it does frequently happen that in retrospect one can see that there was a point or phase where an overall shift in trajectory toward healing can be discerned. It is essential to note: these turning points are usually moments terrible to experience and witness and, understandably, loved ones or the sufferers themselves try to avert such pain. But in so doing they may also prevent the reckoning moment that can fire a change of course toward healing. As in recovery from addiction, many soul-sufferers must "hit bottom" before the enormous self-regulation needed for recovery can be

---

3. Martha Manning, *Undercurrents: A Therapist's Reckoning with Her Own Depression* (San Francisco: HarperSanFrancisco, 1994), 111–12.

marshaled. With heartrending frequency, nothing short of a life-and-death crisis forces the choice for life rather than death and rallies determination enough for the arduous journey that sustains the choice. The bottom has its power to transform because it is a crisis involving some core value—like life or love—and is, therefore, a spiritual crisis. Sufferers sense that without radical redirection, they will die, spiritually or physically.

Sometimes the death threatened is a spiritual death. Daniel Friend worked for the CIA when he found himself hospitalized and diagnosed with bipolar disorder. "What is the bottom? For me," Friend writes, "it was the loss of everything that I valued in life, beginning with my carefully crafted self-image." Friend also lost his career, his wife and children, most of his friends, and important financial resources.

> I was at the intersection where the conflict in values between what I was and what I was trying to be finally collided. There was only one road leading out of this intersection. Who would leave the scene of this terrible collision: the spiritual me that I was, or the me that I was trying to be, the one who was trying desperately to fit in?[4]

Sometimes the death threatened is physical death, and suicide attempted or accomplished by someone near becomes a "death scare," comparable to "suffering a heart attack or undergoing a cancer operation."[5] Journalist Tracy Thompson describes such an experience when, in a suicidal crisis herself, she learned that an accomplished reporter she admired had shot herself to death. *"This*, I thought, *is what waits for you if you aren't careful.* I felt like a soldier in a trench who had just seen the person next to him get blown to bits." The jolt caused Thompson, shortly after, to turn to her "remote last resort": she called the therapist she had left and asked for the medication she had previously refused.[6]

While a rudimentary amount of self-love can cause the turn, for some sufferers it is the power of love for others—especially their chil-

---

4. Daniel C. Friend, "Finding Your True Self: You Must First Hit Bottom," *The Journal of the California Alliance for Mentally Ill* vol. 8, no. 4 (December 18, 1997): 51, 52.

5. Edward Hoagland, *Tigers and Ice: Reflections on Nature and Life* (New York: Lyons Press, 1999), 29.

6. Tracy Thompson, *The Beast: A Journey through Depression* (New York: Penguin; Plume, 1995), 79–87. The quotations are from pages 82 and 87.

dren. "In the last days," Martha Manning says, "I kept going only for my daughter." Every morning, Manning leaned against the bathroom door listening to Keara sing in the shower, "let[ting] her voice invite me to try for one more day." But then,

> [o]ne morning, finally convinced that suicide was an act of love, not hate, I leaned for what I thought would be the last time against the door. I tried to memorize that voice, with all of its exuberance and hope. And then I realized that ending my life would silence that voice, perhaps forever. And I knew what I had to do. I would finally agree to electroconvulsive therapy (ECT), which had been recommended to me for several weeks. I had always said I'd step in front of a moving train for the sake of my child. Now it was time to prove it.[7]

The renewed realization of love for self and others that turns some toward healing exemplifies that some turning points are not strictly trauma but a remarkable combination of despair *and* hope, pain *and* benevolence. Rose and William Styron agree that he was pulled back from the brink by a melding of art and love: he was roused out of a suicidal reverie by a soaring passage from Brahm's *Alto Rhapsody,* probably because, before his mother died when he was thirteen, he heard her sing it.[8] Likewise, Parker Palmer's reaction to an experience of sacred grace convinced him of the seriousness of his condition.

> I heard a voice say, simply and clearly, "I love you, Parker." . . .
>
> It was a moment of inexplicable grace—but so deep is the devastation of depression that I dismissed it. And yet that moment made its mark: I realized that my rejection of such a remarkable gift was a measure of how badly I needed help.[9]

Not all turning points are dramatic. Some of our memoirists choose a new path because they refuse to let go of what Meri Danquah calls her "chipped and fractured" dreams. She remembers a particular day when, as she puts it, "I gave myself my word."

---

7. Martha Manning, "The Legacy," *Family Therapy Networker* (January–February 1997): 40.
8. Rose Styron, "Strands," in *Unholy Ghost,* 133.
9. Palmer, *Let Your Life Speak,* 65.

There was no master plan, no bolt of lightning from the sky, no cryptic calling. I was sick and tired of waiting for miracles, waiting for approval, waiting for happiness. For years I had been waiting, asking over and over and over and over, "Why me?" and I never found the answer so I figured what the hell, and decided to try asking, "Why not me?"[10]

Dramatic or not, nowhere in memoirs of soul-suffering do turning points serve as master plans, bolts of lightning, cryptic callings, miracles, or unmitigated happiness. They are fleeting sources of energy, opportunity, and limited insight. The sufferers who can in retrospect see a juncture in their path are those for whom the momentum of those experiences translates into a period of doing whatever it takes to save their lives. Healing's impetus can sometimes be traced to particular turning points, but healing itself is not a moment but a process—a slow, meandering process, as Rae Unzicker describes.

When I speak across the country, people always ask, directly or indirectly, "what was the one thing that changed your life?" For me, and I believe for most people, it is rarely one thing. It's a process, like life is a process. It was a thousand events, people, challenges, and mysteries.[11]

The first step in the process is acceptance of the need for it. This could be considered part of the overall "healing work" required if survivors are to thrive. We consider it separately, however, because without acceptance of the need for it, healing work is thwarted or never begins.

---

10. Meri Nana-Ama Danquah, *Willow Weep for Me: A Black Woman's Journey through Depression—A Memoir* (New York: W.W. Norton, 1998), 230.

11. Rae Unzicker, "On My Own: A Personal Journey through Madness and Re-Emergence." *Psychosocial Rehabilitation Journal* vol. 13, no. 1 (July 1989): 75.

ACCEPTANCE AND SMALL STEPS

For most survivors, the first step in the process of healing is acceptance of the reality of one's suffering and one's need and desire for healing, whatever it takes. It is difficult to use the word "acceptance" here, but it is the word many memoirists use. The meaning of acceptance in their stories of healing bears no hint of welcoming suffering, or of passive reception—quite the opposite. Healing requires acceptance as the opposite of denial. It is acceptance as in recognition, as in acceptance of a challenge. The lack of acceptance means no improvement and, for some, enormous loss or death. What happened to the England family after Steve's diagnosis of schizophrenia is fairly common. His mother, Rev. Margaret England, writes that

> While we were stunned by the diagnosis, our son refused to accept it. The stigma of schizophrenia is too great a burden. He chose to leave home rather than accept the diagnosis and undertake treatment. He returned to San Diego where he had grown up and would slowly lose everything, jobs, friends, places to stay and even his car, so that he finally became homeless.[12]

As for many other families, the alternative to acceptance is that Steve and his family were constantly under the threat of crisis, loss, and death. In fact, for not a few primary sufferers who are reluctant to accept that they have a condition in need of treatment, it is seeing the cost of their refusal

---

12. Margaret England, "A Family's Spiritual Journey," *The Journal of the California Alliance for the Mentally Ill* vol. 8, no. 4 (December 18, 1997): 12.

to accept their illness that becomes a turning point for them; they move toward acceptance for the sake of their loved ones, if not themselves.

As Sharon O'Brien says, acceptance requires a shift toward the pragmatic.

> Accepting depression as part of your life—something that can be managed, but that, as in my case, still appeared particularly in stressful times—is a long journey, marked by shifts in identity along with ever-deepening stages of rebellion and acceptance. Like many people with depression, I kept drawing lines in the sand, me on one side, my illness and some form of medication on the other.
>
> By now I've stepped over enough lines that I don't need to draw them any more. . . . I've become pragmatic: whatever works.[13]

Sufferers realize that they can no longer afford wishful thinking about the nature of life or to stand on imagined ideal principles. They require principles for living that provide humanitarian and authentic support and are pragmatically focused on saving human lives.

The first, unglamorous step of acceptance is to try not to make one's suffering worse. Reflecting on the difference between her "healed" psychiatric illness and the "unhealed" illnesses of her patients, psychologist Lauren Slater suggests a modest but crucial difference.

> What sets me apart from these "sick" ones—is simply a learned ability to manage the blades of deep pain with a little bit of dexterity. Mental health doesn't mean making the pains go away. I don't believe that they ever go away. . . . Only the muscles to hold things in check are stronger. I have not healed so much as learned to sit still and wait while pain does its dancing work, trying not to panic or twist in ways that make the blades tear deeper, finally infecting the wounds.[14]

Karen Armstrong says her suicide attempt was her "watershed." It proved to be a turning point for her, she said, because she gave up fighting her illness. Instead of fighting her illness, she determined to turn her

---

13. Sharon O'Brien, *The Family Silver: A Memoir of Depression and Inheritance* (Chicago: University of Chicago Press, 2004), 266–67.
14. Lauren Slater, *Welcome to My Country: A Therapist's Memoir of Madness* (New York: Random House, 1996), 192.

attention from her deficits to her capacities, and this led in relatively short order to what she describes as "the first flicker of true recovery." Healing requires identifying that one has, as she puts it, some "potentially powerful tool, a weapon that would help me to fight my way out of this apparent impasse."[15] For her, it was her intelligence.

Another aspect of acceptance is acceptance of mystery. Many memoirists speak of striving to embrace the many unknowns that pervade not just soul-suffering but life in general. The humility of not-knowing that they appreciate in their caregivers becomes a crucial aspect of their self-care. Self-assurance and certainty have their places in well-being, but when healing and health are found and maintained, mystery has been allowed a place of honor as well. Parker Palmer is describing the realistic embrace of mystery from the perspective of depression, but his words apply to many other forms of psychic turmoil as well.

> Embracing the mystery . . . does not mean passivity or resignation. It means moving into a field of forces that seems alien but is in fact one's deepest self. It means waiting, watching, listening, suffering, and gathering whatever self-knowledge one can—and then making choices based on that knowledge, no matter how difficult.[16]

As Palmer notes, acceptance need not be fatalism or passive resignation. Healing is furthered by respectful acknowledgment of the power of illness, but also by deliberate cultivation of powers that compete with the power of illness. So it is that another task of healing acceptance is that the sufferer must embrace the power of humble determination, which allows one to start simply, as healing from soul-suffering usually requires. "Long journeys don't have to start with noble motives. They just have to start."[17] It also enables perseverance through periods of discouragement, when illness—one's own or others'—is not yielding to psychopharmacological, spiritual, or other therapeutic interventions. As Sharon O'Brien puts it,

> Journeys can be long, outcomes uncertain, recoveries incomplete. Beginning the effort is important, though, as is remembering

---

15. Karen Armstrong, *The Spiral Staircase* (New York: Alfred A. Knopf, 2004), 135, 139, 137.
16. Palmer, *Let Your Life Speak*, 60.
17. Thompson, *The Beast*, 184.

that we make our way through the world with wandering steps and slow.

Baby steps.[18]

Once an illness has been accepted, small steps can bring surprising comfort and encouragement for primary sufferers and their loved ones. For families like the Hansons and the Govigs, the acceptance of ongoing disability means that, as Stewart Govig puts it, after a decade of psychiatric *treatment*, "a different angle of the story, namely, psychiatric *rehabilitation*, beckons our family." "Eventually we lowered our expectations and managed to abandon a few of the cultural dictates of success. It was then that we caught our first glimpse of the banks of Jordan." "Jordan" came, for the Govigs, in the guise of the Pacific Community Mental Health Center's Rose Club, where Jay was a *member*, not a *patient*, and where the emphasis was on employment and community-building.[19] Especially when illness leads to nonrational thinking, families are challenged to accept the alternative worldview of the primary sufferer. Dan and Sue Hanson have learned that trying to see the world from J's point of view—that he is God—is often more healing than is fighting it. As long as he is not hurting himself or others, relinquishing him to his way of being in the world enables them to sustain a deeper relationship with him and to give him a sense of belonging that eases his suffering. Dan speaks of the connection that can come amid acceptance:

> I frequently go on long walks with J and we talk about all the "regular" kinds of things fathers and sons talk about. How can he find meaningful work? How can he find someone to love and be loved by? Why are we here? J finds it easy to talk about being God and he readily shares his vision of creating a better world. I used to tune out at those times. J's bizarre dreams of being God and the Universe were more than I could handle. But that was before I learned to see beyond J's words and to begin to listen with my heart instead of my head. Then I began to hear J telling me that he wants my respect, that he wants to be seen as signifi-

18. O'Brien, *The Family Silver*, 272.

19. Stewart D. Govig, *Souls Are Made of Endurance: Surviving Mental Illness in the Family* (Louisville: Westminster/John Knox Press, 1994), 87, 50, 56.

cant and someone who counts in this world. That is when I hear him telling me he is tired of being treated as if he were a child.[20]

A subtle thread runs through these accounts—acceptance and compassion are inseparable. Acceptance breeds compassion, compassion facilitates acceptance. After her travels around the country interviewing other young people with bipolar disorder, Lizzie Simon was asked what insight she gained. "I learned that compassion for yourself is incredibly important and powerful, and that most of us lack it."[21] The capacity to offer compassion to yourself and to others, the capacity to remain empathic when the work of suffering and healing sets us back—these are hallmarks of acceptance.

---

20. Hanson, *Room for J*, 105.
21. Lizzie Simon, "A Conversation with Lizzie Simon," in *Detour: My Bipolar Road Trip in 4-D* (New York: Washington Square Press, 2002), 213.

HEALING WORK

Describing her life after her son's suicide, Lois Bloom emphasizes that grief is work. Grief work "has to do with the effort of reliving and working through in small quantities events which involved the now-deceased person and the survivor. . . . Each item of this shared role has to be thought through, *pained* through."[22] In a similar way, healing is work. It requires "reliving and working through in small quantities" all the ways that suffering robs soul and life. "One begins the slow walk back to health by choosing each day things that enliven one's selfhood and resisting things that do not."[23]

With compassion toward oneself as a foundation, many memoirists provide in their writing a no-nonsense discussion about the need to take responsibility for one's healing. This is not simply soothing self-care, but what Tracy Thompson calls "tough self-love." Thompson bought herself a novelty button ("probably intended for parents of small children," she notes) imprinted with the words "No Whining Allowed." It "became my new liturgy," she writes. "I repeated it a lot; I had to."[24] As parents of small children know, whining often substitutes for making harder choices; throughout the memoirs there is the refrain that healing requires tough choices. Thompson's words provide one example of the many survivors who trace their healing to a moment or ongoing process of choice. For Thompson, there is selfhood and dignity at stake. "If I

---

22. Lois A. Bloom, *Mourning, After a Suicide* (Cleveland: Pilgrim Press, 1986), 6. Citing Erich Lindemann, *Beyond Grief: Studies in Crisis Intervention* (New York: Aronson, 1979).

23. Palmer, *Let Your Life Speak*, 60.

24. Thompson, *The Beast*, 274, 225–26.

wanted to say simply that my brain was sick, I could stop there and dis-
avow responsibility . . . but if I did that, . . . I would be simply a product
of some chemical abnormality in a lumpy gray organ between my ears."

> At one crucial point, I chose life. It was an arduous choice, and I
> tried my best to avoid it. When I could avoid it no longer, it came
> down to the realization that I owned a moral responsibility for
> my life. The question then became: how do I live now? And
> then, having faced that question, I realized something else: every
> day, the question is asked again.[25]

That such a question—how do I live now?—should be so persistently
necessary is, in part, because expert help has been directed more at treating symptoms than at living well amid chronic psychic turmoil. This
means that most sufferers have had to find their own way toward healing, at least initially. But in the memoirs are common themes in the work
a person must do if healing momentum is to be sustained.

CONNECTING WITH FAMILIES OF BIRTH AND CHOICE

After a survivor has accepted the need for healing, part of recovery is
tending to relationships. On the one hand, this means being willing to ask
for and respect the help offered by one's family and friends; real turning
points and genuine acceptance make a dent in the resistance of primary
sufferers to asking for help. This is more work for primary sufferers than
their friends and family normally comprehend or easily accept. Survivors
have to overcome the shame and stigma of asking for help. Many also
have to contend with the fact that they have been taught by religious
upbringing or other cultural sources that it is better *not* to ask for help,
better not to *need* help, better to *give* than to receive: as Rev. Welton
Gaddy had to learn for his recovery, such religious teaching is dangerously one-sided. Sometimes "it is better to receive than to give."[26]

But primary-sufferers have to learn not only to ask for and accept
help but to give it as well. Very few soul-sufferers find healing without
at least one loving relationship in which they give as well as receive loving regard. Most survivors are doing this with their families of birth, but

---

25. Thompson, *The Beast*, 190, 285–86.
26. C. Welton Gaddy, *A Soul Under Siege: Surviving Clergy Depression* (Louisville: Westminster John Knox Press, 1991), 127–39.

sometimes it is with families of choice that survivors in recovery do their part to tend relationship: whether it is to other patients in the hospital, other members of a support group, or within a congregation or monastic community, giving back, even modestly, sparks healing. Whether with families of birth or of choice, sufferers who are healing are sufferers who work at helping to create and sustain the steady, loving connections that make survival possible. The end of her memoir has Lizzie Simon driving back to her family, her "original herd," preparing to rebuild the bridges she had burnt with them.[27] Working at these connections heals "inside." That is, the giving and receiving of love builds up the internal resources that fuel the work of making healthful choices amid the ups and downs of psychic turmoil. When we give and receive resilient love, inside of us "a factory has been built to manufacture creative survival techniques," as Simon puts it.[28] Another product manufactured when survivors tend their relationships is the dignity that comes back to us when we are givers as well as recipients of love and service.

Also, loving connections help us heal "outside." That is, as countless memoirs attest, suffering people who stay related to loving and tenacious advocates are more assured of receiving good care from professionals and social systems.

BUILDING HABITS OF HOLISTIC HEALTH

Lizzie Simon is on her road trip, pushing herself hard. She wakes up in the middle of the night, panicked: "something is resisting my progress."

> It's my faulty body that's not handling this stress or this lack of sleeping or this lack of eating right.
>
> During these moments, I want to spend the rest of my life safe, in a big sweater on a big bed with a big dog, waiting for a big man to return from work to give me a big hug. Because I am terrified at how disabled I can become, and how quickly.[29]

Chronic psychic turmoil is a formidable opponent that, when given the toeholds of stress and neglect, can quickly overwhelm well-being and discourage the intention to heal. So the work of healing requires build-

---

27. Simon, *Detour*, 205.
28. Simon, "A Conversation with Lizzie Simon," in *Detour*, 213.
29. Simon, *Detour*, 158–59.

ing habits of holistic and wholesome living. One emphasis here is on habit: identifying and establishing routines to rebuild one's strength. Meri Danquah notes that she had previously been guided by her passions and was not one to "abide by schedules or plans," so learning to be consistent with her strategies was essential for her healing.[30] Tracy Thompson, too, argues that learning constancy in one's self-care is essential for change, not only comfort. For healing, "the single most valuable tool," Tracy Thompson says, "was the one that sounds the most mindless: rote repetition."[31] David Karp says "rituals, even unhappy ones"—he mentions keeping regular appointments with his psychiatrist for medication oversight—"provide a measure of comfort."[32] We normally think of ritual as a religious matter, but memoirists who find healing typically have brought to even the most everyday aspects of their lives the intentionality and long-term commitment we associate with spiritual devotion. At one point, Thompson scrawled on a sheet of green steno paper "The Rules"—six goals for recovery. "On a daily basis, my job was to do *one thing* that would advance one of those six goals. I didn't have to succeed; all I had to do was seriously try." She ends her memoir by noting that every now and then she encounters this much-folded paper in the bottom of her purse. "Every time, I look at it, thinking I should toss it. And then, after a minute, I fold it up and put it back."[33]

A second emphasis is on wholeness in these habits. ECT resolved the crisis of his clinical depression, but after his crisis abated, William Hulme dedicated himself to self-care on many fronts—spiritual, social, physical, and mental. "A healthy lifestyle is an effective antidepressant," he says.[34] For many survivors, this sort of dedication to overall well-being requires a radical reorientation of one's life.

> I have altered my lifestyle drastically to allow for therapy twice a week, a lot of rest, careful eating habits, and avoidance of crowded or loud places. My work ambitions are considerably different (once I would have said "lowered," but I no longer

---

30. Danquah, *Willow Weep for Me*, 255.

31. Thompson, *The Beast*, 233.

32. David Karp, "An Unwelcome Career," in *Unholy Ghost*, 147.

33. Thompson, *The Beast*, 231, 286.

34. William Hulme and Lucy Hulme, *Wrestling with Depression: A Spiritual Guide to Reclaiming Life* (Minneapolis: Augsburg Books, 1995), 77.

think of it that way). I have slowed myself down considerably, and changed my values so that relationships have become very important. I am also a more actively compassionate person. I attend 12-step meetings regularly for support and guidance, and I have learned how to avoid worsening my symptoms.[35]

Meaningful work is part of wholeness. Memoirists say repeatedly that persons recovering from psychic anguish, "just as much as any of us," as Dan Weisburd puts it, "need success and satisfaction that comes only from meeting real and meaningful challenges."[36] Some survivors can testify to the power of meaningful work because in the early stages of their recovery, someone trusted them. Nancy Mairs' tribute to her boss at the Smithsonian Astrophysical Observatory, who held her job for her during the time she was ill, is unequivocal: "This calm man . . . rescued my shambled life."[37] Martha Manning is moved to tears when, even as she is struggling with depression, her therapist affirms her abilities by referring a client to her.[38] Michael Norlen was not able to return to his previous work as a lawyer, but implies that he has found values more relevant to his healing in far humbler work: amid his depression, he found that the physical work and the people he came to know while delivering newspapers at night helped his recovery.[39]

EDUCATION

Soul-sufferers say that an essential aspect of healing is educating oneself about one's illness. Being self-motivated in seeking out education about one's suffering is crucial not only to compensate for any mental health care providers who share insufficient information with their clients. It is also a crucial part of one's overall well-being—being an active learner, informed and thus empowered in one's own healing processes. It takes effort on the part of sufferers *and* professionals to stay abreast of mushrooming insights about the brain, the neurology of emotion, costs and benefits of treatments, spiritual practices and religious insights that help. But, as Tracy Thompson's comments show, being educated about one's

---

35. "Anonymous," "Birds of a Psychic Feather," *Schizophrenia Bulletin* vol. 16, no. 1 (1990): 167.

36. Dan E. Weisburd, "Planning a Community-Based Mental Health System: Perspective of a Family Member," *American Psychologist* vol. 45 (November 1990): 1245.

37. Nancy Mairs, *Plaintext: Essays by Nancy Mairs* (Tucson: University of Arizona Press, 1986), 148.

38. Martha Manning, *Undercurrents: A Therapist's Reckoning with Her Own Depression* (San Francisco: HarperSanFrancisco, 1994), 73–74 and 146–47.

39. Michael Norlen, "Healing Myself with the Power of Work," *Newsweek* (25 Oct. 1999), 12.

condition yields profound benefit—it promotes dignity as well as wise response to one's suffering.

> Learning more about my illness gave me some sense of mastery and control. . . . It also helped me grasp a counterintuitive idea: that there were occasions when my emotions might actually be caused by something happening *inside* my head, not by anything outside. Always before, I had struggled to make sense of my black periods by finding a "reason" for them in people or events. . . .
>
> Now, . . . feeling the familiar sense of brooding hopelessness, I could try out an alternate explanation. *It's the sickness*, I would say silently to myself. *Just wait it out. It's the sickness.*[40]

More surprisingly, quite a few primary sufferers speak of having to *learn* how to be well. This is the case if they have been ill for a long time, and especially the case if they have been subject for a long while to the health care system's capacity to make coping with illness one's whole identity or at least a full-time job. While reflecting in part 4 on problems associated with hospitalization, we noted Lauren Slater's observation that it takes time and effort to learn not to be sick, to move from an illness-based identity to a health-based identity. Having been weighed down with psychic turmoil since she was a child, Slater writes in her *Prozac Diary* about the challenges of being suddenly much improved, relatively speaking, and knows this sounds strange.

> The Judeo-Christian tradition, of which I am firmly a part, views health as a gift from God and therefore decisively good. The Western medical profession, which grew directly out of our Judeo-Christian culture, takes things one step further, claiming health is not only good but natural. After all, when you are sick, there are plenty of places (insurance willing) where you can go to get healed, but when you are healed are there any places you can go to learn not to be sick? The very idea of having to learn the landscape of health sounds vaguely ridiculous, so ensconced are so many of us in the notion that health is as organic as grass, in the right conditions growing green and freely.[41]

---

40. Thompson, *The Beast*, 220.
41. Slater, *Prozac Diary*, 35–36.

But she is not alone. A few memoirists speak of having to learn how to curb the impulse to do too much too soon. Some, especially those who have experienced hospitalization, tell of having to learn how to be well and stay well in the face of stereotypes and the fact that illness is now, as Martha Manning put it, part of their permanent record.

MOURNING AS PART OF HEALING WORK

Yes, healing requires sustained positive attitudes and is undermined by preoccupation with the pain of soul-suffering. At the same time, if it is to be authentic, memoirists say that healing work includes grief work. Soul-suffering causes many losses, and healing will not be sustainable unless those losses are acknowledged and mourned. Ironically, once recovery begins, many sufferers become more aware of what was lost—those who heal mourn their lost time, lost opportunity, lost relationships. Many say that while there is appreciation for the improvement drugs bring, there is often also grief for what medications take away—an ability, perhaps, like creativity, or some aspect of temperament, like the zest of mania or the introspection of melancholia. Soul-sufferers trying to heal after the suicide of a loved one arguably most exemplify the necessity of mourning in the reconstruction of one's life. As Lois Bloom puts it, "The mourning period is a time of convalescence."[42] Obviously, if healing is to be found in their case, they must move from being overpowered by their bereavement to the ongoing work of active mourning, the "grief work" mentioned earlier. Wisely, suicide survivors are among the most vociferous opponents of the notion that "successful" mourning brings "closure"—Albert Hsu says, sharply, "We can close on a house, but we can't close on a person's life."[43] They are also among the most knowledgeable about how we can find new life among the blows our souls sustain.

Two powerfully healing modes of active mourning used by suicide survivors who find life after death are lament and remembrance. Lament has dignified and redeemed human grief throughout human history. It is not uncommon, for example, for soul-sufferers to turn to Psalms of lament as a vehicle for expressing the deepest agony of loss. In his mem-

---

42. Bloom, *Mourning, After a Suicide*, 9.
43. Albert Y. Hsu, *Grieving a Suicide: A Loved One's Search for Comfort, Answers, and Hope* (Downers Grove, Ill.: InterVarsity Press, 2002), 136.

oir, Stewart Govig refers to biblical texts often. Not surprisingly, this famous lament is among his quotation of the Psalms.

> Out of the depths I cry to you, O Lord,
>> Lord, hear my voice!
> Let your ears be attentive
>> To the voice of my supplications! (Psa. 130:1–2, NRSV)

Grieving for his father, Albert Hsu wished for something like a Christian version of the Jewish tradition of sitting shiva, where lament is shared—and ameliorated. Lament was powerful for Albert as he sought healing after his father's suicide, because it felt to him to be an expression of love, some balance to the anger that was also predominant in his expression of grief. "The agony we undergo is the score on which our love ballad is written."[44] Lament is a part of healing insofar as it serves as an outlet for the pain of loss that would otherwise undermine our capacity to do the work of rebuilding our lives.

Remembrance is another form of active mourning exemplified by suicide survivors. Sometimes healing requires that we remember past pain. A well-meaning friend suggested to Lauren Slater that she have cosmetic surgery to erase the scars from the cuts Slater inflicted on herself during her illness. Slater is upset by the idea—and surprised that she is upset. Observing herself, she muses about why it would upset her to erase the scars: "Every day she takes pills whose purpose is to hide her history. She needs some sign, some inscription. Even if no one can see it, the truth is there."[45] But, in the midst of suffering, often what is more important is to remember that which in the past brought joy, even fleetingly. Slater testifies to the healing power of remembered joys.

> Why—how—have I managed to learn these [healing] things
> while others have not? Why have I managed somehow to leave
> behind at least for now what looks like wreckage, and shape
> something solid from my life? . . . I believe my strength has
> something to do with memory. . . . For while I recall with clarity
> the terror of abuse, I also recall the green and lovely dream of
> childhood, the moist membrane of a leaf against my nose, the

---

44. Hsu, *Grieving a Suicide*, 42, 52.
45. Slater, *Prozac Diary*, 136.

toads that peed a golden pool in the palm of my hand. Pleasures, pleasures, the recollections of which have injected me with a firm and unshakable faith. I believe Dostoevski when he wrote, "If one has only one good memory left in one's heart, even that may be the means of saving us."[46]

Sometimes cultural tradition provides us such mechanisms: as he mourned his father, Albert Hsu realized anew the comfort provided through the Chinese custom of having at the funeral and afterward in the home a prominent portrait of the deceased. Whatever their specific forms, age-old practices of lament and remembrance provide structures that help make the expression of grief life-giving and not only a reckoning with death.

PREPARATION FOR RECURRENCE

The work of healing involves preparation for cycles of well-being and illness. Healing in contexts of soul-suffering is an archetypal embodiment of progress won by the proverbial two steps forward and one step back. Thus, healing requires confidence in one's capacity to be well, but soul-sufferers who find healing also build confidence in their capacity to hold on to the healing trajectory when anguish flares. In this context, healing means, in part, that one has prepared for the common, painful setbacks. To plan for reoccurrence may seem negative, but those plans become comforting in the crisis. Martha Manning had a recurrence not long after her discharge from the hospital, as her daughter had feared: "[Keara's] fears of depression invading our family again were confirmed so quickly that in some ironic way she got to really learn the drill and find comfort in the evidence that our plans worked."[47] An unblinking stance about recurrence also serves healing by functioning as an early-warning system. Rose Styron captures the goal in artful metaphors. "Perhaps the best thing one can do is to act on intuition. And keep intuition's third eye open forever, after recovery, to note the first trembling turning leaves of a change of season."[48] Early intervention is likely to make the recurrence less extreme and thus less damaging to overall healing.

---

46. Slater, *Welcome to My Country*, 192–93.
47. Manning, "The Legacy," 41.
48. Rose Styron, "Strands," in *Unholy Ghost*, 137.

RESPITE

Because healing is work, primary sufferers and loved ones who are recovering need occasional breaks from tending to the distress. Normally we think of respite as help given to sufferers by caregivers. But sufferers attest to the necessity of giving this gift to themselves and each other. Constant focus on psychic distress is not always helpful; as Anne Handler attests from her experience, "If you keep focusing on your ill relative, it adds to his or her problems."[49] Both the primary sufferer and loved ones need to be, occasionally, "off-duty," for the sake of perspective, rest, and renewal. This is easier said than done, admittedly, so assuring respite is, paradoxically, a kind of work—working to assure that one is not working all the time. Several approaches to this conservation consistently appear among our memoirists. We explored in part 4 some of Dan and Sue Hanson's ways of caring for themselves—time apart from J's illness each day as well as involvement in other relationships and activities. Undergirding the capacity to make those choices is another principle for getting respite: if it isn't an emergency, don't treat it like one, they say. They have learned that if healing is to be cultivated and sustained, they cannot respond to every episode of psychic distress with a crisis-type response.

Respite is sanctuary for the soul. Most sufferers have to find it in leaner circumstances, but Kay Redfield Jamison's description of her study at the University of St. Andrews in Scotland— "I took off a year from the turmoil that had become my life"—captures in bold relief what respite can accomplish. She writes lyrically of the gifts of study, North Sea winds, Sunday services in old cathedrals, the magic of Scottish tradition, and late nights of singing and talking with her Scottish roommates.

> St. Andrews provided a gentle forgetfulness over the preceding painful years of my life. It remains a haunting and lovely time to me, a marrow experience. For one who during her undergraduate years was trying to escape an inexplicable weariness and despair, St. Andrews was an amulet against all manner of longing and loss, a year of gravely held but joyous remembrances. Throughout and beyond a long North Sea winter, it was the Indian summer of my life.[50]

49. Anne C. Handler, "Living on the Edge: Experiences of Family Members," in *New Directions in the Psychological Treatment of Serious Mental Illness*, ed. Diane T. Marsh (Westport, Conn.: Praeger, 1994), 147.
50. Kay Redfield Jamison, *An Unquiet Mind* (New York: Random House, Vintage Books, 1995), 39, 52.

HEALING MENTAL HEALTH SERVICES

In part 4, we explored problems sufferers experience with the mental health system. But it is also the case that many survivors find mental health treatment an essential partner in healing, and sometimes it is lifesaving.

HOSPITALIZATION

It is true that even with modern improvements, a few tell tales of harrowing hospitalizations under horrible conditions. It is also true that our memoirists speak often of the need for sanctuary from social and personal sicknesses, and that when hospitals provide such an environment, they assist healing. This may be a surprising claim to the general public; most of us can feel only horror and humiliation at the thought of psychiatric hospitalization. But though loved ones and primary sufferers do not take hospitalization lightly, the memoirs describe some benefits. For example, the need for hospitalization can signal the crisis of hitting bottom and provide a relatively safe environment in which to give way to the crisis and let it do its work, as was the case for Daniel Friend, whose story we considered previously while reflecting on the role of hitting bottom in healing. Hospitalization can also provide true asylum, refuge from life-threatening situations in the world, akin to the political asylum sought by refugees. As Nancy Mairs puts it, "No one could enter the ward unless invited. Thus, the terrible, complicated, demanding world, fear of which made me flush and tremble with feverish nausea, was kept at bay."[51] When primary sufferers endangered by illness are hospitalized, it often

---

51. Mairs, *Plaintext*, 125.

aids the healing of those who love the primary sufferers to the extent it provides some reassurance of their loved ones' safety and respite while their loved ones are in the care of others. Those of us habituated to what Clifford Beers calls the "constant friction"[52] between ourselves and the world—or within ourselves—are unable to comprehend either the visceral suffering that friction inflicts on some sufferers or the protective respite a hospital can provide. William Styron found this to be so.

> This refuge, while hardly an enjoyable place, is a facility where patients still may go when pills fail, as they did in my case. . . . The hospital was my salvation, and it is something of a paradox that in this austere place with its locked and wired doors and desolate green hallways . . . I found the repose, the assuagement of the tempest in my brain, that I was unable to find in my quiet farmhouse.
>
> This is partly the result of sequestration, of safety, of being removed to a world in which the urge to pick up a knife and plunge it into one's own breast disappears in the newfound knowledge, quickly apparent even to the depressive's fuzzy brain, that the knife with which he is attempting to cut his dreadful Swiss steak is bendable plastic. But the hospital also offers the mild, oddly gratifying trauma of sudden stabilization—a transfer out of the too familiar surroundings of home, where all is anxiety and discord, into an orderly and benign detention where one's only duty is to try to get well. . . .
>
> The hospital was a way station, a purgatory.[53]

Survivors value hospitals not only when they serve as relatively safe space for being ill but also when hospitalization offers an environment for recuperation. In recalling the eventual abatement of her illness during hospitalization, Tracy Thompson also remembers how challenging it was to consider life after discharge. "I regarded [the world outside the hospital] with a kind of wary interest, the way someone recovering from the flu might eye solid food."[54] A bout with acute soul-sickness can, like the flu,

52. Clifford W. Beers, *A Mind That Found Itself: An Autobiography,* 5th ed. rev. (Garden City, N.Y.: Doubleday, Doran & Co., 1944), 67.
53. William Styron, *Darkness Visible: A Memoir of Madness* (New York: Vintage Books, 1990), 68–69.
54. Thompson, *The Beast,* 172.

weaken a person. The sanctuary of hospitalization can help rebuild the capacity to digest the "solid food" of life outside the hospital through a gradual resumption of activity and by working on the project we mentioned previously—the development of a health-based identity. Thompson's description of how she worked her way toward discharge is very much an illustration of what Lauren Slater described as the value of convalescence. Thompson's time in the hospital gave her time to educate herself about her illness, to cultivate a more accurate understanding of the physical nature of her illness. But—after she gave up her defensive and superior airs—the community of patients also became a place to practice for a better way of living on the outside. Like a twelve-step group, the other patients saw through her denial and bravado and waited for her to do an *honest* inventory of herself. And it was by entering another patient's isolation—Hugo, of all people—that she got a fragment of the kind of connection she had searched for desperately, unsuccessfully, on the outside.[55] Welton Gaddy makes a similar testimony—that the community of patients is for some sufferers a notable part of hospitalization's healing power. Rev. Dr. Gaddy was hospitalized due to an acute depression. A successful pastor, he says it was a measure of his effort to distance himself from his depression and from the other patients that he took his briefcase to the hospital with him. He was there only seven days, and still he describes his stay as "life-altering in the most positive sense." His memoir movingly describes how his "colleagues in care" demonstrated, more vividly and consistently than he had ever before experienced, values prized within Christianity: compassionate acceptance and tolerance, whatever his mood; pervasive equality, no matter one's emotional or social state; commitment to honesty, especially about difficult emotions and relational encounters; meaningful rituals that welcomed newcomers, structured the community's daily life, and bid farewell to those departing; group activities that stressed mutual helpfulness across all boundaries.[56]

Finally, a notable number of memoirists attest to the healing power of a treatment some sufferers receive during hospitalization—electroconvulsive therapy, or ECT. The general public is still at the mercy of negative stereotypes and media hype that haven't advanced beyond the

---

55, Thompson, *The Beast*, 151–202.
56. Gaddy, *A Soul Under Siege*, 109, 124.

horror portrayed in *One Flew over the Cuckoo's Nest*. Desperate sufferers, however, cannot stop there. Thankfully, they do not need to. So many improvements have been made in ECT in recent years that, remarkably, many contemporary memoirists who have this treatment express appreciation for it. This is the case for several reasons. The treatment typically is used only when other options have failed, and so those who benefit are grateful to have finally found relief, even if under difficult circumstances. But also, on the whole, treatments are given under mild sedation, using lower amounts of electric current, and in fewer numbers, all of which causes ECT to have fewer negative side effects. When she had no further choices, Martha Manning fearfully agreed to ECT.

> ECT was the tractor that pulled me out of the mud. Its power was hard to believe. Within several treatments, I was adding 20 to 30 minutes to my sleep per night. Having lost 30 pounds in three months, I began to look forward to meals. My face, which felt like a mask, regained its elasticity. It was as if several heavy backpacks had been taken from my shoulders.[57]

"Based on my experience," William Hulme writes, "there is no reason to fear shock treatments or to have any sense of shame for having taken them."[58]

DIAGNOSES AND MEDICATIONS

While there are problems associated with diagnosis, a few of our memoirists have suffered from the opposite problem—not receiving the benefit of a diagnosis. David Hilfiker, as previously noted, says, "Since no one stumbled onto [my] diagnosis for the first twenty years of my illness, I was left without a name for my experience, which is almost worse than the experience itself."[59] Sharon O'Brien articulates the comfort and hope a diagnosis can bring:

> I was relieved to know I *had* something, a condition, an illness. . . . "Clinical depression" . . . sounded like a category that other people

---

57. Manning, "The Legacy," 40.
58. Hulme and Hulme, *Wrestling with Depression*, 74.
59. David Hilfiker, "When Mental Illness Blocks the Spirit," *The Other Side* (May and June 2002), 12.

had occupied, and so instead of feeling erased by the classification I felt consoled. I was part of a community of sufferers. Doctors knew about dreadful illness, and I would be cured.[60]

She would soon learn that the doctors had no cures. (As we will see, she did find the community she needed.) But there *are* treatments, and diagnoses help lead the way to them. And while there is ambivalence about them, psychotropic medications do alleviate soul-suffering for many people.

Loved ones of the primary sufferer tend to be less conflicted about medication than the primary sufferers, though most are concerned about physical and psychosocial side effects of the medications. When medications are effective, family members get respite from constant oversight of their loved one's safety. And, where illness has seemed to transmogrify their loved ones, family members get a glimpse of the person they had loved and lost, extended versions of Dan and David Weisburd's one good day. The primary sufferers consistently address both the positives and the negatives in their experience with medication. Even among those to whom the positive effects of medication are now obvious, or among those who are admittedly grateful for medications, they are a necessary evil. No one *wants* to take them, and *everyone* would stop if they could. Lizzie Simon's statement, which seems at first glance to be an unmitigated accolade to medications, also conveys that they overshadow all her ebullient and more personal efforts to reclaim her life: "They have saved me more than I have saved myself."[61] It is not uncommon to find humor mixed with appreciation, as in Kay Redfield Jamison's tongue-in-cheek "Rules for the Gracious Acceptance of Lithium into Your Life." Adaptable to most psychotropic medications, here is a sampling.

1. Clear out the medicine cabinet before guests arrive for dinner or new lovers stay the night.

    . . .

3. Don't be too embarrassed by your lack of coordination or your inability to do well the sports you once did with ease.

    . . .

5. Smile when people joke about how they think they "need to be on lithium."

---

60. O'Brien, *The Family Silver*, 277.
61. Simon, *Detour*, 158.

. . .

10. Always keep in perspective how much better you are. Everyone else certainly points it out often enough, and, annoyingly, it's probably true.
11. Be appreciative. Don't even *consider* stopping your lithium.
12. When you do stop, get manic, get depressed, expect to hear two basic themes from your family, friends, and healers:
    ▪ But you were doing so much better, I just don't understand it.
    ▪ I told you this would happen.
13. Restock your medicine cabinet.[62]

Most memoirists looking back on their experiences with medications' positive effects seem to agree with Tracy Thompson's succinct summary statements of their role. "Life did not get easier. But living did." "Drugs are tools, nothing more—but that is no small thing. To a person scaling a cliff, a grappling hook is the difference between life and death."[63] When they are effective, medications make it more possible for sufferers to do the work of healing—for example, to participate in therapy with more initiative or be more active physically and socially. And, in part because of effective medication, some sufferers are able to become, as Tracy Thompson puts it, "co-investigators": "for the first time, sizable numbers of us can return from that featureless white room to add our voices to the debate about psychotropic drugs and their place in society."[64] Sufferers testify that medications are not the healing itself, usually, but with them, healing comes within reach, for which they are grateful. Like many memoirists, Lauren Slater describes in detail the first realization that the drugs had "kicked in." "It was, to date, the single most stunning experience of my life, although later it would unfold with ever more complexity, even danger." "My remission on the first drugged day—confusing, yes, portending loss, yes—was also a blessing, pure and simple. No, not a blessing, a redemption, both bright and blinding, heaven opening up, letting me in."[65] Slater does not comment on the theological language in her description of Prozac's saving effect, but some sufferers who

62. Jamison, *An Unquiet Mind*, 97–98.
63. Thompson, *The Beast*, 253, 285.
64. Thompson, *The Beast*, 13–14.
65. Slater, *Prozac Diary*, 25–26, 34.

are religious are more direct about how effective medication affects their religious life. Norma Swetnam's sentiment is typical of such sufferers: "I am deeply grateful for the miracle God brought to my life in the form of a prescription drug."[66]

PSYCHOTHERAPISTS AND PSYCHOTHERAPY

Many of our memoirists testify to what research has shown: the combination of psychotherapy and medication is more healing than either one alone. "Pills cannot, do not, ease one back into reality; they only bring one back headlong, careening, and faster than can be endured at times," says Kay Redfield Jamison. "But, ineffably, psychotherapy *heals*." It is a "sanctuary" and a "battleground." "But, always, it is where I have believed —or have learned to believe—that I might someday be able to contend with all of this."[67] Soul-sufferers cherish psychiatrists and psychotherapists who challenge the system's fragmentation and help their clients create the holistic habits they need. Kathleen Norris's doctor saw her not only in her depression but in her wholeness.

> Drugs, therapy, someone might suggest. The last time it got this bad I did consult with a doctor. We discussed many options, and what she suggested to me I treasure still: exercise, she said, and spiritual direction.[68]

Just as sufferers criticize mental health professionals who fail to provide adequate education, they treasure those who are willing to be educators, providing information that empowers the sufferer's intellect and actions in life-giving directions. Tracy Thompson found her second therapist more effective than the first because the second went beyond psychodynamic interpretation to provide her information about the biology of her depression, information without which her self-care and healing had previously been impeded. Well-rounded education about medication is similarly crucial. Those sufferers for whom medication is a necessity say that it is healing when caregivers are empathically respectful of the difficulty of taking medication and, at the same time, represent in a straight-

---

66. Norma G. Swetnam, "My Journey through Hell," in *Presbyterians Today Online* (August 1998), http://www.pcusa.org/today/archive/features/feat9808d.htm (accessed August 1, 2006), 2.
67. Jamison, *An Unquiet Mind*, 89.
68. Kathleen Norris, *The Cloister Walk* (New York: Riverhead Books, 1996), 133.

forward, nonmanipulative way the costs of not taking it. Kay Redfield Jamison's psychiatrist contributed to her healing in this way; he was, she says, able to combine "clarity of thought," "obvious caring," and "unwillingness to equivocate in delivering bad news."

> My psychiatrist, who took all [my] complaints [about medication] very seriously—existential qualms, side effects, matters of value from my upbringing— . . . refused, thank God, to get drawn into my convoluted and impassioned web of reasoning about why I should try, just one more time, to survive without taking medication. He always kept the basic choice in perspective: . . . The choice . . . was between madness and sanity, and between life and death.[69]

Ultimately, though, while psychiatrists and psychotherapists have valuable training in complex theories and techniques, memoirists pay tribute to those who have kindness and steadfastness beyond their technical brilliance. Sufferers say psychotherapists heal by way of what we called in our reflections on care the "ministry of presence." Of her psychiatrist Jamison says, "He kept me alive a thousand times over."[70]

> I remember sitting in his office a hundred times during those grim months and each time thinking, What on earth can he say that will make me feel better or keep me alive? Well, there never was anything he could say, that's the funny thing. It was all the stupid, desperately optimistic, condescending things he *didn't* say that kept me alive; all the compassion and warmth I felt from him that could not have been said; all the intelligence, competence, and time he put into it; and his granite belief that mine was a life worth living. He was terribly direct, which was terribly important, and he was willing to admit the limits of his understanding and treatments and when he was wrong. Most difficult to put into words, but in many ways the essence of everything: He taught me that the road from suicide to life is cold and colder and colder still, but—with steely effort, the grace of God, and an inevitable break in the weather—that I could make it.[71]

---

69 Jamison, *An Unquiet Mind*, 87, 102.

70. Jamison, *An Unquiet Mind*, 87.

71. Jamison, *An Unquiet Mind*, 118.

COMMUNAL APPROACHES TO MENTAL HEALTH CARE

For people who do not need them, support groups are fodder for amusing sarcasm and satirization. Until she needed one, Sharon O'Brien says, she, too, was entertained by such jokes. But then, desperate for help, she takes herself—reluctantly—to a support group for people with depression and bipolar disorder and also finds herself moved—surprisingly—just by people's introductions of themselves and their initial, immediate comprehension of her suffering. The internal dialogue she has while sitting there demonstrates the thought process that is unfortunately required of sufferers in order to fight external and internalized stigma. But her closing remark also testifies to the need for and healing potential of supportive community groups to override stigma:

> As I say the words "I'm Sharon" to a group of strangers, I know I'm doing something that some people, including many of my academic colleagues, would satirize. Support groups are easy targets for people who find the verb "share" humorous. I've heard the phrase "Thank you for sharing" used ironically hundreds of times. . . . I've listened to many jokes beginning with "I'm [name]" that mock the classic support group introduction, and in the past I've probably laughed at them. Maybe right now I am doing something that other academics would find self-indulgent or laughable or politically retrograde.
>
> I have to say, I really don't care.[72]

Groups and community-based treatment programs play a stunningly prominent role in almost every memoir where healing is recounted. Of course, communal approaches are not helpful automatically. Some do not have the qualities of authentic accompaniment that we will be detailing in this section and thus can be harmful. But when groups and community-based programs have some or all of the characteristics we will explore, our memoirists attest to the value of many types—educational and therapeutic groups, groups for the primary sufferer and groups for loved ones, advocacy programs run by laypeople and treatment programs run by professionals, groups for short-term treatment or for long-term "maintenance." These communal approaches to care over

---

72. O'Brien, *The Family Silver*, 252–53.

the long haul are not emphasized in mental health services as much as individual care, by a professional, for the purposes of progress. But according to most of our memoirists, they ought to be, because they offer healing dynamics difficult to create otherwise.

What makes communal approaches so radically healing? Initially, supportive groups and community-based programs are healing because they provide safe harbor, respite from the stigma. Only by remembering the blunt statement made about the extent of the pain caused by stigma—"the stigma is worse than the illness itself"—can we begin to grasp the sanctuary for sufferers of being among people who know firsthand, and provide asylum from, the fears and prejudices of outsiders. Sharon O'Brien:

> "The stigma," a woman in my group says. "If it just weren't for the stigma." It could be anyone speaking. Everyone nods, and as we do, we look at her and then we look at ourselves around the circle. The stigma shimmers and fades in the light of our eyes and we sit there, a visible community, fragile and temporary and real.[73]

Communal approaches tend to be healing also because they emphasize the value and capabilities of the sufferers *as persons*, the healing power of mutual respect, human connection, and meaningful activity. Dan Hanson comments on how, for his son, J, community-based programs provide "the bridge to life outside the vicious cycle of mental illness."

> Some community-based programs consist of teams made up of a social worker, a psychiatrist, a therapist, and a trained support person who can intervene in an emergency or act on behalf of the patient if necessary. In some community-based programs the support person spends time with the patient much the same as a friend might. The support person can serve a critical role here by approaching the relationship as a friendship between equals. Often just spending time with someone, going to a movie, or taking a walk while listening helps. A key ingredient of these programs is respect. Patients like J want to be treated as individ-

---

73. O'Brien, *The Family Silver*, 262.

uals not as "patients" and given the respect they deserve. This is an important point that is too often overlooked.[74]

The mutual respect embodied in a staff person and a sufferer sharing a movie or otherwise relating in a friendly, everyday way exemplifies the healing power of caring human presence that we discussed in part 4. When sufferers heal, it is also because communal approaches tend to provide validation of one's suffering and guidance for healthy identity development when one's identity now includes psychic turmoil.

At first, Sharon O'Brien's reaction to attending a support group as part of her treatment for depression was that it seemed a measure of failure—"a sign that depression would be a permanent part of my life instead of a mind storm just passing through."[75] But, after experiencing support groups held by the Boston chapter of Manic-Depressive and Depressive Association (MDDA),[76] gratitude leads O'Brien to write an eloquent reflection on their healing power.

> MDDA meetings are . . . democratic: mental illness is the great leveler, and the class distinctions that privately obsess American society, despite our public ideology of classlessness, are momentarily erased here. In the "Depression" group you can see a Harvard grad student sitting next to a Vietnam vet who's living in subsidized housing, a therapist who is having a bad reaction to a new medication being encouraged by a nurse's aide whose week has been "pretty level, thank God." Sometimes I think that John Winthrop's long-ago utopian vision of Boston as the "city upon a hill," where people would gladly help others in need, is realized not in space but in time, every Wednesday from seven to nine o'clock at McLean [Hospital].[77]

Communal approaches so often heal because they are so often made true democracies by the "great leveler" of illness. This inherent equality does

---

74. Daniel S. Hanson, *Room for J: A Family Struggles with Schizophrenia* (Edina, Minn.: Beaver's Pond Press, 2005), 119.

75. O'Brien, *The Family Silver*, 250.

76. See the website of the Manic Depressive and Depressive Association of Boston: http://mddaboston.org/index.html. See also the website of the Depression and Bipolar Support Alliance (http://www.dbsalliance.org/).

77. O'Brien, *The Family Silver*, 260.

not smother difference but it does breed mutuality—each has needs that can be met and each has resources that can be shared—such as wisdom honed from years of battling soul-suffering in private and public. When communal approaches heal, they do so because of this sharing of resources, perhaps even more than the meeting of needs. It is touching how often our memoirists say that their need to have solutions drops away in the presence of true community. Heartbroken over their son's diagnosis and refusal of treatment, Rev. Margaret England and her husband found their way to their first National Alliance on Mental Illness conference.

> [O]ur spirits were lifted as we sat with 2,500 other people who shared the pain and the suffering. There would be moments when a speaker would touch that pain and everyone in the room was united in a holy moment of identity with the suffering caused by these mental illnesses.[78]

---

78. England, "A Family's Spiritual Journey," 13. See the appendix for more information about the National Alliance on Mental Illness.

HEALING MIND, BODY, AND SOUL

The remainder of this portion of our study is dedicated to a broader horizon of healing, one that includes the physical but also the metaphysical. We will attend to ways that sufferers use traditional forms of religion and broader conceptualizations of spiritual values to construct meaning in their lives, a meaning that includes their suffering but is not held captive by it. Here the question moves beyond "How will I deal with my anguish?" to "How will I deal with the whole of my life?" Soul-sufferers make excruciatingly clear that suffering is hell, that there is nothing good about the suffering. The notion that soul-suffering imparts special insights or sensibilities is, as Martha Manning says, "romantic nonsense" that stands only until the next crisis arrives.[79] At the same time, most sufferers testify with Stewart Govig that, "On the inside, I cannot help raging against chronic mental illness, but at the same time I will admit to strange blessings in its wake."[80] Some sufferers find meaning, or make it, despite the suffering, or in the midst of suffering, but never instead of suffering. These are hard-won blessings, wrested from an adversary, but significantly, many of our memoirists speak of similar blessings. Appropriately, Rev. Susan Gregg-Schroeder calls these "gifts of the shadow" and "treasures of the darkness."[81] In and through their suffering, survivors find the sacred,

---

79. Manning, *Undercurrents*, 173.
80. Govig, *Souls are Made of Endurance*, 95.
81. Susan Gregg-Schroeder, *In the Shadow of God's Wings: Grace in the Midst of Depression* (Nashville: Upper Room Books, 1997), 59, 60. The phrase "treasures of the darkness" is taken from Leslie Weatherhead, source not identified.

have moments of profound tenderness with others, grow in their appreciation of everyday pleasures, and see through the sham of many dominant values. Not as some simplistic notion of healing but for the sake of their dignity, most sufferers would agree with David Karp that they "do [their] best to live gracefully in the present moment."

> The recognition that the pain of depression is unlikely to disappear has provoked a redefinition of its meaning, a reordering of its place in my life. It has taken me more than two decades to abandon the medical language of cure in favor of a more spiritual vocabulary of transformation.[82]

---

82. David Karp, "An Unwelcome Career," in *Unholy Ghost*, 148.

HEALING RELIGION

In the next section, we will widen our scope beyond religion to spirituality, but here we focus on testimony in our memoirs to the healing capacities of religious tradition. For some, religious concepts, practices, and professionals—so often disparaged and disregarded by the healthy and the healers—enable healing. It is often thought that people in psychic turmoil tend to have extreme or otherwise unreliable religious experiences. Actually, most survivors who find healing have only the most ordinary spiritual resources on which to rely.

RELIGIOUS CONCEPTS

We have noted earlier that some sufferers struggle with religious concepts that contribute to their suffering and, in some cases, critique and revise those concepts in ways that are more humane and healing; we will not revisit those discussions here. Instead, in this section we will focus on religious concepts in which sufferers find consolation and healing ready and waiting. Space does not allow us to address all the concepts that appear in the memoirs. So we will first address two areas that are addressed by numerous memoirists: ideas about G-d in light of suffering, and biblical language and images. Then we will reflect on a few themes not addressed by many memoirists but of notable importance to a few: resurrection, detachment, and a theology of disability. The theme of hope, touched on by most memoirists, religious or not, we will address at the conclusion of part 5.

G-d, in Light of Suffering

Ideas and experiences of G-d sustain some of our memoirists. For a fortunate few, psychic anguish does not damage or even challenge faith in G-d, and some sufferers' notions of G-d remain steady and encouraging. So it was for Lucy Hulme, even during the acute phase of her husband's depression: "In the background of the day-to-day hospital visits was my faith that I was in God's care."[83] For some in psychic anguish, as for Florence Lerrigo, assurance of divine acceptance is a counterweight to human rejection. Early one Sunday morning, she was rereading the Gospel of John.

> "The light shines in the darkness, and the darkness has not overcome it," . . . The light which is the life of Jesus shines in this darkness I know so well. . . . The gloom of fear surrounding me lifted for a moment. . . .
>
> I began to remember how it felt before the darkness of mental illness had fallen. . . .
>
> I am acceptable to God, I thought, not to myself, not to society, but to God; . . . This is a constructive fact I can hold on to.[84]

However, because suffering raises such profound questions about traditional teachings—especially that G-d is all at once loving and all-powerful—many memoirists tell of ways that soul-suffering precipitated change in their notions of G-d. As Lois Bloom found, after her son Sammy committed suicide, what she calls her "preconceived answers" to theological questions didn't seem like answers at all. The predominant question is: "Where is G-d in relation to my suffering?" Lois Bloom's questioning eventually brought her to a theological position common to most memoirists who find religion healing. "Where was God?" "Why hadn't God intervened?" To other suicide survivors she testifies that

> I believe that when God created us, we were given the power to reason and the freedom to make choices—even to live or die. Unfortunately, our loved ones made a decision we did not agree with. I suspect it was not God's choice either.[85]

Many memoirists whose belief in G-d remains unchallenged by suffering accomplish this in a similar, straightforward way. It is incomprehensible to them that the G-d they believe is love would allow their suf-

---

83. Hulme and Hulme, *Wrestling with Depression*, 14.
84. Florence Lerrigo, "What the Christian Faith Can Mean to a Deeply Troubled Mind," unpublished essay, 3.
85. Bloom, *Mourning, After a Suicide*, 18, 4, 15–16.

fering to continue if G-d had the power to change it. So, God must not have the power to change it. Nor does God judge the suffering. Lois Bloom affirms Lloyd Carr's study of biblical passages on suicide: "no place in the Bible are any . . . persons [who committed suicide] recriminated against for their suicidal act." She also writes that, though she has found answers to some of her questions, "others have ceased to be important."[86]

Notions of G-d's immanence often bring comfort to memoirists previously more mindful of G-d's transcendence. For example, in struggling with his depression, Parker Palmer found that "the way to God is not up but down." The image given to Palmer by his therapist—the friend pushing him toward ground safe to stand on—enabled Palmer to reclaim his life, in part, he implies, because it also eventually transformed his comprehension of G-d.

> I had always imagined God to be in the same general direction as everything else that I valued: up. I had failed to appreciate the meaning of some words that had intrigued me since I first heard them in seminary—Tillich's description of God as the "ground of being." I had to be forced underground before I could understand that the way to God is not up but down.[87]

And the way to G-d is not answers but mystery. Our memoirists speak of G-d, but not with smug certainty.

> Depression demands that we reject simplistic answers, both "religious" and "scientific," and learn to embrace mystery, something our culture resists. Mystery surrounds every deep experience of the human heart: the deeper we go into the heart's darkness or its light, the closer we get to the ultimate mystery of God.[88]

Some sufferers are fortunate to find holiness in surprising places. G-d— and Jesus—are found in their suffering. Indeed, for most memoirists, suffering has little religious value except that the sacred is sometimes found there.

---

86. Bloom, *Mourning, After a Suicide*, 16, 18.
87. Palmer, *Let Your Life Speak*, 69. Palmer is referring to Paul Tillich, *Systematic Theology*, vol. I, II, & III (Chicago: University of Chicago Press, 1951, 1957 & 1963).
88. Palmer, *Let Your Life Speak*, 60.

Where is God when it hurts? He is with us when life seems darkest.... At these times God draws closest to us in unexpected and mysterious ways. Our grief journey may be much like that of the disciples on the road to Emmaus. In our grief and loss, Jesus comes alongside us. He is not intrusive, but he is available to break bread with us and rekindle our hope.[89]

But soul-suffering reveals that the unexpected places in which the immanence of holiness appears are also beyond the self. Sometimes one's own soul-suffering leads to greater openness to the possibility that sacred light can be found in other troubled and troubling people. As part of her healing, Florence Lerrigo tried to see others through the lens of those words from the Gospel of John that had been such an assurance to her.

Nineteen years have now gone by since that moment of illumination on the darkness of a mental hospital life. I am still a student, but I look now for God and find him in many places—in people who seemed to misunderstand me, in those whom I have misunderstood, and in troubled people who, as I once was, are raw and open and ready to receive the Gospel because, as Jesus said, "Blessed are the poor in spirit, for theirs is the kingdom of heaven."[90]

Martha Manning describes an incident in which the holy is revealed in an anonymous act of thoughtfulness and the exquisitely detailed beauty of the natural world.

After a morning of errands, I come home to find a bunch of tulips stuck in our mail slot . . . without a note. . . . They are breathtaking—a fiery red-orange opening to reveal the most incredible golden stars in their centers. Each time I catch sight of them, I am enthralled. I lose my focus, my balance. No matter what I'm doing, I have to stop and go over to peek inside to assure myself that the gold stars are still there. They always are, and for a moment I let myself believe in God again.[91]

---

89. Hsu, *Grieving a Suicide*, 122.
90. Lerrigo, "What the Christian Faith Can Mean," 4.
91. Manning, *Undercurrents*, 167.

Biblical Language and Imagery

Nearly every survivor, even those who are not religious, references biblical language and imagery. Bible is shared language dramatic enough to communicate the profundity and value of life in the extremity of mental and spiritual anguish. The Psalms, especially those of lament, are arguably the most frequently cited. It isn't so much that biblical texts comfort, as that they dignify the suffering. Indeed, as Stewart Govig puts it, biblical texts "can both sharpen the pain and frame the heartache."[92] While on retreat, Martha Manning is reading the Psalms and says

> It's incredible to me that we never learned the psalms as children. All that time and energy memorizing the catechism when the real thing was right here. It's like memorizing the *TV Guide* rather than watching the show.[93]

She includes in her memoir one she loves, to show us. A portion of Psalm 38:

> O, Lord, all my desire is before you;
> From you my groaning is not hid.
> My heart throbs; my strength forsakes me;
> The very light of my eyes has failed me.
> My friends and neighbors stand back
> Because of my affliction;
> My neighbors stand far off.[94]

Govig tells of an incident when he was embarrassed by his son's rantings in a public parking lot. Later, reading the Psalms, Govig encounters the prayers of other people who "groaned in spirit": Out of the depths I cry to you, O Lord, Lord, hear my voice! Let your ears be attentive to the voice of my supplications! (Psa. 130:1–2 NRSV). The text reframes his son's anguished vocalisms: "Jay was yelping passionately to the Other(s) . . . on a plane of torment completely hidden from his caregiver father and the parking lot spectators."[95] Susan Gregg-Schroeder takes the title of her memoir from Psalm 57, a portion of which reads as follows:

---

92. Govig, *Souls Are Made of Endurance*, 83.
93. Manning, *Undercurrents*, 50.
94. Manning, *Undercurrents*, 50. Psalm 38:9–11, New American Bible, St. Joseph edition. Subsequent Biblical quotations by Manning are also from this version.
95. Govig, *Souls Are Made of Endurance*, 80, 79.

Be merciful to me, O God, be merciful to me,
    for in you my soul takes refuge;
in the shadow of your wings I will take refuge,
    until the destroying storms pass by.
I cry to God Most High,
    to God who fulfils his purpose for me.
He will send from heaven and save me,
    he will put to shame those who trample on me.
God will send forth his steadfast love and his faithfulness.
                     (Psa. 57:1–3 NRSV)

But dozens of other texts and images are referenced in memoirs of soul-suffering: for example, the suffering and defiance of Job, the cries of Lamentations, the rising of Lazarus, Namaan's lack of faith in the means of healing, the bush that burned and was not consumed, the Jordan river, mustard seeds, leprosy, Gethsemane, Paul's conviction that nothing can separate us from God. Implicit in Martha Manning's description of her profound ambivalence about her first ECT treatment is a Calvary-like allusion conveyed in language evocative of biblical expression: "I offer myself up to these strangers in exchange for the possibility of deliverance. . . . Fingers anoint my temples with cool ointment and fasten a plastic crown tightly around my head."[96] In the grip of her depression, Sharon O'Brien stops by her childhood church, though she hasn't been to mass for a year. Drawn to the Stations of the Cross, she walks around the church, remembering the story. Jesus takes up his cross. . . . Some woman wipes his brow. . . . Jesus falls the third time. . . . Jesus dies on the cross.

And then, the last one: *They lay Jesus in the tomb*.

Wow. That's impressive. They didn't go for the Hollywood ending.

I stand there for several minutes, watching Christ's disciples, shoulders bowed in grief, place the lifeless body in the tomb. I am so grateful I could weep.

No one knew about the Resurrection when Christ died. All people knew about was the dying. I leave the church momentarily exhilarated because there's a match between my story and a greater one.[97]

---

96. Manning, *Undercurrents*, 124.
97. O'Brien, *The Family Silver*, 204.

Resurrection

Though not for Sharon O'Brien, for some survivors there is a match between their lives and the notion of resurrection. In some cases, the suffering is so deadening, so life-threatening, that if recovery comes, it is
like being raised from the dead, more like resurrection than healing.
This was the case for William Hulme, who calls his response to ECT
"my resurrection."[98] In other cases, the notion of resurrection offers theological solace to those sufferers burdened by feelings of worthlessness or
hopelessness. This was the case for Professor Roberta Bondi. A scholar
and teacher of the history of the Christian church, Dr. Bondi tells of the
day that her "lifelong depression hit its lowest point." Bone-weary from
both the consciousness of sin and the imperative to serve that she was
taught are the heart of Christianity, she cried out her despair in prayer:
"'the harder I try, the more I worry. There must be something essential
about Christianity I am missing. . . . I can try no longer. . . . I absolutely
give up.' . . . And I did give up, utterly . . . the light of my life went out.
. . . My heart was torn in half . . ."

> How long I sat there in that state, I have no idea. . . . I only know
> that, all of a sudden and without any warning, I woke up. I
> heard my own voice repeating in my mind the words from the
> Roman Catholic eucharistic prayers for Easter, "The joy of the
> Resurrection renews the whole world." Every cell of my body
> heard them and for the first time I knew that these words were
> absolutely true, and that they were true for me.[99]

Over the next hours and days and years, Bondi says, the notion that Jesus
was resurrected—with his wounds—became solace for that which before had fueled only depression rather than joy over the uplifting love of
G-d. "How could I have been a church historian and a person of prayer
who loved God and still not known that the most fundamental Christian
reality is not the suffering of the cross but the life it brings?"[100]

---

98. Hulme and Hulme, *Wrestling with Depression*, 43.
99. Roberta Bondi, *Memories of God: Theological Reflections on a Life* (Nashville: Abingdon
Press, 1995), 167, 169–70.
100. Bondi, *Memories of God*, 170.

Detachment

For writer Kathleen Norris, the religious notion of detachment—in contrast to the modern connotations of aloofness and lack of concern—provided a way of seeing values hidden within the tumult of her husband's sudden hospitalization for depression. Monastic forms of detachment emphasize "being free from [wanting] certain things to happen"[101]—or not happen. Being free from wishing her husband were not ill meant being able to take in more fully—"once the initial shock wore off"—that the situation was the occasion of much caring, healing connection: her husband was getting needed help; Kathleen was being cared for by her pastor, the sisters with whom she was staying, and the monk who was the hospital chaplain; family and friends were offering moral support. From this perspective, "our situation no longer seemed like a disaster" but was a reminder that one "shares in a common human lot." In the upheaval of psychic anguish, the gift of spiritual detachment does not allow "either worldly values or self-centeredness to distract us from what is most essential in our relationship with God and with each other."[102]

Theology of Disability

Although much of our memoirists' reflection on religious and spiritual matters is implicitly a theology of disability, Stewart Govig engages in an explicit and substantial discussion of this theme. Undoubtedly, this is because of his own physical disability, which led him to publish a book about disability and the church—*Strong at the Broken Places*—five years before he published his memoir—*Souls Are Made of Endurance*—about living with his son's schizophrenia. Both books, which we have frequently referenced—as well as a third, *In the Shadow of our Steeples*[103] —are extended theological reflections on disability that cannot be adequately summarized here; a few observations must suffice. First, he shows that a theology of disability is built from a wealth of biblical texts that offer a wealth of respectfulness, solace, and instruction. Above all, he reveals how prominently disability is portrayed in the Bible, and how

101. Kathleen Norris, *Amazing Grace: A Vocabulary of Faith* (New York: Riverhead Books, 1998), 32. Quoting Dorotheus of Gaza, source not provided.
102. Norris, *Amazing Grace*, 32, 34, 35, 36.
103. Stewart D. Govig, *In the Shadow of Our Steeples: Pastoral Presence for Families Coping with Mental Illness* (Binghamton, N.Y.: Haworth Pastoral Press, 1999).

normalizing those portrayals are: disability is treated as a common, expectable part of life; disability is but one of many afflictions, not more or
less weighty or worthy of compassion than any other infirmity; disabled
persons play respected roles in a remarkable number of biblical stories
and images. Govig relentlessly articulates the disparity between the tendency of scripture to normalize and include disability and the tendency
of denominations, congregations, and pastors to both single out and ex-
clude disabled persons. In many religious communities, disability is
treated as an order of suffering different from others; religious communities minister admirably to many people in need, but the disabled are
often conspicuously ignored, even to the extent of ignoring the barriers
to their physical presence in the church building or at worship. But his
main focus, arguably, is to close the gap between the respect shown by
scripture and the stigmatizing disregard shown by many religious bodies. Thus, his theology of disability is not only words and ideas, but a
communication of many concrete and simple acts that can make an inherent and supported place in religious communities for disability, one
that would mirror the inherent and supported place disability—and disabled people—have in creation.

Religious Practices

Objects and actions associated with many kinds of religious practices appear in memoirs of soul-suffering, and appear to sustain: rosary beads
and prayers, a crucifix, meditation alone and in groups, Buddha chants,
recitation of creed, intercessory prayer, biblical reflection, charismatic
groups. Sometimes these objects and actions support healing when done
even occasionally. Sometimes, even when soul-anguish robs religious
practices of their comfort, persisting in the habit of them keeps open a
space for new infusion of meaning, as was the case for Lois Bloom. In
fact, most times, religious practices support healing because they are undertaken ritually, with intentionality, regularity, and devotion—this
harks back to the healing value of habits mentioned earlier. In any case,
four practices with religious significance most often appear in memoirs
of soul-suffering: reflective writing; participating in religious community; prayer or meditation; and worship and other rituals.

Reflective writing has long been a spiritual practice, when it is undertaken to better comprehend life's meanings and to discern the sacred

values and choices that help build an honorable life. We could argue that most memoirs of soul-suffering are, thus, a spiritual if not religious practice, because almost all memoirs seek, in part, to make honorable living more possible. But Henri Nouwen conveys explicitly that the practice of reflective writing was spiritual sustenance for him not just after but also during his anguish of soul. He is grateful—and surprised—that his soul-suffering did not rob him of his ability to write.

> Writing became part of my struggle for survival. It gave me the little distance from myself that I needed to keep from drowning in my despair. Nearly every day, usually immediately after meeting with my guides, I wrote a "spiritual imperative"—a command to myself that had emerged from our session. These imperatives were directed to my own heart. They were not meant for anyone but myself.[104]

As one reads the imperatives that follow his brief autobiographical account of his despair at the beginning of *The Inner Voice of Love*, one can see from their contents how the regular practice of reflective writing became for him a way to get a little distance from the undertow of his despair. But those contents suggest that what kept him afloat was not only distance from himself, but also that through his writing he was speaking to himself from the heart of the ancient comforts and assurances afforded by his religious tradition.

The practices of participating in religious community provide crucial sustenance for some of our memoirists. We noted in part 4 that sometimes the care offered in religious community is harmful, but memoirists also tell of religious communities that uplifted them with sacrificial love. Extensive descriptions of her retreats at a monastery stand like bookends in the early and closing pages of Martha Manning's memoir.[105] A few days after the funeral for their daughter-in-law, though exhausted and wary of people's reactions, Lloyd and Gwendolyn Carr went to church. They remember with gratitude the spacious warmth with which their pastors and congregation greeted them. Relieved that their church

---

104. Henri J. M. Nouwen, *The Inner Voice of Love: A Journey through Anguish to Freedom* (New York: Doubleday, 1998), xvi.
105. Manning, *Undercurrents*, 45–53 and 190–197.

friends were not invasive and did not spout religious platitudes, the Carrs were able to let down their guard and take in the simple expressions of loving support offered amid the painful mystery of tragic death.[106] Living briefly in religious community provides sanctuary to two of our memoirists—Norris and Manning—but it also feeds them the nourishment of loving community and consistent, communal prayer. Kathleen Norris writes of being taken in by Benedictine sisters in the city where her husband is hospitalized, and the sisters enveloped her in the comfort of shelter, worship, daily routine and, even, some laughter.

Some of our memoirists find solace and guidance in religious community when those communities encompass and contextualize prayer practices. Kathleen Norris's telephone conversation with a friend makes clear that community and prayer make a powerful combination, becoming a presence sufficient enough to sustain Norris even amid the crisis of her husband's unexpected hospitalization in a place far from their home.

> One day at the height of the crisis I was talking to a friend in New York City, who asked, "What are you doing for yourself? Are you seeing a counselor? Did you get someone to give you a prescription for tranquilizers?" "No," I replied, and then I startled myself by saying, "I'm OK; I've been praying the psalms." "And that's enough?" she replied, incredulous.
>
> The funny thing is, it was enough. I was not praying the psalms alone but with the Benedictine women who had graciously taken me into their small convent near the hospital, offering me a guest room there for as long as I needed it. There is no way I can measure the help they gave me.[107]

But it is also important to note that religious practices can contribute to healing even when they are not exactly soothing. Sharon O'Brien's experience with meditation makes this point plain. She is trying to meditate regularly as a way of managing her depression—we could understand this as one of those habits of holistic self-care we considered earlier.

---

106. G. Lloyd Carr, with poetry by Gwendolyn C. Carr, *The Fierce Goodbye: Hope in the Wake of Suicide* (Downers Grove, Ill.: InterVarsity Press, 1990), 33ff.
107. Norris, *Amazing Grace*, 33.

I meditate for twenty minutes, struggling just to stay with my breath, the way the books tell you. . . . I make up my own mantra, derived from Dame Julian of Norwich . . . "All will be well, and all manner of thing will be well." I do "all will be" on the in breath, "well" on the out breath.

All of a sudden grief hits. It's a tidal wave that's been waiting; slowing down in meditation has allowed it to surface. I slide to the floor . . . and weep for a long time. I weep because I have never felt so alone. I miss my parents. It's not just the love, it's the silenced wisdom I need. I want my mother to tell me how she faced death, I want my father to tell me about his depression, and how he survived. They don't have to tell me it will be all right: nobody can know that for sure, and I won't believe it anyway. I just want them to tell me what it was like for them, those times when the ropes and bridges broke and they were falling down and down into the dark. I call for them but they do not answer, and I cannot even imagine what they would say.

When I stop crying, I lie on the floor until [my cat] Megan comes in and demands to be fed.[108]

What is the healing value in this experience that looks only like pain? A spiritual practice imbued with religious meaning precipitates weeping unfortunately held off by the pace of contemporary life. Religious people know the power of ancient holy words—in this case, "All will be well . . ." —to evoke deep feeling. We cannot tell from what O'Brien writes whether the grief comes at the assurance of wellness, or because of the gap between the assurance and her depression, or both. But religious traditions of many kinds hallow the soul's weeping, because of its truthfulness and capacity to clean wounds that need to heal. Weeping is not merely a symptom, nor even just a way station on the path to happiness. O'Brien allows the grief to be a stopping point. Prostrate position, unashamed mourning, plaintive longing for the wisdom of her elders— all these are part of spiritual maturation in many religious traditions. The healing possibility is implied more than directly stated, but it appears that the meditation became safe passage into soulful authenticity.

---

108. O'Brien, *The Family Silver*, 200–01.

The power of religious practice to help heal is arguably most often conveyed in memoirists' accounts of worship. Sometimes, even when the mind is numbed by psychic anguish, familiar religious ritual has power to sustain at the level of the unconscious. Lloyd Carr describes an experience in worship—his daughter-in-law's funeral—during which he sensed that the ritual recitation of religious meanings touched him deeply, despite his numbed consciousness.

> The minister's quiet voice rehearsed the familiar words. "Let not your hearts be troubled . . . believe in God, believe in me . . . resurrection and . . . life . . . whoever believes in me . . . though he die will live, and whoever believes in me . . . never die.". . . But while our ears heard them, their very familiarity relegated the hearing to the unconscious.[109]

Other times, worship has the power to jumpstart a spiritual life drained of energy, in part because it can draw people isolated by soul-anguish into experiences of connection—human and divine. Kathleen Norris describes such an experience.

> I have promised to go to services this Sunday, at the modest but spirited Disciples of Christ church where my brother is a pastor. I still feel half-dead but do my best to sing with the congregation. One of the verses of "Spirit of God, Descend Upon my Heart"— "I ask no dreams, no prophet ecstasies, no sudden rending of the veil of clay, no angel visitant, no opening skies; but take the dimness of my soul away"—makes me realize that I am praying for the first time in days, and that it's working. The rest of that service is a giddy blur; I felt alive again, appropriately enough, on a Sunday morning.[110]

RELIGIOUS PROFESSIONALS

In part 2, we reflected on how the frenetic pace of contemporary life tends to undermine human well-being. As an example, we considered a story told by Martha Manning about the effects of busyness on her family's experience one Sunday morning at church. After leading the prayers

109. Carr, *The Fierce Goodbye*, 17.
110. Norris, *Cloister Walk*, 133.

she has hastily written on the back of a grocery store receipt, Manning realizes she hasn't yet planned her Sunday school class, which meets directly after worship. She'll have to think about that during the readings and sermon, she figures. But as the congregation stands for the gospel reading, she realizes it is the story of Mary and Martha. Her attention is caught, first because the priest reads it "with life and passion." But she is also momentarily distracted from Sunday school planning because both Martha and Mary are Manning's namesakes. Manning's mother named her Martha Mary and not Mary Martha as a kind of protest—her mother thought most interpreters of the scripture gave Martha a raw deal: Mary is said to have been right to sit reverently and studiously at the feet of Jesus, Martha wrong to have worried about the meal. Martha Mary Manning has taken in her mother's suspicion of most priests' explanation of the passage.

> As the priest begins the sermon, I am prepared once again to be annoyed. I get ready to organize for Sunday school. One minute into this guy's talk and he has my rapt attention. He has a commanding presence and a great facility with language. There is something electric about him. I can't help myself. For once, I put everything aside and just sit there and listen.
>
> He eschews the typical party line and talks about not choosing between Martha and Mary, but integrating both of those aspects within ourselves. . . . The goal, he says, is for each of us to struggle constantly with the Martha and Mary within ourselves, to balance the real and present demands on our time and energy with the need to let go, to reflect and listen, to be always open to the divine.[111]

Manning says she has an experience she has never had before: she feels that the message is for her, and it makes her uncomfortable. After the mass, she approaches the priest, not knowing why. She introduces herself: "I am Martha Mary."

> He grins and takes both my hands, pulling me close to him. He stares me dead in the eyes and asks, "Did you hear what I said?"
> I nod and tell him it was very good. But he waves away the compliment. Instead, he squeezes my hands and says, "Someday

---

111. Manning, *Undercurrents*, 18.

you will do more than hear. You will understand. And when you do, that message will explode in your head and your life will never be the same again."

I just stand there, staring at him. Other people begin to approach. He kisses my forehead, lightly, almost like a blessing, and says, "Good-bye, Martha Mary."

All I can do is nod. I feel like I have just spent a couple of minutes in the *Twilight Zone*. . . . I know this absolute stranger has told me something important, but I don't know what it really means.[112]

Manning opens her memoir with her slip falling down to her ankles while she is caring for her young patient Stephanie. She closes it by telling us about—after getting back on her feet after her depression—taking a five-day retreat at Holy Cross Abbey. She has been there before and told us near the beginning of the memoir about an earlier retreat. "It is like coming home," she says, and Brother Francis greets her: "You been doin' okay?" At vespers the first night, there is, like always, the ringing of the bells, and the monks chanting "O, Lord, come to my assistance. Make haste to help me." With a voice that is "vibrant and strong," an old monk reads from Psalm 56.

> You have kept an account of my wanderings;
> You have kept a record of my tears;
> Are they not written in your book?
> For you rescued my soul from death,
> You kept my feet from stumbling,
> That I may walk in the presence of God
> And enjoy the light of the living.[113]

I struggle to keep from losing it. I am so moved by the words. Then the second reading: the story of Martha and Mary. Jesus says, "Martha, Martha, you are anxious and troubled about many things . . ."[114]

It was the same reading that had been so important in the powerful but puzzling interaction with the priest that Sunday morning months ear-

---

112. Manning, *Undercurrents*, 19.
113. Psalm 56:8, 13.
114. Manning, *Undercurrents*, 190, 191.

lier! Now, after having been through depression, after having things "explode" in her head, she was embodying the message that she heard as a call to her from within his sermon: more balance, more letting go, more reflection, more openness to the divine.

Religious professionals play intriguing cameo roles like this in the memoirs we have been studying. Not many have the unifying significance played by the priest who preached to Martha Mary about being Martha *and* Mary. Henri Nouwen's two spiritual guides led him through his wilderness: they "did not leave me alone and kept gently moving me from one day to the next, holding on to me as parents hold a wounded child."[115] But most appear in much smaller roles. In all cases, their way of being points beyond human capacities to something greater. William Hulme remembered with appreciation that though in the depth of his depression he sent his pastor away repeatedly, the pastor kept returning, never personalizing the rebuff, his gentle reappearance always suggesting the endlessness of love in the divine.[116] The significance of their pastor's care is signaled by Lloyd and Gwendolyn Carr's dedication of their memoir to him. The few of his activities they mention are notable: he goes with their son to identify their son's wife's body; wordlessly, he embraces and walks with them after the funeral. The pastor's presence points beyond himself to a divine presence that pervades, quietly, faithfully, and with no demands, the most excruciating of our experiences. Albert Hsu is moved to realize that one of his pastors—on the pastor's birthday—traveled a significant distance to attend Hsu's father's funeral, even though his pastor had never met his father. The pastor's generosity and interest point beyond the pastor to the sacred value of every person, including those unknown to us.

---

115. Nouwen, *The Inner Voice of Love*, xvi.
116. Hulme and Hulme, *Wrestling with Depression*, 30, 71.

HEALING SPIRITUALITY

For our memoirists who are religious, spirituality and religion are closely related and complementary. But where memoirists are not religious, or where religion has failed them, "spirituality" addresses a realm of ultimate value much broader than—perhaps even unrelated to—institutional religion. For our memoirists who use the terminology of spirituality or the spiritual, it tends to refer to values and practices that cultivate meaning, help clarify priorities, promote holistic well-being, and honor that which is sacred or otherwise of precious value. Sometimes spiritual values and practices bring comfort, provide connection to caring others, testify to the importance of things unseen. But always spirituality is approached as a means of finding connection to passionate aliveness in and beyond the self. Spiritual matters also give hope, sometimes that their suffering might abate, but always that life can be meaningful despite suffering.

APPRECIATION OF SIMPLICITY

Simplicity is valued in many spiritual traditions and is often one of the first spiritual values to emerge for soul-sufferers in the process of healing. Simplicity is seen when sufferers begin to let go of grandiose dreams of cure and take heart instead in each precious small step of healing. Valuing simplicity enables sufferers to grasp less after sophistication and a relentless upward trajectory of success and accumulation, instead opening themselves to the deeper nourishment of everyday pleasures and modest accomplishments in the face of great odds. When Stewart Govig began to have simpler hopes for his son, he had what he calls "small wonders"—

like being able to see the enormous accomplishment it was for Jay to function well as the luncheonette cashier at the Rose Club, his day treatment program, and the pleasure and pride it gave him. Some days Martha Manning's depression left her unable to do or enjoy the "little things" in life; when the depression began to lift during her hospitalization and ECT treatments, she treasured Darnell, the recreation therapist, because he organized activities for the patients that were pleasurable simply for their everydayness—long walks around the neighborhood, eating popcorn and watching movies, conversations about the challenges and changes they were going through.[117] Because their lives are assailed by the unpredictable winds of psychic turmoil, many of our memoirists speak of heightened appreciation for the simple gift of a serene day. Illness makes wellness more precious: William Hulme was fortunate to find healing, and, the Hulmes say, "Life [after his illness] was so much more precious and enjoyable because of the contrast."[118] Lauren Slater says that when medication began contributing to her ability to heal, there were what she calls "genuine moments" when she experienced in a newly acute way, as if from an inner "ethereal ledge," the beauty of the world—"the purple silk of a plum, sun on a green plate." Maybe such genuine moments had always happened, she muses, "but I had never noticed them or given them their value."[119] Remarkably, more than a few memoirists speak not just of appreciation of the simple things but of considerable *gratitude* for them, and a few speak of consciousness of gratitude as a spiritual practice. David Waldorf, the artist and patient at Creedmoor State Hospital we met earlier, provides a modest and poignant example.

> I was an extremely suicidal person. . . . I could be dead in the bottom of some lake somewhere, I mean, who knows? What changed all that was that I heard a TV preacher—I was switching the channels around—and he said, "before you give into despair, thank God for every little thing." So I began to thank him for cigarettes, and for coffee, and small things like that, and it really helped.[120]

---

117. Manning, *Undercurrents*, 135.
118. Hulme and Hulme, *Wrestling with Depression*, 116.
119. Slater, *Prozac Diary*, 125.
120. Dawn Parouse, prod., Jessica Yu, dir., *The Living Museum* (Filmworks, 1999). Interview of David Waldorf.

HUMOR AND PLAYFULNESS

Humor and playfulness are not frequently seen as spiritual values. However, insofar as they are the tangible result of a sense of perspective and a decision to live life with some lightness and joy, they are precious spiritual values. Given that soul-suffering is sometimes quite disabling, sufferers in the process of healing can see the humor in very simple things, like silliness. Stewart Govig describes an occasion when he and Jay are at a buffet-style restaurant eating, as usual, in silence. All of a sudden, Jay asks his father if he has ever seen anyone slurp Jell-O. When Stewart's reply is no, Jay casts about a furtive glance to be sure no one is looking, lifts a couple Jell-O cubes with his spoon, and slurps them through his lips. "I was awarded with a broad, toothless grin. Childlike behavior for a thirty-something person, . . . yet I could not help joining his simple mirth."[121]

Sometimes the humor is healing because it puts very difficult things in perspective. After her first breakdown, Lizzie Simon is faced with returning to high school, at Providence Academy. Given what she had been through, she dreaded other students' curiosity. She consults a friend from school, Mindy, who has also been in and out of hospitals, for anorexia.

> "What do I tell people?" I moaned to her.
>
> She shrugged her shoulders. "Mitigating circumstances," she offered. "It works pretty good. Mitigating—you know, most people at Providence Academy get thrown off by the word 'mitigating.'"[122]

As we have noted, Sharon O'Brien is surprised that she gets so much out of the support programs run by MDDA—the Manic-Depressive and Depressive Association. One of things she gets out of it is some lightness of spirit about illness. For example, the MDDA logo has two words "unipolar" and "bipolar" (referring to the two types of bipolar illness) and two polar bears. One is seated, shivering, paws over its eyes. The other one is jauntily prancing in the sun, brandishing a walking stick, and looking ready to at any minute erupt into a dance routine. She goes to the annual summer picnic and finds that the centerpiece on the cake is a polar bear and that they are serving—what else?—Polar Cola. But

---

121. Govig, *Souls Are Made of Endurance*, 90.
122. Simon, *Detour*, 24

sometimes the playfulness and humor have a more serious, even political, purpose. As O'Brien's depression continued to abate, she was urged to "graduate" to the wellness group.

> I'd been resisting because I hate the world "wellness," but . . . [m]y depression was lifting a little and I wanted to start focusing more on prevention and coping. Besides, all the bipolars in Wellness gave the group a lot more energy.
>
> Most people in Wellness were suffering from chronic mood disorders and were working on managing them. They were all acquainted with grief but weren't giving up, so there was an atmosphere in the room of, if not hope, at least stubborn persistence, and sometimes a cathartic black humor. . . .
>
> At the break, I'm startled to hear people make mood disorder jokes. How many ECTs does it take to screw in a light bulb? asks Don, the group leader.
>
> I haven't heard the abbreviation before, but I catch on: ECTs must be people who've had electroshock treatments.
>
> "I don't know. How many?"
>
> "I forget." Everybody laughs.
>
> "I don't get it," I whisper to Charlie. "Memory loss, a side effect," he whispers back.
>
> "How many depressives does it take?" Don asks.
>
> "I give up," everybody says, playing the game.
>
> "None. They haven't noticed that the light has gone out."
>
> People say things casually to each other they'd find insulting in the outside world. . . . Making jokes is a way to take our power of naming back from the culture. It's also a way of reinforcing our momentary "outness."[123]

PARADOX

As we discussed in part 1, the capacity to tolerate and live wisely amid the ambiguity and paradox in life is a core characteristic of spiritual life. Where memoirs of soul-suffering describe healing, sufferers have typically found a place for ambiguity and paradox in their well-being. This portion of our study has shown many ways in which this is the case. For example, we have reflected on: the prevalence of hitting bottom as a part

---

123. O'Brien, *The Family Silver*, 254–55.

of climbing out of the tyranny of illness; the need to accept one's illness as a part of getting well; the requirement that healing include preparation for episodes of recurrence; religion's tendency not to vanquish suffering but to weave it into what Sharon O'Brien called "a greater [story]"; the value of playfulness and a sense of humor to contextualize the indisputably serious circumstances surrounding psychic turmoil.

We have also seen that soul-sufferers come to healing in part by coming to terms with the paradox that is part of being human. Whatever equilibrium Dan and Sue Hanson have been able to find in order to live with J's schizophrenia, it seems to have developed in part from receiving meaningful insights about social and religious issues from an illness they lament. Kay Redfield Jamison was able to accept the medication that tempered the most positive aspects of her mania by reckoning with the violence of her mania. Parker Palmer makes the point that making a place in consciousness for paradox is work.

> I now know myself to be a person of weakness and strength, liability and giftedness, darkness and light. I now know that to be whole means to reject none of it, but to embrace all if it.
>
> Some may say that this embrace is narcissistic, an obsession with self at the expense of others, but that is not how I experience it. When I ignored my own truth on behalf of a distorted ego and ethic, I led a false life that caused others pain—for which I can only ask forgiveness. . . .
>
> Others may say that "embracing one's wholeness" is just fancy talk for permission to sin, but again, my experience is to the contrary. . . .
>
> . . . Embracing one's wholeness makes life more demanding—because once you do that, you must live your whole life. . . .
>
> . . . I had failed to understand the perverse comfort we sometimes get from choosing death in life, exempting ourselves from the challenge of using our gifts, of living our lives in authentic relationship with others.[124]

As noted earlier, in wrestling with her depression, Rev. Susan Gregg-Schroeder uncovered several "gifts of the shadow" that ultimately nourished her life—body, mind, and soul. One of those gifts, she says, is

---

124. Palmer, *Let Your Life Speak*, 70–72.

"the gift of learning to live with paradox." Resistance of several specific paradoxes had contributed to her depression; healing required her to come to terms with the values of and interplay between good and evil, the known and unknown, *chronos* time (clock time) and *kairos* time (sacred time), relinquishing power and claiming power, independence and dependence, and doing and being. Like Palmer, Gregg-Schroeder emphasizes the challenge of living wisely with paradox—she reiterates the definition of paradox as "that which cannot be explained." Healing in face of paradox is not attainment "of a perfect balance, for balance is not a static point. It is a dance between two polarities." It requires, she says, tolerating the mystery of life's inconsistencies and contradictions as, when necessary, we patiently discern appropriate choices.[125]

CREATIVITY

Creativity plays a consistently important role in the spiritual lives and healing of soul-sufferers. For example, for many of our authors, the creativity of writing a memoir is not only a result of healing, but part of the process of healing; as we noted in discussing the motivations of memoirists, the memoirs' spiritual value range from profound levels of honesty and empathy to impassioned efforts to create more justice for the sake of the common good. Creativity is shown in the remarkably resourceful advocacy and love provided for primary sufferers by their loved ones. Shortly, we will reflect on the creativity inherent in the natural environment that soothes and inspires soul-sufferers, and on a creative range of ways in which soul-sufferers provide service to others. But most obviously and consistently, the creativity of art plays an enormous role in healing, with spiritual weight.

As is widely recognized, a remarkable number of soul-sufferers are famous, professional artists; less well understood is that many ordinary soul-sufferers become amateur artists. They have created a substantial body of visual art, music, and poetry, including the image on the cover of this book, as well as music and poetry.[126] Some of these artists find that art

---

125. Gregg-Schroeder, *In the Shadow of God's Wings*, 84.

126. See, for example: Parouse and Yu, *The Living Museum;* Nancy Glidden Smith, ed., *Sunshine from Darkness: The Other Side of Outsider Art* (Brea, Calif.: NARSAD Artworks, 1997); Harold S. Koplewicz and Robin F. Goodman, eds., *Childhood Revealed: Art Expressing Pain, Discovery, and Hope* (New York: Harry K. Abrams, 1999). See also NARSAD Artworks, "Museum-Quality Art Products by and on Behalf of Mentally Ill Persons," NARSAD Artworks, https://narsadartworks.org/ Default.aspx (accessed October 27, 2006).

provides them a spiritual value discussed in a later section—the value of doing meaningful work that makes a contribution to society. But the creation of the art is also a spiritual end in itself. Art provides a way to work with and communicate their suffering. Art is also a way of making visible to others the aesthetic that some sufferers experience in or through their suffering and healing. Art also provides a way to concretize their wisdom. This poem, "If I Played My Life," by Elizabeth MacDonell and the title poem of a collection of poetry by people with schizophrenia, illustrates all these purposes.

If I played my life on the viola
I'd scratch and pull
My smooth hair bow
Into tuneless, hopeless
Twentieth century
Disjointed, squealing
Painful music.
I'd play two types—
On and off pills.
On—long notes and sad,
Dreary low notes,
Wasting sounds.
Off medication,
I'd play the roof off
With angry short bursts
Blistering the paint
Like a sailor's language
Lit with liquor.
Music from high notes
Arpeggios down, down
To unmoving rests.[127]

The art world has noticed some of the visual art done by soul-sufferers; they have appropriately included it in the "outsider art" movement and displayed it in shows and galleries.

127. Elizabeth MacDonell, "If I Played My Life," in *If I Played My Life: Poems by People with Schizophrenia* ed. Kate Goldsmith (Calgary, Alberta, Canada: Bayeux Arts Incorporated, 1998), 12.

Whether or not soul-sufferers are artists, art plays an explicitly spiritual role. For a notable number of sufferers, art plays a central role in their spiritual practices. Illustrative of this role are the stories related earlier from Kathleen Norris and Martha Manning about incidents where worship music awakened and moved them at deep levels. Similarly, Meri Danquah tells how she uses music in her spiritual practice to ease the grip of suffering on her consciousness; she has a particular song that she uses as her morning prayer. "I . . . allow [the words] to reach out, like hands, and lift me to a more sacred state of consciousness."[128] For others, like Tracy Thompson, the arts give expression to their depths not because they are part of current spiritual practices but because they reference religious concepts familiar since childhood.

> And yet: I knew I was more than this sickness—though that was an insight that came only sporadically. Sometimes it came in the form of music, which I listened to like an aphasic person—mouth agape, struggling to find a word in the coils of my brain and finding instead a kind of wail. Others had found that wail, too, and transformed it. The "Lacrymosa" from the Berlioz *Requiem*, was my wild grief, the aria from Handel's *Messiah* could temporarily dissolve the stone that was my heart. "Comfort ye, comfort ye my people," sang the tenor, and aching and sweet melody, "and cry unto her that her warfare is ended, and her iniquity pardoned."[129]

But often the value of art to the soul is not limited to what we easily recognize as religion or spirituality. Occasionally, art plays a role in choosing life over death: we noted earlier the ameliorating effect on William Styron's suicidality of Brahm's *Alto Rhapsody*.[130] Sometimes, as in the case we noted earlier of Jane Kenyon's "Having it Out with Melancholy," poetry is powerfully consoling to people in psychic anguish because the poet, too, has been similarly debilitated; thus, the poetry conveys a familiar condition of soul, and also helps alleviate the existential aloneness profound suffering often causes. Similarly, just as her journey into madness was beginning, Kay Redfield Jamison was drawn to "Renascence," which was Edna St. Vincent Millay's first poem, published

---

128. Danquah, *Willow Weep for Me*, 16.
129. Thompson, *The Beast*, 57–58.
130. Styron, *Darkness Visible*, 66, 81.

shortly before the first of her several breakdowns and hospitalizations.[131] For still others, with just an image or a very few choice words, art is a way of visualizing or speaking the most essential aspects of issues in their lives. On a visit to the Frick Collection in New York City, Susanna Kaysen recognizes herself in a painting by Vermeer and finds the title of her memoir in the title of the painting: *Girl Interrupted at Her Music*.

> She was sad. She was young and distracted, and her teacher was bearing down on her, trying to get her to pay attention. But she was looking out, looking for someone who would see her.[132]

Or, creativity momentarily anesthetizes pain: for Roberta Bondi, the beauty of creation in nature and music "got her through" her childhood and adolescence.

> Sometimes, when I hurt so much I could hardly bear it, I would experience something through the medium of beauty that for a moment would simply annihilate my pain and longing and help-lessness. Then, the sunlight coming through a glass of water, or a single note of my flute would flash out with a power that would flood me with fierce happiness.[133]

Karen Armstrong found the title for her memoir and, arguably more significant, "the first flicker of true recovery"—in a poem. Not too long after her suicide attempt, she went to hear a lecture on T. S. Eliot's "Ash Wednesday." The lecturer pointed out that though the poet says repeatedly, "I do not hope to turn again," that is exactly what he is doing, slowly turning and gradually gaining perspective, as on a spiral staircase, which thus serves as a symbol of "spiritual progress and illumination."

> But what thrilled me most about Eliot's poem were the words "because" and "consequently." There was nothing depressing about this deliberate acceptance of reduced possibilities. It was precisely "because" the poet had learned the limitations of the "actual" that he could say: "I rejoice that things are as they are."

---

131. Jamison, *An Unquiet Mind*, 72–73.
132. Susanna Kaysen, *Girl, Interrupted* (New York: Vintage Books, 1993), 167.
133. Bondi, *Memories of God*, 154–55.

Because I cannot hope to turn again
Consequently I rejoice, having to construct something
Upon which to rejoice[134]

"Having to construct something upon which to rejoice"—the phrase described just what she felt herself to be doing, and it also reflected the realism and effort required for rebuilding her life.

The story of David Waldorf shows most of these themes woven together. As noted previously, for most of his adult life he has been a patient at Creedmoor State Hospital in Queens, New York. In the mid-1980s, two artists-turned-psychologists employed at Creedmoor started a program in which patients were invited to spend most of their time making and talking about art. The project mushroomed—soon so many patients were participating and creating so many sizable and interesting pieces of art that an old dining hall on the campus was converted to a larger studio and art storage facility. They also decided to make the art available for viewing at what they called the Living Museum; some of the art was also shown at a gallery in New York City. The Academy Award winning documentary filmmaker Jessica Yu made a film about the program, and Waldorf was one of the artist-patients featured. "Art is very prayerlike for me," he says. "I see no difference in praying and art because I try to celebrate life with prayer." In his interview, he addresses not only how art can be both means and end to spiritual expression and growth, but also how the last theme we addressed—living with paradox—is at the heart of his artistic mission.

> Art reminds us that our lives are beautiful, that our lives are spiritual, that our lives have meaning. I think that's what art is all about. I think it's just about living . . .
>
> Art helps me to see the trial and error of living, the trial and error of spirituality. In art there is trial and error. It's the whole process of making something out of nothing, or good from evil. My artwork is an attempt to show the beautifulness of ugliness. I try to get a raw edge and yet I try to somehow make an aesthetic of beauty out of it.
>
> Beauty is always involved with ugliness, and life is always involved with death. We have to find out the harmony and the

---

134. Armstrong, *The Spiral Staircase*, 139–44. The quotations are from pages 140, 141–42.

balance to make it . . . artful. The ugly poor person, the old ragged woman, is really a beautiful thing. There is good from evil. The sinner should be forgiven.[135]

NATURE

Like creativity, the natural environment is referenced often as a source of spiritual value in the lives of numerous memoirists. It is often the subject of the artistic creativity we have just noted: Zelda Fitzgerald, for example, became a prodigious artist in the last fourteen years of her life; after three breakdowns, she spent the remainder of her life at Highland Hospital in Asheville, North Carolina, where she painted the nearby mountains in which she hiked most days.[136] In something like an extended walking meditation, Terry Osborne ended up mapping his internal landscape, which was shaped by depression, through twelve years of intense exploration of the Vermont landscape around his home, and vice versa.[137] Physical activity in nature was partly responsible for John Tsai finding some degree of healing; suffering from schizophrenia, he was coaxed back to meaningful activity and relationship largely by his sister Tammie's encouragement to hike, with her and as part of the Chinese-American Outdoor Club.[138] Nature provides elegant and stirring beauty, which can soothe the deepest despair, as was the case when Martha Manning's belief in G-d was nourished again and again by the sight of those stars deep inside red tulips. Nature gives images for healing meaningful enough, for example, to be chosen as title for a memoir: melancholia is *Where the Roots Reach for Water*.[139] In the grip of postpartum depression, the simple act of washing Swiss chard, and appreciation for its loveliness, helped Kimberlee Conway Ireton glimpse a world far outside the terror in which she was trapped.

---

135. Parouse and Yu, *The Living Museum*. Interview of David Waldorf.

136. Eleanor Lanaham, ed., *Zelda, An Illustrated Life: The Private World of Zelda Fitzgerald* (New York: Henry N. Abrams, 1996), 62–69.

137. Terry Osborne, *Sightlines: The View of a Valley through the Voice of Depression* (Hanover, N.H.: University Press of New England, Middlebury College Press, 2001).

138. Tammie Tsai, "Climbing to the Summit with My Brother John," *Journal of the California Alliance for the Mentally Ill* vol. 10, no. 1 (March 28, 1999): 48–50.

139. Jeffrey Smith, *Where the Roots Reach for Water: A Personal and Natural History of Melancholia* (New York: Farrar, Straus and Giroux; North Point Press, 1999).

I became aware of how beautiful it was—the crinkly green leaves with their bright red veins, the thick yet silky texture of the leaf as I gently pulled apart each fold to wash inside it, the way the leaves glistened in the sunlight slanting through the kitchen window. . . . Time seemed to stop—or at least cease to matter—as I wondered at the beauty of the chard. . . .

It didn't instantaneously end my depression and bring me to a place of joy. But it stirred my desire to live. It enticed me to notice and pay attention to the world around me. And at a time when I felt hopeless, this moment of mystery gave me hope that there is more to life—my life, the life of the world—than usually meets the eye, or the ear, or any of my physical senses. In the moments when the veil parts, we see the not-yet now, we glimpse the mystery and beauty at the heart of all that is, we see things as they really are and not as they usually appear.[140]

Some reach beyond the beauty and life in nature for nature's full ecology; seldom referenced in a romantic way, nature is drawn upon often for its complexity—full of extremes, paradoxes and, especially, its cycles of dying and rebirth. When Kathleen Norris's depression cycles into activity, she says, "I die down to the roots to wait it out."[141] When Albert Hsu offers to other sufferers an image of what to expect from their grief and how to make their way through, he turns to Minnesota winters.

The wind-chill factor falls so far below zero that merely taking a breath brings sharp pain to your lungs and makes your nostrils freeze up. . . . The dark skies, icy streets, and arctic winds [make] it nearly impossible to travel anywhere or even to see where to go. . . .

. . . It can be hazardous to venture outside after a new snow. . . . If the top layer of the snow is crusted over with ice, the surface appears deceptively solid. . . .

. . . It's always easier to walk through snowdrifts if you place your feet in the footsteps of those who trudged through earlier.[142]

---

140. Kimberlee Conway Ireton, "Waking to Mystery," *Weavings* vol. 21, no. 1 (Jan./Feb. 2006): 19, 22.
141. Norris, *Cloister Walk*, 130.
142. Hsu, *Grieving a Suicide*, 11–12.

Singer/songwriter Judy Collins lost her son to suicide. She composed a haunting song about her grief and struggle to survive, and it centers on nature's use of lying fallow. Wise farmers know that fields must sometimes go unplanted, unproductive, and "wasted," their nutrients waiting to be renewed by the cycle of seasons. Her lyrics capture that, as a field lies fallow, even in the harshest winter conditions, the soil is preparing itself for new life. This natural phenomenon seems to show Collins a way to survive but perhaps also to hope for some healing in herself—during her harsh winter season, the fallow earth "dreams of violets."[143]

As she drives through them during her road trip, the canyons of the Southwest put Lizzie Simon's struggle into a bigger context, and teasingly summon her to life. "Things are really different after my detour, mostly because I am ready for them to be different. I feel a solid foundation within me; I remember the canyons."

> The canyons are gorgeous. They're sitting there where they've been forever, watching kids like me roll by, and they're like, yup, dummy, it's your life; take it easy, all right?
>
> The canyons communicate with me:
> You're in charge, they say.
> We trust you.
> We know you know how to get things done. . . .
> You know how to say no and how to say yes. . . .
> You can let the right people in.
> You can show the wrong people out.
> We know you can ask for help. And for company. . . .
> This is an adventure. Your adventure. You can enjoy this.
> You have the power to forgive yourself.
> To stand by yourself.
> To be close to people.
> To cry all you want. We don't care.
> You have all the wisdom you need.
> Just listen harder.
> Look more closely.[144]

---

143. "The Fallow Way," music and lyrics by Judy Collins, from the album *Forever* (The Wildflower Company/ASCAP, 1997).
144. Simon, *Detour*, 203, 174, 197–98.

GENUINENESS

The message Lizzie Simon took from the canyons—"You have all the wisdom you need. Just listen harder. Look more closely"—suggests a recurrent theme in memoirs of soul-suffering. If it is sincerely engaged, soul-suffering can sometimes assist in the development of genuineness, integrity, authenticity—qualities understood by many religious traditions to be fruits of spiritual practice and maturity. Many soul-sufferers find that in order to be well, they must fight for honesty, which means fighting against the socialization so many of us receive to be less than we are and can be. Most of us have experienced some form of proscribing, cultural indoctrination; Tracy Thompson describes hers.

> My indoctrination as a Southern female had taught me there was no benefit in real honesty when something more comfortable would suffice. Better to keep quiet—or, if you had to talk, to say something that someone wanted to hear, something that might get you what you wanted. This approach to life didn't actually ban honesty outright; what you meant to say and what the other person might find pleasing could occasionally coincide. But the main thing was to say what was necessary, or socially acceptable, or expedient.[145]

Like the writer Lesley Dormen, who says depression "was the crucible, the rite of passage, that allowed me to create my life,"[146] some memoirists convey that if they wrestle with their soul-sickness, it can make them less false, more genuine. Parker Palmer:

> When people ask me how it felt to emerge from depression, I can give only one answer: I felt at home in my own skin, and at home on the face of the earth, for the first time.
>
> Florida Scott Maxwell put it in terms more elegant than mine: "You need only claim the events of your life to make yourself yours. When you truly possess all you have been and done . . . you are fierce with reality."[147]

---

145. Thompson, *The Beast*, 177.
146. Lesley Dormen, "Planet No," in *Unholy Ghost*, 241.
147. Palmer, *Let Your Life Speak*, 70, citing Florida Scott Maxwell, *The Measure of My Days* (New York: Penguin Books, 1983), 42.

Rev. Susan Gregg-Schroeder found that wrestling with her depression eventually yielded genuineness—which she calls "the gift of authentic self." Healing from her depression required mental health treatment, but it also involved the spiritual work of re-creating a holistic consciousness aware of connections between parts of herself that dualistic thinking had made to seem opposed. Several approaches fueled the fire of genuineness, she found: living in ways that respected the unity between her mind, body, and spirit; showing honor toward herself; observing the renewing practices of Sabbath time; developing ways to listen to her inner process, such as through dreams and reflective writing; building relationship with selected symbols that spoke to her and pointed the way to deeper understandings and continued the growth of her genuineness.[148]

SERVICE

One of the spiritual values that predominates in our memoirists' processes of healing is the importance of meaningful work and service to others. In a remarkable number of cases, survivors find ways to make a contribution to the common good; this service to others both enables and sustains their recovery. As one survivor put it, "I am coming to believe that the best way to accept my illness is to make it useful."[149]

Of course, our memoirists serve the community of soul-sufferers by producing their memoirs. But most of them do more. Some offer service through their employment, others through volunteer work. Some do service not directly related to their experience with soul-suffering; when the journalist Tracy Thompson found that her healing was yielding extra energy, she volunteered to mentor a high school student. But the work was part of her healing, too, because it kept her wrestling honestly with both her abilities and limitations to be of help.[150] However, the majority of our memoirists who find some degree of healing offer their efforts in the area of mental health. These efforts range from one-time projects to careers, from simple tasks to complex organizations, from local contributions to more far-reaching ones. The size or sophistication of the service does not matter much relative to the healing, and its value is more profound than

---

148. Gregg-Schroeder, *In the Shadow of God's Wings*, 69–77.
149. "Anonymous," "Birds of a Psychic Feather," *Schizophrenia Bulletin* vol. 16, no. 1 (1990): 168.
150. Thompson, *The Beast*, 269ff.

even the self-respect, structuring of time, or income made possible by service to others. The value of service is healing at the level of soul—it gives purpose to lives pervaded by suffering, it enables sufferers to give help and not only receive it, it provides a meaningful and dignified connection to others, and it yields a more whole and complex perspective on human experience and one's place in the human community. Jay Govig's work in the café associated with his day treatment program illustrates the most fundamental level of the value of work and service to others. Again we encounter a situation where the spiritual practice of appreciating simplicity is part of healing: the achievement of this kind of work and service is simple by worldly standards. But the memoirists in our study who are parents of adult children with schizophrenia have made this point consistently and emphatically: the importance of meaningful work to persons most disabled by their illnesses cannot be overstated.

For most of our memoirists, a first step in providing service to the community of survivors is being willing to "come out" as a person who has a psychiatric disorder or has survived some other form of debilitating soul-suffering. Sharon O'Brien was encouraged in her willingness to tell her story by the remarkable example set by her father. In 1952, just as he was getting back on his feet again after two years of disabling depression, he was asked to write a report of his activities for the reunion of his graduating class from Harvard University. As we would expect, most reports from his classmates were jocular accounts of professional and social accomplishments. Though directed to start their accounts with "Career," her father began his by relating a passage from a book he was reading, Marquand's *Melville Goodwin, U.S.A.* The narrator of the book makes a statement that, her father noted, "certainly applies to me": "Life makes almost everyone into something that he never exactly wanted to be, and then the time comes when he can't very well be anything else." He goes on:

> If a depression had not rooted me out of Boston and advertising work and transplanted me to Elmira and radio broadcasting, I shouldn't have met and married an Elmira girl with whom I have been living happily ever after, together with three increasingly congenial children. And if I hadn't guessed badly in the choice of a new job, . . . I probably shouldn't have dipped as deeply into matters spiritual as I have since, to my ever increas-

ing inner satisfaction. So, although J. P. Marquand's quotation has reminded me that Life seems to have made me into something that I never exactly wanted to be, I have no kicks.[151]

Sharon's father's testimony exemplifies the service done through the countercultural act of telling, simply and with genuineness, the story of one's suffering and what one has learned from its course. A proud daughter comments on the service her father provided through telling his story to his Harvard classmates:

> For my father to have written about the dark side of the American dream in a class report—a genre in which men even more than women tend to list their professional accomplishments, or not respond to at all—that's gutsy. To admit to the stigmas of depression and unemployment in 1952—that is to honor the truth of one's experience more than the opinions of others. My father must have decided that if he were going to write this report at all, he would have to write something real. I also believe he knew that others in his class might share parts of his story, and so he might be able to put into words something they could not express but would understand, and be comforted by.[152]

Sharon O'Brien implies that when it was time for her to "go public" with her illness, her father's example gave her courage. When it was "MDDA Night" at a concert of the Boston Pops orchestra, Sharon O'Brien went and sat with the group from her chapter of the Manic-Depressive and Depressive Association. Well aware of the stigma, she still found herself "hardly daring to hope" that there would be a banner proclaiming their presence, just like those announcing the presence of "Raytheon" and "The Matignon Alumni Association." "Would MDDA really be that bold, to have a banner spread out over the second balcony in snooty Symphony Hall . . . ?" She was relieved when she saw it draped in front of the MDDA section: *Depression: It's an illness, not a weakness.*[153] Telling their stories is an important part of battling both social stigma and internalized stigma for many of our memoirists. For example, psychologist Frederick Frese says he

151. O'Brien, *The Family Silver*, 164, 169.
152. O'Brien, *The Family Silver*, 170–171.
153. O'Brien, *The Family Silver*, 261–62.

published his story about living with schizophrenia in a national magazine as "an attempt to make one little step toward breaking through the walls of silence that have been standing between us and the world of those of you I have come to call *'chronically normal people.'*"[154]

Many memoirists make direct contributions to the mental health of others. Lois Bloom, who encourages suicide survivors to "grab hold of what has happened to you and to do something in spite of it,"[155] has spent the decades since Sammy's death participating with her husband in suicide research and support groups for survivors. People moved by William Styron's memoir wrote and telephoned him; "Almost every day," Rose Styron wrote before his death in 2007, "Bill is in contact with fellow depression sufferers."[156] As in the case of Frese and Norma Swetnam, some survivors become mental health professionals because of their experiences with psychic turmoil. Similarly, Marie Balter, who is diagnosed with schizophrenia and spent the first twenty years of her life on the back wards of a psychiatric hospital, determined to become a mental health professional and has served as a noted consumer-advocate for change in the treatment of the chronically mentally ill.[157] The memoirs of psychologists who become ill and then return to work—Manning, Slater, Jamison—show the many ways they use what they learn through their suffering to improve mental heath care for everyone. The same happens in another professional field—ministry—as we have seen in the witness of Anton Boisen, Lucy and William Hulme, Stewart Govig, Parker Palmer, Roberta Bondi, and Howard Stone. Similarly, Rev. Harry Emerson Fosdick was among the first to articulate that preaching offers opportunity for, among other things, a ministry of counseling; his commitment to offer such a ministry through preaching was undoubtedly a service made important to him by his own breakdown.[158] Having experienced how much help religious communities need to respond more appropriately to soul-sufferers, Rev. Susan Gregg-Schroeder has developed

---

154 Frederick J. Frese, III, "A Calling," *Second Opinion* 19 (January 1994): 12.
155. Bloom, *Mourning, After a Suicide*, 20.
156. Rose Styron, "Strands," in *Unholy Ghost*, 136.
157. See Marie Balter and Richard Katz, *Nobody's Child* (Reading, Mass.: Addison-Wesly, 1987). Balter's life was portrayed by Marlo Thomas in *Nobody's Child* (Gaylord Productions, 1986).
158. Harry Emerson Fosdick, *The Living of These Days: An Autobiography* (New York: Harper and Brothers, 1956).

a new organization, Mental Health Ministries, which offers a growing body of educational and liturgical resources to congregations.[159]

Primary sufferers and their loved ones also join together to provide service to others. The National Alliance on Mental Illness (NAMI), which is said to be the largest advocacy and support organization dealing with mental illness, was founded and is staffed mostly by primary sufferers and family members. Primary sufferers and their loved ones have also founded and/or worked with similar organizations that address specific illnesses. Such organizations provide the service of national networks of advocacy and support that offer to survivors the profound comfort of realizing they are not alone in the struggle with psychiatric disorder. But such organizations also become powerful forces for systemic change as family members and primary sufferers speak publicly—to mental health professionals, the media, lawmakers, religious leaders—about the dearth of services, unjust distribution of public funds, and the myths and mentalism that lead to the stigma they and their loved ones suffer. Family members and primary sufferers also organize to assure needed research happens. They organize fund-raising walks all over the country, for example, but they also use their personal resources and connections. For example, in recent years several parents of autistic children set in motion a chain of events that raised private and public funds to form the M.I.N.D. (Medical Investigation of Neurodevelopmental Disorders) Institute in Sacramento, now one of the leading autism research facilities in the United States.[160]

Dr. Frederick Frese's delusional paranoia surfaced in the form of a belief in his being called to special missions; later he lets go of his delusions but not of his belief in his having a mission. "I am quite certain we each have our own Inner Light. We are each given our special mission; finding it can be a most wonderful, but also perhaps terrifying, experience."[161] Frese is right that sometimes the sense of having a mission, the intuition that one can and wants to try to make a difference for others, is unnerving, in part because healing is often partial. But what is more re-

---

159. See the appendix for more information about Mental Health Ministries and other religious advocacy and support ministries.

160. For more information, see the website for the M.I.N.D. Institute at the University of California at Davis: http://www.ucdmc.ucdavis.edu/mindinstitute (accessed August 29, 2006).

161. Frese, "A Calling," 25.

markable is how so many people who have been brought low by psychospiritual suffering—primary sufferers and family members—find the generosity and strength to work on behalf of others. Service to others is for some soul-sufferers a result of healing, but for many, it is also a means of healing.

HOPE

Throughout our discussion of what soul-sufferers have found to be the building blocks of healing amid chronic psychic turmoil, we have implicitly been building a case for hope. As we noted early on, many of the building blocks of healing amid soul-suffering can seem to be relatively small steps, not very significant in themselves. But now at the end of our discussion of healing, looking back, we can say that when put together, step after step after step, they constitute something quite remarkable and, from a spiritual point of view, essential for life: the construction of meaning, the accumulation of reasons to go on living and, thereby, the strengthening of one's hope. Given the devastating and chronic nature of soul-suffering, it is not surprising that the issue of hope is threaded through many memoirs. Soul-sufferers who speak of hope usually make the point that their soul-suffering has forced them to see hope in new ways. Most memoirists who discuss hope take pains to differentiate their hope from wishful thinking, as is demonstrated in the comments below from Albert Hsu and Dan Hanson: hope must take fully into account the realities of mental illness and other forms of soul-anguish. But neither need hope be captive to those realities. Albert Hsu summarizes the newness in his understanding of hope as seeing the difference between hope as a verb and hope as a noun, a differentiation that his religious orientation helps him to grasp.

> Most people use *hope* as a verb: "I hope things will turn out better" or "I hoped he wouldn't do this." When *hope* is a verb, it is usually just wishful thinking on our part. We crank up our feelings and try to generate enough emotional or mental energy to bring something into reality. Such hope is only a human activity, limited by our finitude.
>
> But the Bible uses *hope* as a noun. "For most people, hoping is something that they *do*, but the Bible talks about hope as some-

thing they can *possess*." Hope, in the Christian sense of the word, is far more than a wish or a dream. It's a tangible thing, as real as any object. *"We have this hope* as an anchor for the soul, firm and secure" (Hebrews 6:19). Our hope is a noun, as solid as a cast-iron anchor.[162]

For Hsu, the "anchor" of his hope is the promise of resurrection. For Dan Hanson, the cast-iron anchor of his hope is love. Hanson captures the evolution in hope experienced by many soul-sufferers.

> When J was first diagnosed with mental illness we hoped that he would recover from his illness and become just like the rest of us. How naïve we were to think that we could mold someone into our likeness! Through our struggles we have learned to accept J and his beliefs and a new definition of hope has emerged. The hope that I am referring to is closer to love than it is to wishful thinking. It is a hope grounded in reality, yet lifted by a vision of a world wherein there is room for J and others like him. It is a way of looking at hope that is best described by the Biblical evangelist Paul when he writes, "Love bears all things, believes all things, hopes all things, endures all things . . . love never ends."
>
> Our love for J will never end, and therefore our hope will endure.[163]

Hanson emphasizes the hope engendered by his family's love for J, but embedded in his words are another dimension of the love that is a bedrock for hope—the contribution that any of us can make through our loving concern to creating "a world where there is room for J and others like him." Discussions of hope often assume that the responsibility for reason or capacity for hope lies with the sufferer. But as in any situation where hopelessness is created or exacerbated by marginalization, the responsibility for hope lies as well with those who can help increase reasons for hope by diminishing our bigotry and indifference and increasing the resources—caring relationship, work, housing, treatment—that make healing and hope more possible.

❁

---

162. Hsu, *Grieving a Suicide*, 134.
163. Hanson, *Room for J*, 120.

Every small or simple step toward healing—all these bits of acceptance, healthy habit, purpose, connection, professional help, authenticity, loveliness, value—they become little things to believe in, reliable articles of faith. In a realm of life in which so much is unknown, this is not a faith based on certainties, but it is a sturdy commitment nonetheless. As Joshua Wolf Shenk puts it,

> I look for help in therapy, in relationships, and faith in its broadest sense—the faith of the gardener, the faith of the lover, the faith of the writer. The faith that I can experience what is real about the world, that I can hurt plainly, love ravenously, feel purely, and be strong enough to go on. . . .
>
> In contrast to the smug assurance that passes for faith on the "700 Club," the truest faith reckons with uncertainty. It must account for the inevitable mystery, must survive the tension between the familiar and the shocking unknown (and the shocking unknowable).[164]

Shenk's words reflect the promise, poignancy, and unpredictability of healing. Healing is a delicate subject because it is so elusive for so many. But it is also true that many soul-sufferers do find different kinds and degrees of healing. In so doing, they build meaningful lives, and, in some cases, attribute a good portion of that meaningfulness to their struggle with suffering. In fact, more times than most of us would expect, memoirists say that their lives are more meaningful because of their illnesses and, for that reason, they would not give up their illnesses if they could. This is a remarkable claim, that soul-suffering can yield a life so worth living that some sufferers would not surrender their suffering, and we will explore it more extensively in the epilogue. Especially in the light of such affirmations, it is intriguing to consider what any of us might gain by considering the lessons learned from soul-suffering and the work of healing, and it is to that final question we now turn.

---

164. Joshua Wolf Shenk, "A Melancholy of Mine Own," in *Unholy Ghost*, 254, 255.

Epilogue:
Spiritual Wisdom for All of Us

*Please dig deeper and spend time
to understand the delicate information of
the delicate topics I write about.*

**—J Hanson, as quoted in his
father's memoir, Room for J**

In his memoir, Dan Hanson includes some of J's writings. Because J's sense of reality is not typical, some of his meaning is difficult to understand. As J himself observes, "I know that my writing style is not what most people consider perfect English literature." But, as in the experience of madness itself, clarity sometimes breaks through J's writing and delicate topics are broached.

> [Y]ou all have a hard time with change and proper growth.... The past here on earth is not that good so why do you rely on it so much and neglect and abuse the gifts of the present and the future as you do not create your own language, nor do you honor, respect and understand mine well enough. You all are so scared because you [do] not realize well enough that fear is ultimate evil....
>
> I know, and it has been said, that ignorance is the opposite of love; there is no love in ignorance. I believe that! If one ignores

something they cannot understand it ever, for they are pushing, sometimes, good things that are necessary to better their lives away from them.[1]

Understandably, most of us push madness away. We have seen that out of love for his son, Dan Hanson works diligently to overcome his ignorance about mental illness. In so doing, he has developed a growing sense that there might be something in the insights of those in psychic turmoil that the rest of us actually *need*.

> We call people like J "mentally ill." By labeling them, we excuse ourselves from their world. More importantly, we keep them from disrupting our well ordered and "in control" world. We fear the chaos that might ensue if we allowed them "in." But I am growing to believe with each passing day that our world needs to be disrupted. Perhaps we need people like J to remind us that we are not in control regardless of how much we'd like to think we are. Perhaps we need people like J to remind us that we truly are connected to the Universe, and that we do possess the power to change the world.
>
> I once heard a priest talk about his work with the poor. He said something I will never forget: "When Jesus reminded the disciple Judas that the poor are always with us, he was not saying this so that we should go out and save the poor, but rather that the poor might save us."[2]

Just as the capacity of the poor to save others in no way idealizes poverty, Dan's implication that something in the lives of soul-sufferers might "save" others in no way changes the fact that living with J's schizophrenia is mostly agonizing. Even with their love for him, it is hard to see anything of value in J's condition, much less to be open to any spiritual insights in it. But, amid the strain of loving and living with someone who resists treatment for schizophrenia and who thinks he is God, still, Dan says something meaningful beckons him from within J's experience. Dan does not claim to be sure of what it is. But interacting with J's world has

---

1. Daniel S. Hanson, *Room for J: A Family Struggles with Schizophrenia* (Edina, Minn.: Beaver's Pond Press, 2005), 96–97. Quoting from J[oel] Steven Hanson, "Guide to the Universe."
2. Hanson, *Room for J*, 100.

drawn Dan's attention to things of spiritual significance that are off-kilter in his own world. For example, as Dan says, most of us don't act with adequate mindfulness of the interconnectedness at the heart of the Universe, or of the extent to which we cannot exert control, or of the power we do have to create change.

Throughout this book, we have sought to better and more compassionately understand those affected by psychospiritual anguish. We have sought to identify wise insights and practices, in full consciousness of the anguish in which they are honed. The insights and practices soul-sufferers have developed for their own well-being are valuable and worthy of consideration in their own right. Still, we have also, indirectly thus far, studied memoirs produced by soul-sufferers in order that we might learn from them something of value for all of us, any person or community, whatever our relationship to soul-suffering. We have considered issues of identity: implicitly, we have been reminded to consider how any of us are more than the illnesses we have, and we have been offered social analysis to advance our ability to see when human sickness is not simply personal but also collective in its causes or effects. We have considered the suffering encountered in psychic turmoil: implicit in our examination of the nuances of soul-suffering are insights that equip us to engage all forms of suffering with more detailed understanding and, thus, more sensitive response. We have considered caregiving and care receiving: many insights have been implied about how to recognize when something intended as care might actually do harm, and about how to lend our support in any circumstance to the healing synergy of caring human relationship. We have considered healing itself: don't romanticize it, we are implicitly advised—then we might better discern when healing is emerging in humanity's lowest points and from modest but hard and steady work on many fronts—simple habits, strengthened relationship, care of mind, body, and soul.

As the book comes to a close, building on our work thus far, we will now consider more explicitly what insights and values encountered in the struggle with soul-sickness might yield spiritual wisdom that speaks to the soul of any person or community. Again, to pursue this line of inquiry is not to sidestep the fact that psychic turmoil is devastating. To the contrary, we will continue to respect the devastation by considering that the experience of soul-suffering, or those who endure it, might have something to teach all of us. Thinking in this more general way will draw our attention to several overarching themes. Some of the values we will consider we have encountered previously. Others have been threaded through our analysis in more subtle ways. Not surprisingly, spiritual wisdom excavated from soul-suffering tends to emerge as counterpoints to mainstream values.

- clarity, and also mystery
- center, and also margin
- health, and also infirmity
- ability, and also limits
- safety, and also sanctuary
- sanity, and also "divinest sense"

CLARITY, AND ALSO MYSTERY

Clarity plays a significant and valued role in the spiritual life. Not infrequently, clarity is a future consolation promised by spiritual teachings, as in this text so familiar to Christians—"For now we see through a glass, darkly; but then face to face: now I know in part; but then shall I know even as also I am known" (1 Cor. 13:11 KJV). Obviously, it is valuable to the life of the personal and communal soul to have a growing clarity about the world around us, to seek and develop deep knowledge of the many contexts in which we are located. Similarly, it is valuable to seek and develop clarity about the world within, to cultivate honest knowledge of our internal landscapes. Most personal and corporate prayer practices and other forms of meditation have clarity as at least one goal, partly because living without clarity is so difficult, but also as a way of growing toward this promised future understanding. Moreover, decisiveness and right action are essential aspects of a consistently spiritual life, and clarity of vision and conviction show the way to such action. In the same book in which he writes about his depression, Parker Palmer describes such a meditative process—the clearness committee—which he used to find clarity when faced with a difficult vocational decision.[3] In the Quaker tradition, when individuals are faced with a crucial decision, they are encouraged to assemble a group of selected advisors, with whom

3. Parker J. Palmer, *Let Your Life Speak: Listening for the Voice of Vocation* (San Francisco: Jossey-Bass, 2000), 44–46.

to meet. By interweaving questions, quietness, and conversation, the group constructs a discernment process that seeks that person's "truth and the right course of action."[4] It is often of life-saving importance not to settle for obfuscation where clarity is possible: for example, many of our memoirists told of refusing to give in to the confusion of the mental health system but rather pressing to get the information and treatment options they needed.

The value of clarity notwithstanding, it is also true that our lives are marked as much by mystery as by clarity. Life requires all of us to live with a discomforting amount of mystery in many areas of our lives. For example, so much about suffering is mysterious—its causes, timing, degree, and duration. Many of us live with the specific suffering of mysterious illness—pain in body and mind for which no name, cause, or treatment is known. Curing and healing is mysterious—why do some people heal when others don't? With so much mystery, some of which we expect, but some of which brings into question things we thought for sure were certain, is anything reliable? How are we to trust even love, given the frequency with which it falters? Some of us live with spiritual mysteries that cause turmoil in our souls: There is the mystery of purpose—does our living make any difference? The mystery of death is especially impenetrable—what happens to our loved ones and to us when breath leaves our bodies? Holiness is a mystery—is there a power greater than ourselves, and if so, what is its nature? Given their prevalence and seriousness, it is no wonder that most of us find it difficult to face directly into these mysteries. It is a challenge not only for "our culture," as Palmer describes, but also for us as persons, families, and communities.

> Our culture wants to turn mysteries into puzzles to be explained or problems to be solved, because maintaining the illusion that we can "straighten things out" makes us feel powerful. Yet mysteries never yield to solutions or fixes—and when we pretend that they do, life becomes not only more banal but also more hopeless, because the fixes never work.[5]

---

4. Jan Hoffman, "Clearness Committees and Their Use in Personal Discernment," Friends General Conference of the Religious Society of Friends, http://www.fgcquaker.org/library/fosteringmeetings/0208.html (accessed October 16, 2006).

5. Palmer, *Let Your Life Speak*, 60.

Yet memoirs of soul-suffering bear witness to the spiritual wisdom of engaging the true mysteries in our lives. Palmer's observation of the costs associated with trying to impose a resolution on that which is irresolvable—"life becomes not only more banal but also more hopeless, because the fixes never work"—turns us toward the potential of mystery's spiritual value. Those memoirists who have found some healing have developed the wisdom to know the difference between things that can be changed and things that cannot be changed. Like them, all of us do well to be continuously differentiating problems to be solved—that which can be "fixed"—and mysteries to be pondered, where "fixes never work." We all do well to follow our memoirists' example and never settle for uncertainty where care and healing are simply hidden. But we also do well, once mystery is discerned, to desist from trying to, as Palmer puts it, "straighten things out." This is because, as the lives of soul-sufferers remind us, our time is limited and our energy too precious to waste. From our memoirists we can learn the practical wisdom of discerning and engaging mystery for pragmatic reasons—we need to conserve, not throw ourselves away on "fixes" that aren't fixing anything. But there are also more beguiling reasons to stop fighting the mystery of life and to try to engage it: unexpectedly, mystery, once befriended, can make life less banal and more hopeful. Through the lives of our memoirists shines the paradoxical world of the spiritual: we tend to think that life is hopeless where human power is thwarted, but in and through mystery, we can sometimes find powers and other consolations.

We met Kimberlee Conway Ireton in our discussion of healing, where we reflected on the contrast between her postpartum depression and another dimension she glimpsed, unexpectedly, through the simple act of washing Swiss chard. That moment attuned her to others like it.

What I have since realized is that I do have these glimpses of the glory beyond, and that they are a mixed blessing. The parting of the veil fills me with awe and delights my soul, but it also opens in me a yearning, a deep and almost painful desire. For in glimpsing this fleeting beauty, I become aware of a mystery: I begin to sense that there is more to life than usually meets the eye. And in sensing this, I begin to yearn to enter more deeply into that mystery and to live in those moments that shimmer with a radiance beyond what we usually see or know.[6]

Mystery can lend to life an enticing profundity, a beguiling depth that is obscured where human knowledge prevails. Mystery can reveal that where we think we are broken or abandoned, something beyond human capacity holds us. The consolation of mystery can be so powerful that, once we have experienced it, we want more. Mystery is a mixed blessing in the life of the soul. But none of us can avoid it, and the shimmering moments it sometimes brings are a priceless counterpoint to the banality and hopelessness that infect us after desperate attempts to control the uncontrollable fail.

CENTER, AND ALSO MARGIN

The motif of "centering" is threaded through ancient and modern discussions of spirituality. Centeredness in image (mandalas, for example), centered consciousness (centering prayer, for example), centeredness in identity and action (centering oneself and focusing one's energies, for example)—all these speak to the priceless capacity of the center to provide stability amid hardship, focus amid distraction, and wholeness amid polarities. Similarly, we point toward the spiritual value of the center when we speak of creating more social justice so that those who have been marginalized will again have access to the center—to the center of community, center of concern, center of power.

The value of center notwithstanding, it is also true that marginality pervades life for most of us. Many of us are marginalized by systemic oppression and discrimination. Some of us live at the margins of our own communities because of shunning, banned by those at the center because of moral or other social judgments. More and more people are marginalized by the complex effects of immigration and now live far from the centers of power in both their old and new lands. Many are marginalized because their education is substandard. Still others have ample access to the centers of social life and power, but feel strangely marginalized because they find the life of privilege they lead dishonorable: empty of meaning, full of pretense, riddled with corruption. Of course, like our

---

6. Kimberlee Conway Ireton, "Waking to Mystery," *Weavings* vol. 21, no. 1 (Jan./Feb. 2006): 20.

memoirists, many of us are marginalized because we are ill, or marginalized by our illnesses. It is difficult to face into the extent of our marginality, much less to consider it a source of spiritual wisdom; most of us wish only to flee it and, to the degree that it is unjustly imposed upon us, we should flee it, if we can. As Emily Dickinson put it, sometimes we are unjustly marginalized—"handled with a Chain"—because we have dissented in some crucial way from the mainstream—"the Majority."

Yet memoirs of soul-suffering bear witness to the spiritual wisdom of engaging some of the marginality of our lives. As stories from other marginalized people and communities show, memoirs of soul-suffering provide evidence that marginal consciousness or marginal people sometimes discover and embody profound principles and practices, even under enormous duress, to an unexpected and valuable extent. Though most persons in psychic turmoil are socially ostracized to one degree or another, many have remarkable capacities to live faithfully, despite their decentered, marginalized condition. We began our reflections on identity in part 2 with reference to actor Margot Kidder's public breakdown, during which she wandered the streets in a mania-induced delusional state.[7] She wandered in the urban wilderness of Los Angeles for almost forty miles over about five days. With no food or money, she was fortunate to meet on the streets, as she describes them, "some of the most terrific people I've ever known," homeless people who, in spite of her delusions and vulnerability, she says, "absolutely took care of me." She remembers one man in particular, Charlie, whom she "would like to find and thank." She remembers Charlie saying to her gently, "You've been very confused" and offering to take her in for the night. On the way to his home, walking through poor urban neighborhoods, she remembers with some chagrin a few of her words to him—"Look, I don't know how to behave, I'm not from this kind of neighborhood"—and his reply—"*None* of us are *from* here." They arrived at Charlie's home, a cardboard shelter, and Kidder says, tearfully and with wonder in her voice, that he gave her all his blankets, and held her. We are told that the majority of homeless persons are crazy and, indeed, at the margin of society, Kidder runs into a person who does something that seems crazy by "normal"

7. Barbara Walters, "Interview of Margot Kidder," *20/20*, American Broadcasting Company, September 6, 1996.

standards—he gives shelter and other comfort to Kidder, a disheveled and troubled stranger: "I was in worse shape than most of them." And Kidder was drawn into the sacrificial generosity. Laughing, she says "the great tragedy" of the experience was that she exchanged "my best Armani suit—my *only* Armani suit!" for a homeless woman's used clothes. These persons at the margins of sanity and society practice classical spiritual values—giving shelter and clothing to people in need, giving away all one has to the poor.

Though not always so dramatically, memoirs of soul-suffering show that by engaging our marginality, we may find profound experiences for which we have yearned. None of this is rationalization for the bigotry and stigma that marginalizes sufferers. Rather, it is to say that in some contrast to common preferences for the center, at the margins, despite social disregard, soul-sufferers practice values worthy of emulation—as Kidder's story illustrates. There are many such stories. When Welton Gaddy and Tracy Thompson embraced the marginalization of being hospitalized, they found in a hospital with other psychiatric patients a quality of community and connection hard to find elsewhere. Kay Redfield Jamison's tribute to her mother is but one illustration of the deep love embodied by families who engage the turmoil rather than turn away from it; families' faithfulness to ill loved ones who are frequently in marginal as well as marginalized conditions sets an extraordinarily high bar for relational commitment. The sheer determination with which many primary sufferers who acknowledge their marginality work toward healing and make meaningful contributions to their families and communities far exceeds the contributions of some people who are not weighed down by illness and loss. When primary sufferers and their loved ones embrace their psychospiritual and social marginalization, they are more likely to benefit from or even join with vital communities, like NAMI, that provide many forms of support to consumers and their families. Time and time again soul-sufferers report that by joining such organizations they find hope and help beyond their expectations.

Engaging marginality often strengthens the whole and the center. As the prophetic tradition illustrates, we are more likely to work on behalf of the common good if we engage our marginality; when needed critique and/or reform of the center and social change happens, it is almost always because persons on the margins have ceased to be ashamed of their marginality and instead, with dignity and some pride, used it as a site of resistance and reform. Our discussion in part 5 of the service undertaken by soul-sufferers in the process of their healing illustrates vividly such work on behalf of the common good by marginalized persons. Remember, for example, the social advocacy organizations composed of people who have engaged the struggle of psychic and social marginality, which boldly work from the margins to critique and better equip mental heath professionals and religious communities to respond sensitively and effectively to soul-sufferers. Such groups are also steadily breaking down stigma against mental illness and other forms of emotional difference and speaking out about social sicknesses that cause or at least complicate psychic turmoil.

While these values can theoretically be embodied and enjoyed at the center, they tend to proliferate in conditions of marginality. One thinks of Jesus saying that it is not impossible for rich persons to enter the realm of G-d, but our possessions make it very difficult—like a camel passing though the eye of a needle (Mark 10:25). In our marginal and marginalized state, we have been relieved of many "possessions" but, with our social capital diminished and our needs more conscious, we are also likely to be freer to embody and expect principles and practices that honor the sacred nature of life.

HEALTH, AND ALSO INFIRMITY

It is of great spiritual value to practice good stewardship of our minds and bodies by warding off illness and pursuing health. Cultivating physical and mental health demonstrates appropriate respect for the gift of life. In a state of health, we have the potential to be less encumbered with self-care and therefore more engaged in the nurturance of the common good. It is not surprising that researchers can document the health benefits of prayer and participation in a congregation: for centuries, meditative spiritual practices and regular involvement in religious community have been developed to support health. We are fortunate to live in a time where our medical opportunities for health are regularly advanced, and our spiritual maturity is demonstrated in part by wise use of these resources: genetic testing for those who do not wish to pass on inheritable diseases through pregnancy; more effective approaches to cure and treatment of disease; not only traditional medical philosophies and practices, but alternative medicine. Good stewardship of the life entrusted to us involves trying to digest at least some of the avalanche of information provided to us about how we can protect the health we have or try to recover health if we have lost it—the best nutrition, forms of exercise, sleep patterns, amount of sun-exposure, environmental protections, even the patterns of relationship that seem to promote health. We have available to us myriad ways of pursuing spiritual health—better-than-ever access to the variety of the world's most enduring religious traditions as well as a plethora of new forms of spirituality. Spiritual wisdom requires that we not neglect the responsibility and means we have to cultivate health.

The value of health notwithstanding, it is also true that infirmity characterizes our lives at least as much as health. There is hardly a family anywhere that isn't coping with serious physical or psychiatric illness, and these illnesses actually dominate life for many of us. If we are not ourselves ill, then we are likely to be caring for a friend, child, partner, parent, sibling, or other relative that is ill. Many of the treatments we use to control or cure one form of illness make us ill in some other way. Ironically, the increasing capacity of medicine to extend our lives means that if we are not yet ill, our odds of living with illness steadily increase as we age. Beyond the illnesses close to home, our lives are affected by the illnesses of friends, neighbors, co-workers, and people at church—communities rally to help care for the sick, or pay for treatment insurance won't cover; even when we don't know the victim well, it can still break our hearts when others are struck down. The difficulties associated with being ill make it completely understandable not only that we avoid infirmity but also, if we cannot avoid it, we resist full consciousness of it.

Yet, memoirs of soul-suffering bear witness to the spiritual wisdom inherent in squarely facing our infirmity, and that of others. As we explored in part 5, their lives are clear evidence that, if illness of some kind has come into our lives, our healing depends to a large extent on our acknowledging and engaging our infirmity. The healing we find by engaging our illness is another way in which there can be spiritual wisdom in engaging our marginal and marginalized condition. As we have also seen, it is sad but true that illness sometimes makes us wiser about how to appreciate and make the most of health and healing; at least in periods when it is not completely disabling, being fully conscious of our infirmity may well motivate us to engage life with more focus and drive. In reflecting on a comment one of her friends sometimes makes to her—"You're one of the most amazingly productive people I know"—Lauren Slater says that it isn't so much her "partial 'cure'" that makes her productive but having experienced the marginalizing capacity of illness itself.

> It could be that my "amazing" productivity (completion of a doctoral program in two years, becoming a psychologist, director of the clinic where I now work, lecturer, writer, and furniture refinisher) is not so much due to my partial "cure" but to the experience of illness, of incapacitating OCD [obsessive-compulsive disorder], which still sometimes cripples me, and the full-time return of which I fear to the point of nightmares. My firsthand knowledge of psychological paralysis and death, and the sense I have that they may return, means that I must move, move now, grasp whatever I can, take in time as though it were in short supply. Which it is. Hungry and grateful, I feast.[8]

Similarly, infirmity can chip away at our tendency to deny our mortality, take the future for granted, and procrastinate about things that matter deeply. It can remind us that our time is limited and of the preciousness of every day. Suicide is incomprehensible to many of us, but many of us throw away our lives in other ways, at least to an extent, assuming that we can put off until tomorrow appreciation of the "small things" that we have noted are not at all small, in the light of infirmity. Edward Hoagland:

> What is more remarkable than that a tiny minority of souls reach a point where they [commit suicide] is that so few of the rest of us will splurge an hour of a summer day gazing at the trees and sky. How many summers do we *have*?[9]

Given these stakes, it is a bit less unpalatable that soul-sufferers bear witness to the possibility that our infirmity can be of some value to us. Lee Stringer, who has written about the twelve years he spent drug-addicted and homeless in New York City, says infirmity has some value if it forces us to reckon with time and the state of our souls. He uses one of his infirmities—depression—as an example.

---

8. Lauren Slater, *Prozac Diary* (New York: Random House, 1998), 194–95.
9. Edward Hoagland, *Tigers and Ice: Reflections on Nature and Life* (New York: Lyons Press, 1999), 39.

We, all of us, suffer some from the limits of living within the flesh. Our walk through this world is never entirely without that pain. It lurks in the still, quiet hours which we, in our constant busyness, steadfastly avoid. And it has occurred to me since [my depression] that perhaps what we call depression isn't really a disorder at all but, like physical pain, an alarm of sorts, alerting us that something is undoubtedly wrong; that perhaps it is time to stop, take a time-out, take as long as it takes, and attend to the unaddressed business of filling our souls.[10]

Of course, as our study has asserted many times, this "time-out" must not be romanticized, as it certainly was not for Stringer. Our constant busyness, our reluctance to pay attention to the alarm of illness is understandable in a way because, if illness becomes our teacher, it almost certainly will teach us truths that radically reform our lives, truths we would not have engaged voluntarily, as Parker Palmer found.

Finally, blessedly, I found a counselor who understood what was happening to me as I needed to understand it—as a spiritual journey.

Of course, it was not the sort of spiritual journey I had hoped some day to take, not an upward climb into rarefied realms of light, not a mountaintop experience of God's presence. In fact, mine was a journey in the opposite direction: to an inner circle of hell and a face-to-face encounter with the monsters who live there.[11]

Even more common than these essential values is that soul-sufferers who engage their infirmity often discover new kinds, and sometimes greater amounts, of intimacy in relationship. As we saw in our reflections on care that helps, we are more likely to experience profound connections with one another when we engage infirmity, rather than futile efforts to resist or resolve it. The notion that it is always better to give than to receive is instilled in many of us. That this is not always true confronts

---

10. Lee Stringer, "Fading to Gray," in *Unholy Ghost: Writers on Depression*, ed. Nell Casey (New York: Harper Perennial, 2002), 112–13. Among other works, Stringer is the author of *Grand Central Winter: Stories from the Street* (New York: Washington Square Press, 1999).
11. Palmer, *Let Your Life Speak*, 66.

sufferers who engage their infirmity; they find, as Welton Gaddy did when he confronted his depression, that sometimes it is as spiritually blessed to receive help as to give it.[12] Similarly, when family members engage infirmity, and offer to help with illness rather than fix it, very often their acceptance allows greater intimacy, as Martha Manning and her therapist-husband found.

> It was only when we both gave up the expectation that my husband could somehow "cure" me that we moved from pseudo therapy to true support. Instead of reaching out with well-intentioned "therapeutic" interventions, he shifted to questions like, "What would help right now?"[13]

Infirmity is always difficult. But memoirs of soul-suffering serve to remind us all of the irony that, when we face them, illness and other infirmities can bring us closer together, give us opportunity to give and receive profound levels of care, and in other ways awaken our souls to the preciousness of life. Since few of us will leave this life without knowing ill health or frailty of some kind, the spiritual wisdom of engaging infirmity is wisdom for all of us.

ABILITY, AND ALSO LIMITS

One of the goals of the spiritual life is to exercise to the extent of our abilities the gifts we have been given. In the previous section we noted that health has spiritual value, and this is in part because of the role it plays in our capacity to develop and exercise our abilities. It is a core value of human life that we mature those abilities, partly as ends in themselves— for the sheer delight of a task well done, artistry creatively accomplished, athleticism matured, intellect used in discovery. Our abilities also have spiritual value because, when exercised, they make it possible for us to take responsibility for the material support of our own lives and to make a contribution to the common good. Whether these contributions to the common good are local and modest or global and revolutionary, those who labor to develop what many see as "God-given" talent are rightly appreciated and honored.

---

12. C. Welton Gaddy, *A Soul Under Siege: Surviving Clergy Depression* (Louisville: Westminster John Knox Press, 1991), 127–39.
13. Martha Manning, "The Legacy," *Family Therapy Networker* (January–February 1997): 38.

The value of ability notwithstanding, it is also true that our lives are affected as much by our limits as by our abilities. Illness is a prevalent limit, as we noted in the previous section, but there are many others. Most of us are quite average in ability. Very few people's lives mirror the popular trajectory of success—a steady climb upward in our economic, educational, professional, and social capital. Most of are far more marginal than that; we are coping instead with plateaus and setbacks. These "failures" are sometimes due to limits in our abilities. But they are also due to real limits imposed upon us from external circumstances—economic downturns, unaffordable education, professional politics, social discrimination—to name a few of the forces that hem us in and limit our opportunity to fully develop our capacities. People with extraordinary ability or people who appear to be have limitless possibility are often idolized—the very rich, very talented, very powerful—but it is not uncommon that they seem to sabotage their own accomplishments: they live shallowly, expose themselves to addictions, spend themselves into bankruptcy, risk their freedom with criminal actions. We are constantly buffeted by existential limits: some relationships thrive and others fail, despite our best efforts; despite our desire that children should be able to live in safety, our capacity for peace is limited by our tendency to war; despite religion's power to do good, some people pervert religion into violence. We have many abilities, but human beings are also weak, vulnerable, and fragile. It is difficult to face into these limits. We perpetuate what is, for all but the most extraordinary, a myth: that "you can do anything you set your mind to."

Yet, memoirs of soul-suffering bear witness to the spiritual wisdom of engaging "life within limits," as Stewart Govig puts it. It was right to continue to seek the best treatment for his son Jay's schizophrenia, but eventually he found that it was also spiritually valuable to stop constantly expecting things of their son and of themselves that weren't possible. Unrealistic expectations wasted their energies, strained their relationships, bruised their spirits. For Govig, the religious notion of acknowledging human limits and trusting in a sacred benevolence made it more possible to mourn the loss of his son's emotional health and relinquish "the cultural dictates of success." But acceptance of limits did more: he found a sense of rebirth within a different framework of values.

Life within limits has become a vital reality and slowed down my pursuit of religious and psychological crutches. Anger recedes and the strangest reframing of all has taken place: rebirth within the boundaries of God's salvation. Lament has given voice to suffering and becomes the means to approach the One who can take it away. It spurs a movement toward God.[14]

Life within limits gave them their "first glimpse of Jordan"—the start of a new life on the other side of the death-dealing effects of schizophrenia—which was to begin to set new horizons within what was possible, and to value those more limited possibilities.

But our memoirists also note that what appears from outside an experience to be only disappointing limits and disability is often from within the experience a different and potentially grace-filled way of living. Henri Nouwen first says that it was strange that his breakdown occurred shortly after he had decided to live and work at L'Arche, a community where people with and without developmental disabilities live in mutual support of one another. But he also says some things that explain this "strange" concurrence. He found "true home" among these persons: "I had been received with open arms, given all the attention and affection I could ever hope for, and offered a safe and loving place to grow spiritually as well as emotionally." "Going to L'Arche and living with very vulnerable people, I had gradually let go of many of my inner guards and opened my heart more fully to others."[15] He elected to live within the limits imposed by developmental disability, with people in some ways quite vulnerable, fragile, and weak, and there Nouwen found an authentic, noncompetitive space that evoked new levels of honesty and authenticity in him.

The year that Martha Manning experienced her hospitalization was a hard year for almost every member of her family, she says—"the dissolution of a marriage and an engagement, depression, addiction, life-threatening illness, accidents, and the estrangement of one family member." On Thanksgiving Day that year, the whole family gathers, except

---

14. Stewart D. Govig, *Souls are Made of Endurance: Surviving Mental Illness in the Family* (Louisville: Westminster John Knox Press, 1994), 84.
15. Henri J. M. Nouwen, *The Inner Voice of Love: A Journey through Anguish to Freedom* (New York: Doubleday, Image Books, 1996), xiii–xiv, xv.

for the estranged one, and after the feast is on the table, Manning describes the family's efforts to pray. Her father makes the sign of the cross and expresses gratitude for the food. Then he says, "Lord, we thank you for the many ways in which you have blessed our family this year. . . ." Martha's sister Rachel tries to restrain herself but then bursts into laughter. "Dad, I'm sorry, but what are you talking about? This is the worst year this family has ever had!" For several minutes, others around the table express agreement with Rachel, and then Martha's mother says, "Well, at least we're all together." General agreement with her statement seems at first to settle things down, and they all bow their heads again. But then Martha's brother Chip protests, given that Sarah, one of the sisters, didn't show for the family gathering: "Wait a minute, . . . We're not all together." Martha remembers: "We laugh self-consciously, acknowledging the pain of the estrangement and the futility of our attempts to deny it." Several more minutes of discussion ensue about whether there is anything for which they can pray their thanks. Finally, Martha's brother Mark says, "I'm thankful that I survived this year. And I thank God that you all did too."

> My brother-in-law Darrell, who at the tender age of forty is recovering from vascular surgery, responds with a resounding "Amen!"
>
> We sit in silence for several moments, each of us absorbing my brother's words and applying them to our own situations. One by one, we offer our personal assent to his declaration. Chip yields the floor to my father, saying, "Take it, Dad. . . ."
>
> For the third time, my father bows his head, inhales cautiously, and prays, "God, we give you thanks that we survived this year. We pray for those who didn't and we ask for the strength to survive another year." We answer with a unanimous and enthusiastic chorus of amens.
>
> The food, by this point, is stone cold. But no one moves. We just look at each other, holding on to this moment, this connection, this prayer-by-consensus.[16]

Engaging the limits of the human condition can bring relief to our souls in many ways. It can give us rest from the relentless pursuit of being

---

16. Martha Manning, *Undercurrents: A Therapist's Reckoning with Her Own Depression* (San Francisco: HarperSanFrancisco, 1994), 147–49.

in some condition other than where we are. It can make it safer to be honest. It can foster an atmosphere characterized as much by relaxed humility as by hard-nosed competence. Instead of always working to develop our abilities, engaging our limits invites us to play more often. Engaging our limits encourages interdependence as much as self-reliance, and expands our attention beyond our own abilities toward powers beyond ourselves.

SAFETY, AND ALSO SANCTUARY

The spiritual value of safety is inarguable. Much spiritual teaching suggests that safety is an attribute of holiness or a consequence of being in the presence of the divine. Many religious practices have as an important goal the cultivation of the nonviolent human spirit that makes safety possible. One of the highest standards for human love is that we strive to provide safety to the ones we love—physical safety but also safety for the heart and soul. The provision of safety to children and other vulnerable people is a moral obligation—and in some countries, a legal obligation—binding on all societies and all responsible adults. Safety is the ideal condition for evoking honesty, deep reflection, and learning.

The value of safety notwithstanding, it is also true that danger and risk pervade our lives. Children and adults alike are regularly harmed by other people in places where they were supposed to be safe—homes, schools, churches, no-fire zones. Some of us have greater safety because others sacrifice theirs—soldiers, police officers, firefighters, for example—but still, there are accidents, natural disasters, illness, and many other kinds of violence from which we cannot protect one another. It is difficult to face into the full reality of our vulnerability. But perhaps the language of safety peppers our speech—safe spaces, safe houses, safe sex, safe conduct; safety belts, safety nets, safety valves, safety zones—precisely because we know the desirability but elusiveness of safety, because we live amid so much danger and risk.

Yet, memoirs of soul-suffering bear witness to the spiritual wisdom of facing into the reality of danger because it shows us the need, where utter safety is not possible, of giving to one another the holy gift of sanctuary. The intentional act of providing sanctuary to persons who are suffering or in danger is a highly valued practice in many religious traditions. Our memoirists have been confronted rather brutally with their incapacity to keep themselves or their loved ones safe from harm of psychic turmoil. But the lives of our memoirists remind us that, precisely because suffering and danger cannot always be averted, sometimes the most precious thing we have to offer one another is shelter in the storm. Perhaps it is the enormous grace of sanctuary that accounts for why some traumatized people survive and thrive if they have even one reliable, loving person in their lives. We noted earlier that when Lauren Slater tries to understand why she has found some healing in her illness, especially given the fact that so many others do not, she concludes that it has something to do with memories of even fleeting experiences of pleasure. But she also says that her capacity can be traced to another factor: "I had the extreme good fortune to be placed in a foster home where I stayed for four years, until I turned eighteen, where I was lovingly cared about and believed in."

> Even when my behavior was so bad I cut myself in their kitchen . . . or when, out of rage I swallowed all the Excedrin in their medicine cabinet, . . . my foster parents continued to believe in my abilities to grow, and showed that belief by accepting me after each hospital discharge as their foster child still. That steady acceptance must have had an impact, teaching me slowly over the years how to see something salvageable in myself. Bless those people, for they are a part of my faith's firmness. Bless the stories my foster mother read to me, the stories of mine she later listened to, her thin blond hair hanging down in a single sheet. The house, old and shingled, with niches and culverts I loved to crawl in, where the rain pinged on a leaky roof and out in the puddled yard a beautiful German shepherd, who licked my face and offered me his paw, barked and played in the water. Bless the night there, the hallway light they left on for me, burning a soft yellow wedge that I turned into a wing, a woman, an entire army of angels who, I learned to imagine, knew just how to sing me to sleep.[17]

Lauren Slater's foster parents could not guarantee her safety. But they were for her a modest and still more-than-adequate sanctuary in the

---

17. Lauren Slater, *Welcome to My Country: A Therapist's Memoir of Madness* (New York: Random House, 1996), 193–94.

storm. Responding to her need to be cared for body and soul, they gave her physical sanctuary but also psychospiritual sanctuary.

For many of our memoirists, such sanctuary becomes time and space in which, though it is transient, the presence of loving others provides profound and precious comfort. But beyond the comfort, the loving sanctuary provided by others can make it more possible to weather the dangers. Sanctuary can increase "faith's firmness," as Slater put it. It does this, in part, by embodying care made holy by its reliability, simplicity, and perseverance. But such care can also be internalized—an "entire army of angels" inside. In this sense, relational sanctuary is something like the physical sanctuaries built by religious communities. Sanctuaries of religious centers are spaces for the worship of G-d, but they are also intended to shield us for a while from the demands and dangers of the world, so that our souls can be consoled and strengthened in preparation for engaging those demands and dangers once more. (Of course, sometimes religious sanctuaries are not safe either.) Political asylum is powerful solace to refugees seeking sanctuary from governmental persecution, and space to heal from torture and other persecutions. Similarly, relational sanctuary provides profoundly comforting haven, but it also assuages our wounded spirits. We often cannot protect ourselves and our loved ones from harm; even in the peaceable realm described in the Bible (Isa. 11:6–9), sheep and wolves lay down together; wolves do not transform into sheep. But if we have the spiritual wisdom to recognize our limited ability to create safety, we may well discover our much less limited capacity to be for one another not only a refuge and shield, but sanctuaries of peace and healing.

SANITY, AND ALSO DIVINEST SENSE

Spiritual teachings and practices have failed their purposes if they do not assist us in the cultivation of sanity. Being of right mind is a fundamental aspect of the health and ability that we have previously noted are important values in spiritual life. When our capacities for intellectual and emotional logic are well-developed, they prove to be invaluable tools in discernment. Humans have always needed common sense to navigate complex and ambiguous life situations in ways that reflect their highest values. Diplomatic, peaceable human relations—whether in families or between cultures—will always depend to a large degree on the calming effect of reasonableness, the clear thinking of negotiation, the equitable understanding of empathy. Arguably, our growing capacities in science—for example, information technologies, biomedical innovations, nuclear power—require of us more and more sanity if those capacities are to be used safely and fairly. Ethical and moral decision making of the scale we face requires wisdom, which is one reason why religious traditions have always called their adherents to a lifetime of study and practice in spiritual life, so as to mature our intelligence and good sense into sanity in its wisest forms—profound levels of perception and understanding.

The value of sanity notwithstanding, it is also true that we live amid much madness. The prevalence of psychiatric disorder, though significant, is but the tip of the iceberg. There is the madness of violence against and between children—at home, in schools, in the streets, in war. There is the madness of all forms of violence—assault, murder, war, genocide. Ill-planned and underfunded, the "reform" of the mental health system in the United States has led to a massive increase in the numbers of persons who are both homeless and mentally ill. In light of global hunger, it is madness that farmers are paid not to plant crops and food overstocks are destroyed. The disparity between localized wealth and globalized poverty is madness. Nuclear "defense" can be argued to be madness—either because it might be used, or it might not be used and thus is a waste of billions of dollars desperately needed for humanitarian purposes. There are the social madnesses we explored earlier—racism, sexism, other systemic forces of bias and subjugation. There is the madness of violence in the name of religion. Understandably, it is difficult to face into the amount of madness around us. Perhaps we perseverate on the madness in persons because, however difficult or frightening, it is more bearable than seeing the madness in our societies.

Yet, memoirs of soul-suffering bear witness to the spiritual wisdom of engaging madness. Indeed, incredibly, some soul-sufferers encounter in and through madness experiences of such profound or ultimate value—what Emily Dickinson called "divinest Sense"—that, even if they had a choice, they would not give up their illnesses. Claims like this are startling, and not universal, but also not unusual. Anton Boisen, for example, felt that the divinest sense in his suffering was that it might serve a larger good. As mentioned earlier, Boisen founded the method of theological education called CPE—Clinical Pastoral Education. He worked as a chaplain and later as a seminary professor, but Boisen's first profession was forestry, and the anecdote he relates in the following passage from his autobiography comes from that period of his life.

> Sanity in itself is not an end in life. The end of life is to solve important problems and to contribute in some way to human welfare, and if there is even a chance that such an end could best be accomplished by going through Hell for a while, no man worthy of the name would hesitate for an instant.
>
> I often think of a little incident which occurred when I was in Washington. One of the old Forest School men had just returned from two years in the North Woods and a lot of his old class-mates were gathered around him while he dished out yarns about his experiences in the wilds. Finally one of the men asked, "Say, Bill, have you ever been lost?" Bill straightened up, glared at him, and replied with some heat: "Lost! Of course I've been. It's only the dubs who never go five miles from camp who don't get lost sometimes."
>
> I agree with Bill. The kind of sanity which has to be preserved by sticking close to camp and washing dishes for the rest of my life is not worth preserving. I could never be happy or contented in such a course, especially when I feel that the particular territory in which I lost my way is of greatest interest and importance. I want to explore and map that territory.[18]

Boisen's position that "no man worthy of the name would hesitate for an instant" to undergo the suffering of psychic turmoil exudes more bravado and is more proscriptive than that taken by most other memoirists we have been studying. But otherwise, he is not alone in his sentiment. As we saw in earlier reflections, occasionally sufferers will choose some aspect of the suffering as a way of doing good for others. Some sufferers imply this stance when they decide to endure the side effects of medications or undergo ECT despite their reluctance, because to do so will better the lives of their loved ones. Other sufferers imply this stance when they participate in drug trials without any assurance that they will benefit, because the research might help someone else.

Many memoirists would not relinquish their illnesses because they feel strongly that without psychic anguish we would have less art, intel-

---

18. Anton T. Boisen, *Out of the Depths: An Autobiographical Study of Mental Disorders and Religious Experience* (New York: Harper and Row, Publishers, 1960), 132.

lectual accomplishment, and deep human relations. Susanna Kaysen articulates this point of view so well that, though we have noted earlier her claim that "melancholy is useful," it bears repeating here.

> I think melancholy is useful. In its aspect of pensive reflection or contemplation, it's the source of many books (even those complaining about it) and paintings, much scientific insight, the resolution of many fights between couples and friends, and the process known as becoming mature. . . .
>
> Those feelings are unpleasant, but they spur change. What would we be without self-doubt and despair? . . .
>
> If the price of being happier is an occluded worldview, I don't want to pay it. I'd rather see things clearly.[19]

Other memoirists say that illness and their struggle with it have made them a better person, and it is worth the cost of the illness. Comments like Meri Danquah's are representative of such views.

> Before, I used to wonder what my life would have been like had I not gone through my depressions; now, I don't know if I would trade those experiences. I love who I am. And without those past depressions, I wouldn't be the same person. Through the depressions, through therapy, I have learned to speak out, to claim the life that I want, and to cherish the people with whom I choose to share it. Having lived with the pain, having felt/heard/seen and tasted it, I know now that when you pass through it, there is beauty on the other side.[20]

David Waldorf echoes Meri Danquah's closing point. We met Waldorf in our reflections on healing—the artist and long-time patient at Creedmoor. Like him, some soul-sufferers haven't healed much but are still reluctant to surrender their illnesses, because the "divinest sense" they have discovered through it has brought something precious into their lives. For Waldorf, his suffering has brought to him art, and more community through making art with other artists, and as he put it, made it possible for him to see beauty in ugliness.

---

19. Susanna Kaysen, "One Cheer for Melancholy," in *Unholy Ghost*, 38, 39, 40.
20. Meri Nana-Ama Danquah, *Willow Weep for Me: A Black Woman's Journey through Depression—A Memoir* (New York: W.W. Norton, 1998), 265–66.

> I think if an angel came up to me and said, "David, you can be healed of mental illness, but you'll never again know the worth of life again like you did when you were ill," I think I'd have to pick the mental illness. 'Cause that's just how I feel, that it does show me a beautiful, enchanting side of life that I never saw before.[21]

Kay Redfield Jamison takes a similar perspective. In the epilogue to her memoir, Jamison says that she often asks herself whether she would choose to have manic-depressive illness. If lithium were not available or did not work for her, the answer would be a "simple no," she says, partly because she finds the depressions that are part of her illness so awful that she would not go through an extended one again. But her feeling about mania is different. Since lithium works for her, "Strangely enough," she says, "I think I would choose to have it. It's complicated."

> I honestly believe that as a result of it I have felt more things, more deeply; had more experiences, more intensely; loved more, and been more loved; laughed more often for having cried more often; appreciated more the springs, for all the winters; worn death "as close as dungarees," appreciated it—and life—more; seen the finest and the most terrible in people, and slowly learned the values of caring, loyalty, and seeing things through. I have seen the breadth and depth and width of my mind and heart and seen how frail they both are, and how ultimately unknowable they both are. Depressed, I have crawled on my hands and knees in order to get across a room and have done it for month after month. But, normal or manic, I have run faster, thought faster, and loved faster than most I know. . . .

> The countless hypomanias, and mania itself, all have brought into my life a different level of sensing and feeling and thinking. Even when I have been most psychotic—delusional, hallucinating, frenzied—I have been aware of finding new corners in my mind and heart. Some of those corners were incredible and beautiful and took my breath away and made me feel as though I could die right then and the images would sustain me.

---

21. Dawn Parouse, prod., Jessica Yu, dir., *The Living Museum* (Filmworks, 1999). Interview of David Waldorf.

Some of them were grotesque and ugly and I never wanted to know they were there or to see them again. But, always, there were those new corners and—when feeling my normal self, beholden for that self to medicine and love—I cannot imagine becoming jaded to life, because I know of those limitless corners, with their limitless views.[22]

Importantly, Jamison chose these words to close her memoir. She is careful to qualify her assertions. As she says, she is beholden to medicine: she has an effective treatment that keeps her depressions and manias from destructive extremes. She is beholden to love: she implies that there are people who care for her through the periods when her symptoms are strongest. She is selective: though she speaks with appreciation of being manic, she finds no divinest sense in her depressions. She finds the best moments ambiguous: psychotic moments that give her breath-taking images also give her grotesque ones. She is speaking only for her self and her illness: other people with other illnesses have other experiences. But still, her last words, along with those of Boisen, Kaysen, Danquah, and Waldorf, stand for other memoirists who say that the values and experiences they have had in and through madness are so precious and so powerful that, even if they had the choice, they could not easily surrender their illnesses.

Of course, not all our memoirists hold this most radical position—many of them would give up their psychic turmoil in a second, if they could. But neither do all the memoirists need to take this most extreme position for the point to be made: many of our memoirists bear witness to the surprising fact that they would be reluctant to relinquish some of the insights, practices, and experiences their soul-anguish has taught them. This can be understood as sobering witness that, for all of us, spiritual wisdom consists of something more than sanity—at least if by sanity is meant rationality, measured emotion, and prudence. In addition to those valuable mentalities, spiritual wisdom is composed of the capacities to envision as well as see, to see what is needed and not only what is reasonable, to reason with the heart and soul and not the intellect only. Maturation of such capacities will sometimes take us beyond the parameters of human sanity to divinest sense—a sensibility of a different and yet valuable kind.

---

22. Kay Redfield Jamison, *An Unquiet Mind* (New York: Random House, Vintage Books, 1995), 217, 218–19.

Appendix

American Association for Marriage and Family Therapy
Telephone: 703-838-9808
http://www.aamft.org/index_nm.asp

American Association of Pastoral Counselors
Telephone: 703-385-6967
Internet: http://www.aapc.org
To find a pastoral counselor/center: http://www.aapc.org/centers.cfm

American Psychiatric Association
Telephone: 703-907-7300
http://www.psych.org

American Psychological Association
Telephone: 202-336-5500; 800-374-2721 (toll-free)
http://www.apa.org

Anabaptist Disabilities Network: Mental Health
Telephone: 877-214-9838
http://www.adnetonline.org/ADNet_Home/Awareness/MH_Awareness

Association of Brethren Caregivers
Telephone: 847-742-5100, ext. 300
http://www.brethren-caregivers.org

Congregational Resource Guide
http://www.congregationalresources.org/mentalhealth.asp

Depression and Bipolar Support Alliance
http://www.dbsalliance.org

The Episcopal Mental Illness Network
Telephone: 501-661-0384
http://www.eminnews.org

Families USA
http://www.familiesusa.org/resources/faith-based-resources

Faith-Net: Outreach to the Faith Community
http://www.nami.org/faithnet

Jewish Association for the Mentally Ill
Telephone: 020 8458 2223 (U.K.)
http://www.jamiuk.org/index.cfm

Lutheran Network on Mental Illness/Brain Disorders
http://www.elca.org/disability/mentalillness

Mental Health America
Telephone: 703-684-7722; 800-969-6642 (toll-free)
TTY 800-433-5959
http://www.nmha.org

Mental Health Chaplaincy
http://www.mentalhealthchaplain.org

Mental Health Ministries
http://www.mentalhealthministries.net

The Mental Illness Network (United Church of Christ)
Telephone: 216-736-3848
http://www.min-ucc.org

Muslim Mental Health
http://www.muslimmentalhealth.com

The National Alliance for Research on Schizophrenia and Depression
Telephone: 800-828-8289
http://www.narsad.org

National Alliance on Mental Illness
Help-line: 888-999-NAMI (800-950-6264)
Telephone: 703-524-7600
TDD: 703-516-7227
For general information: http://www.nami.org
To find your local chapter:
http://www.nami.org/Template.cfm?Section=Your_Local_NAMI&Template=/
CustomSource/AffiliateFinder.cfm

National Association for Rights Protection and Advocacy
Telephone: 205-464-0101
http://www.narpa.org

National Consumer Supporter Technical Assistance Center
Telephone: 800-969-6642
http://www.ncstac.org

National Depressive and Manic-Depressive Association
Telephone: 800-82-NDMDA (800-826-3632)
http://www.ndmda.org

National Institute of Mental Health
Telephone: 301-443-4513; 1-866-615-6464 (toll-free)
TTY: 301-443-8431; 1-866-415-8051 (TTY toll-free)
http://www.nimh.nih.gov

Pathways to Promise (Interfaith Coalition)
http://www.pathways2promise.org

Presbyterian Serious Mental Illness Network
http://www.pcusa.org/phewa/psmin.htm#list

Substance Abuse and Mental Health Services Administration, Center for Mental
Health Services
http://www.stopstigma.samhsa.gov/index.html

Suicide Prevention Action Network USA
http://www.spanusa.org

Suicide Prevention Lifeline
1-800-273-TALK

United Methodist Caring Communities Program
http://www.umc-gbcs.org/site/pp.asp?c=fsJNK0PKJrH&b=942829

Virginia Interfaith Committee on Mental Illness Ministries
http://www.vaumc.org/gm/micom.htm

ACKNOWLEDGMENTS AND PERMISSIONS

ACKNOWLEDGMENTS

I am grateful for opportunities I have been given to present and receive response to this work in different venues:

- The project received substantial early support when I was named one of the 1998–1999 Henry Luce III Fellows in Theology. The fellowship resulted in the first publication of material from the project: "'Dark Nights of the Soul': Meaning and Ministry in First-Person Narratives of Severe Psychospiritual Suffering and Healing," in *The Papers of the Henry Luce III Fellows in Theology,* vol. 5, ed. Christopher I. Wilkins (Pittsburgh: Association of Theological Schools in the United States and Canada, 2002), 23–45.

- Several academic organizations invited presentation of the work: American Academy of Religion (Person, Culture, and Religion Group and the Religion and Ethics in Health Care Group); American Association of Pastoral Counselors—Pacific Region; Association of Practical Theology; International Academy of Practical Theology; Society for Intercultural Pastoral Care and Counseling.

- Portions of the research were presented at the request of mental health organizations: Pacific Clinics, Inc., Arcadia, California; Christian Counseling Service, Redlands, California; the Pomona Valley (Calif.) and Orange County (Calif.) affiliates of the National Alliance for Mental Illness; the annual conference of the National Alliance for Mental Illness California.

- Several churches supported presentation of the research: Claremont United Church of Christ, Congregational, Claremont, California; First United Methodist Church, Ventura, California; First United Methodist Church, Phoenix, Arizona; Presbyterian Church of the Master, Mission Viejo, California; Trinity United Presbyterian Church, Santa Ana, California.

- Portions of the work were presented at the invitation of several educational institutions: The Anna Howard Shaw Center at Boston University School of Theology; Claremont School of Theology; Loma Linda University; Women's Studies in Religion Program, Claremont Graduate University.

I am grateful for the many individuals at these events and in other contexts who have given feedback and support. I am particularly thankful for the many primary sufferers and family members who, at these events and in my clinical work, and through memoirs I have studied but not cited in this work, have shared their stories with me and in other ways motivated, inspired, and encouraged this work. Special thanks are due to Gunnar and Susan Christiansen, Sophie Williams, and Joretta

Marshall. I am fortunate to have had the help of three extremely competent research assistants—Claremont School of Theology students Shannon Ulrickson, Dan Sharp, and Jill Snodgrass—and I thank them for their careful attention to locating texts, securing permissions, and otherwise dealing with details associated with the project.

I am deeply indebted to Ulrike Guthrie, who has been an exemplary editor. Her wisdom about the content of this book and about the process of writing any book has played a crucial role in bringing this work to publication. Her collegiality and encouragement have been of inestimable value. I have been very fortunate to work with a production staff at The Pilgrim Press who have been not only competent but collaborative, and I thank Timothy Stavetig, Janice Brown, Kristin Firth, and Frederick Porter.

Family and friends arguably play the biggest role and pay the biggest price in the process of bringing most books to publication, and that is certainly the case with this book. My dedication to this subject was born in the struggle my family-of-origin has waged amid the effects of serious mental illness. My determination to address this subject has continued to be fueled by the friends who courageously and honestly wrestle with anguish of soul, and by their loving partners, families, and friends. That my own soul-suffering has guided this work and not sunk it is due in large measure to Jane, whose love is the closest and most consistent embodiment in my life of divinest sense. All these people, over the past few years especially, have given me leave to do this work, with much understanding and graciousness, and I am grateful.

PERMISSIONS

Grateful acknowledgment is made for permission to reprint previously published materials from the following authors/artists:

ANONYMOUS: "Adagio, A Movement in Slow Time," chalk pastel by anonymous in *Childhood Revealed: Art Expressing Pain, Discovery and Hope*, edited by Harold S. Koplewicz and Robin F. Goodman, published by Harry N. Abrams, Inc. Copyright © 1999 by New York University. Reprinted by permission of New York University Child Study Center.

GWENDOLYN CARR: Excerpts from *After the Storm* by G. Lloyd Carr, with poems by Gwendolyn C. Carr, published by Inter-Varsity Press Ltd. (Later published in the United States as *The Fierce Goodbye*.) Reprinted by permission of Inter-Varsity Press Ltd.

NELL CASEY: Excerpts from *Unholy Ghost*, edited by Nell Casey, published by HarperCollins. Copyright © 2001 by Nell Casey. Reprinted by permission of Nell Casey.

MERI NANA-AMA DANQUAH: From WILLOW WEEP FOR ME: A BLACK WOMAN'S JOURNEY THROUGH DEPRESSION by Meri Nana-Ama Danquah. Copyright © 1998 by Meri Nana-Ama Danquah. Used by permission of W. W. Norton & Company, Inc.

JYL LYNN FELMAN: Excerpts from "Nurturing the Soul" by Jyl Lynn Felman in *Tikkun* vol. 11, no. 4 (August 1996). Copyright © 1996 by Jyl Lynn Felman. Reprinted by permission of Jyl Lynn Felman.

STEWART D. GOVIG: Excerpts from "Chronic Mental Illness and the Family: Contexts for Pastoral Care" by Stewart D. Govig in *The Journal of Pastoral Care and Counseling* vol. 47, no. 4 (Winter 1993). Reprinted by permission of *The Journal of Pastoral Care and Counseling*. Excerpts from *Souls Are Made of Endurance: Surviving Mental Illness in the Family*. ©1994 Stewart D. Govig. Used by permission of Westminster John Knox Press.

DANIEL S. HANSON: Excerpts from *Room for J: A Family Struggles with Schizophrenia* by Daniel S. Hanson. Copyright © 2005 by Daniel S. Hanson. Reprinted by permission of Beaver's Pond Press and Daniel S. Hanson.

DAVID HILFIKER: Excerpts from "When Mental Illness Blocks the Spirit" by David Hilfiker in *The Other Side* (May & June 2002). Copyright © David Hilfiker. Reprinted by permission of David Hilfiker.

ALBERT Y. HSU: Excerpts taken from *Grieving a Suicide* by Albert Y. Hsu. Copyright (c) 2002 by Albert Y. Hsu. Used with permission of InterVarsity Press, PO Box 1400, Downers Grove, IL 60515. www.ivpress.com.

WILLIAM E. HULME: Excerpts from "Our Daughter Need Not Have Died" by William Hulme. Copyright 1974 *Christian Century*. Reprinted with permission from the December 4, 1974 issue of the *Christian Century*. Subscriptions: $49/yr. from P.O. Box 378, Mt. Morris, IL 61054. 1-800-208-4097.

KAY REDFIELD JAMISON: Excerpts from AN UNQUIET MIND by Kay Redfield Jamison, copyright © 1995 by Kay Redfield Jamison. Used by permission of Alfred A. Knopf, a division of Random House, Inc.

JANE KENYON: Excerpt from "Having It Out with Melancholy" by Jane Kenyon. Copyright 2005 by the Estate of Jane Kenyon. Reprinted from *Collected Poems* with the permission of Graywolf Press, Saint Paul, Minnesota.

ELIZABETH MACDONELL: "If I Played My Life," by Elizabeth MacDonell from *If I Played My Life: Poems by People with Schizophrenia*, edited by Kate Goldsmith. Copyright © 1998 by Bayeux Arts. Reprinted by permission of Bayeux Arts, Inc.

NANCY MAIRS: Excerpts from "On Living Behind Bars" from *Plaintext* by Nancy Mairs. Copyright © 1986 ARIZONA BOARD OF REGENTS. Reprinted by permission of the University of Arizona Press.

MARTHA MANNING: Quotations totaling 2754 words from *Undercurrents* by Martha Manning. Copyright © 1995 by Martha Manning. Reprinted by permission of HarperCollins Publishers. Excerpts from "The Legacy" by Martha Manning from *Psychotherapy Networker* (January/February 1997). Copyright © *Psychotherapy Networker*. Reprinted by permission of *Psychotherapy Networker*.

SHARON O'BRIEN: Excerpts from *The Family Silver: A Memoir of Depression and Inheritance* by Sharon O'Brien. Copyright © 2004 by Sharon O'Brien. Reprinted by permission of University of Chicago Press and Sharon O'Brien.

PARKER J. PALMER: Excerpts from *Let Your Life Speak: Listening for the Voice of Vocation* by Parker J. Palmer. Copyright © 2000 by John Wiley & Sons, Inc. Reprinted with permission of John Wiley & Sons, Inc.